Theology after Ricoeur

Theology after Ricoeur

New Directions in Hermeneutical Theology

DAN R. STIVER

Westminster John Knox Press
LOUISVILLE
LONDON • LEIDEN

Book design by Sharon Adams
Cover design by Kathy York

First edition
Published by Westminster John Knox Press
Louisville, Kentucky

This book is printed on acid-free paper that meets the American National Standards Institute Z39.48 standard.∞

PRINTED IN THE UNITED STATES OF AMERICA

01 02 03 04 05 06 07 08 09 10 — 10 9 8 7 6 5 4 3 2 1

Library of Congress Cataloging-in-Publication Data

Stiver, Dan R.
Theology after Ricoeur : new directions in hermeneutical theology / Dan R. Stiver.— 1st ed. p. cm.
Includes bibliographical references and index.
ISBN 0-664-22243-9 (alk. paper)
1. Theology—Methodology. 2. Hermeneutics—Religious aspects—Christianity. 3. Ricoeur, Paul. I. Title.
BR 118.S74 2001
230′.092—dc21 2001017792

To My Parents,
Bernie and Wilma Stiver

CONTENTS

LIST OF ILLUSTRATIONS

PREFACE

My first encounter with Paul Ricoeur occurred while I was doing special studies for my graduate work at the University of Chicago Divinity School in the fall of 1981. My focus at the time was on the theology of David Tracy, Langdon Gilkey, and Hans Küng (who was teaching there during that semester). Ricoeur was of interest because of his influence on Tracy and Gilkey. I attended a lecture by Ricoeur, ending up sitting on the floor with many others due to the overflow crowd. Despite the great interest and "buzz," most found him difficult to follow. I concluded that in order to appreciate what he was doing, I would have to give his lectures much more time than I had—and thus I did not continue with the lectures.

I then began to teach in the area of Christian Philosophy at Southern Baptist Theological Seminary in Louisville, Kentucky, in 1984. As I focused on phenomenology, hermeneutics, religious language, and postmodernism, I kept running into Ricoeur's work. In exploring areas such as phenomenology, symbol, metaphor, and narrative, I found him providing insights that were especially illuminating. One illustration relates to my attempt, after a few years, to teach a course on Ricoeur, due to my own interest and the enthusiasm of a number of students. The course was almost not approved because colleagues thought it was too narrow for a master of divinity course. What I only realized in actually teaching the course was that to understand Ricoeur, we needed an introduction to the history of philosophy, not to mention philosophy of religion. The course, ironically, ended up being almost too broad! Along with this breadth, however, what also struck me was that despite his great influence in various areas, there were few attempts to understand Ricoeur comprehensively. Indeed, it seemed to many that he was not offering a comprehensive philosophy.

As I continued to consider his work, however—and as he continued to write—a fuller pattern began to be discernible, particularly with the publication of his Gifford lectures, *Oneself as Another.* This work seemed to pull together in significant ways various strands of his thought. Particularly, it returned to the focus of his first major book, *Freedom and Nature,* namely, the nature of the self, providing a kind of bookend to his work.

Especially as I tried to find my way through the issues raised for philosophy and theology by postmodernism, I found this fuller "hermeneutical philosophy" seen in Ricoeur (and also Hans-Georg Gadamer) especially promising and fruitful, better and more balanced than many other postmodern contenders. Yet I was still struck by the typically piecemeal appropriation of Ricoeur and also by the diverse interpretations of his work. Particularly, the tendency to see him as a subjectivist and noncognitivist in the way that many interpreted Friedrich Schleiermacher and Rudolf Bultmann I found surprising and difficult to defend in his work.

This book is consequently an attempt to offer to others my understanding of what I consider to be one of the major, if not the best, postmodern philosophies that can serve as a resource for the doing of theology in our challenging time. It is also a response to so many students and colleagues who have asked me to "explain Ricoeur" or to point them to a particular book that would "give Ricoeur" to them. The problem is that there is no one book, no magnum opus, that adequately reveals Ricoeur's philosophy. His thought is difficult and scattered across a lifetime of writing, which is one of the reasons why his work is yet to be fully tapped. In addition, he himself recognizes that he has not "pulled it all together" into a definitive interpretation. Given that his is a hermeneutical philosophy, it is perhaps fitting that the interpretation of his own work is open to diverse interpretations, even a conflict of interpretations.

As a result, my reading of Ricoeur is self-consciously a creative appropriation. I try to defend it in places as the "best" interpretation of Ricoeur; in other places, I indicate that I am modifying his thought. In the latter situation, it is always the case that I thought the change would overcome tensions and better represent the basic flow of his thought. My purpose has been to show that, despite Ricoeur's scattered yet amazingly erudite writings in numerous fields, what has emerged is a comprehensive and impressive philosophy. In many ways, it is as comprehensive as any produced in the last century. It is not a Hegelian system, to be sure, and it retains Ricoeur's characteristic caution and humility before the mystery of reality. But this is exactly part of its attraction. If it is possible to produce a philosophy in a postmodern time—a real question for many—it will likely look like Ricoeur's. His hermeneutical humility is coherent with a time that calls just for such philosophical prudence.

Any book owes huge debts to others, and this is no exception. First of all, I express appreciation to Paul Ricoeur himself, who has been willing to give us the highest quality of philosophical reflection from someone who truly has lived through the major vicissitudes of the twentieth century. Additionally, thanks is given to all who responded to many papers that reflected my ongoing efforts to grasp Ricoeur over many years: the eastern regional of the Society of Christian Philosophy, the Baptist Association of Philosophy Teachers (BAPT), the American Academy of Religion, a conference on evangelical hermeneutics at Gordon College in 1996, and The Scripture and Hermeneutics Seminar at Redeemer College, Canada, in the summer of 2000. I especially appreciate much informal dialogue with former colleagues at Southern Seminary, particularly Richard Cunningham and Charles Scalise. Several former students, now colleagues, have helped me immeasurably by their interest in Ricoeur. They had the virtues of not only listening but being critical of my ideas: Pat Horn, Charles Hawkins, Greg Johnson, Tim Maddox, and Michael Robinson.

Similarly, my editor at Westminster John Knox Press and also former colleague at Southern Seminary, Carey C. Newman, has graced me with his support, his inspiration, and also with his frustrations in trying to get me to explain Ricoeur to someone who is not a Ricoeur specialist. What clarity there is in the book is owed in significant ways to him.

The Southern Seminary that nurtured me and provided such a fertile academic and spiritual environment in my student days and early career, before it went in a different direction, gave me a last gift of a sabbatical in 1997–1998 that enabled focused research on this book. The writing would also hardly have been possible without the gift of a new beginning in the fall of 1998 at the Logsdon School of Theology at Hardin-Simmons University, where I now teach theology and philosophy in the excitement of building a new divinity school. The dean, Vernon Davis, has been especially supportive of writing in the midst of teaching. I have appreciated the support of student assistance, especially the work of Chris Powell and Heather Hood, who helped me a great deal with proofreading and indexing.

Selections from two other works have been incorporated into this book. I am grateful to the editors and publishers for permission to use this material: "Re-figuring Ricoeur," *Southwest Philosophical Studies* 22 (2000), forthcoming and "Ricoeur, Speech Act Theory, and the Gospels as History," in *After Pentecost: Philosophy and Theology of Language and Biblical Interpretation,* ed. Craig Bartholomew, Elaine Botha, Colin Greene, and Karl Möller, The Scripture and Hermeneutics Series 2 (Grand Rapids: Zondervan, forthcoming).

Finally, I dedicate this book to my parents, Bernie and Wilma Stiver, who provided much more indirect but nevertheless much more substantive support. My mother, now deceased, and my father gave me the gifts of presence and freedom to go my own way, balanced in just the right way. As a parent now myself, I increasingly appreciate what they did for me and their "practical wisdom" that I have tried, not always very successfully, to emulate.

Introduction

Theology in the twentieth century reflected the convulsive nature of its time. The twentieth century began in hopes for a Christian century and a war to end all wars and ended in manifold global threats. It began with optimistic and confident theologies, liberal and conservative alike, and ended by fracturing into a host of divergent attempts to gain theological footing in a dramatically altered landscape. In an unsteady situation like this, one looks for a helping hand wherever it can be found. In the past, theologians have commonly looked for help from philosophy, which has played a decisive foundational role. Part of the "shaking of the foundations," however, has been to question the need for such aid.[1] If philosophy can help now, it will have to be a philosophy that looks quite different from philosophies of old and must be appropriated in a way quite different from the usual way. The truth is that philosophy, too, has not come through the reoriented landscape unscathed; it has been shaken to its own foundations by the changes in the twentieth century.

In this light, Paul Ricoeur's hermeneutical philosophy offers just such an altered philosophical resource for the reconstruction of contemporary theology, a partner that self-consciously does not desire to dictate the flow of conversation as much as to help keep it going in interesting and productive ways. Spelling out these ways is the purpose of this project.

Ricoeur's philosophy is attractive for several reasons. For one, with his more recent work, he offers an almost unrivaled combination of breadth and depth as one of the major twentieth-century philosophers. Despite

1. This phrase refers to the title of a famous sermon by Paul Tillich, referring to the unsettled nature of theology in the twentieth century: Paul Tillich, *The Shaking of the Foundations* (New York: Charles Scribner's Sons, 1948).

this, however, his philosophy is still relatively untapped by theologians. A major reason for this odd fact is that, until the emergence of more recent material by him and about him, it was difficult to see his work as a coherent whole.[2] As a result, theologians and others have tended to latch onto individual creative nuggets of insight while ignoring the wider vein that extends into many other areas. For example, some have drawn on his idea of a "second naïveté," others on his work on narrative, and others on his work on metaphor. As a result, his broader philosophical project remains to be explored by theologians.

What also should make his work intriguing for theologians is that it has unusual affinity for theology because its fundamental paradigm is the

2. Three recent works in particular that have focused on the value of Ricoeur's broader philosophical project for theology have encouraged and contributed to this study: James Fodor, *Christian Hermeneutics: Paul Ricoeur and the Refiguring of Theology* (Oxford: Clarendon Press, 1995); Kevin J. Vanhoozer, *Biblical Narrative in the Philosophy of Paul Ricoeur: A Study in Hermeneutics and Theology* (Cambridge: Cambridge University Press, 1990); Mark I. Wallace, *The Second Naiveté: Barth, Ricoeur, and the New Yale Theology,* Studies in American Biblical Hermeneutics (Macon, Ga.: Mercer University Press, 1990). Another book, by Loretta Dornisch, focuses on the connection of faith and philosophy in Ricoeur, but as she says, it is primarily descriptive: Loretta Dornisch, *Faith and Philosophy in the Writings of Paul Ricoeur,* Problems in Contemporary Philosophy 29 (Lewiston, N.Y.: Edwin Mellen Press, 1990). Yet another is by Werner Jeanrond, *Theological Hermeneutics: Development and Significance* (New York: Crossroad, 1991). Jeanrond's focus is on the development of theological hermeneutics in general, although he has great appreciation for Ricoeur and, particularly, for David Tracy's appropriation of Ricoeur. He does not deal with Ricoeur, however, in great detail.

The first three, who offer comprehensive, critical perspectives, spend a great deal of time relating Ricoeur's thought to that of what is often called the Yale School of narrative theology. Of the three, I am closest to Wallace. His work, although very valuable, is brief (125 pages) and focused on arguing that Ricoeur is closer to Karl Barth and the Yale School than is often thought. Additionally, his and Vanhoozer's books were not able to draw on Ricoeur's important *Oneself as Another* and, of course, other, more recent work. While Vanhoozer and Fodor are very appreciative of Ricoeur, in the end they, like the Yale School, tend to see Ricoeur as too subjective when it comes to faith. Despite the fact that I have learned much from Vanhoozer and Fodor, my project differs from theirs in significant ways. First and foremost, I am not so interested in Ricoeur's particular theological views as I am in the value of his philosophical framework as a resource for Christian theologians across the theological spectrum. In other words, one can go in a variety of theological directions on the basis of Ricoeur's hermeneutical philosophy. They focus on Ricoeur's theological forays and end up disagreeing with him on that theological score. As a result, it is difficult to see the value of his philosophy over against his theology. I am interested, conversely, in the contribution that Ricoeur's philosophy can make to a variety of theological standpoints, not whether it is conservative or liberal or postliberal. Second, when it comes to Ricoeur's theological perspective, I do not interpret him in as subjective a way as they do. In that sense, my interpretation of him is similar to Wallace's. Moreover, as all three recognize, Ricoeur is more of a philosopher and an exegete than a theologian; his theological perspective, therefore, is more suggested than developed. It allows, I argue, for a variety of interpretations. While I find Ricoeur's particular religious view more theologically helpful than do Fodor and Vanhoozer (and, in fact, closer to their theological perspectives than they think), I do not put as much weight on it as on his relatively clearer philosophical perspective. Third, I stress more Ricoeur's hermeneutical arc as the fulcrum for his value to the theological enterprise. Finally, I emphasize different works more strongly than these three major critics do. Obviously, I can draw on more recent works that shed light on his project (as we all recognize, this is the risk of interpreting a living philosopher), but as we shall see, I also emphasize more than they older works such as *Freedom and Nature* and *Lectures on Ideology and Utopia.* My agreements and disagreements with them will be made clearer as the book progresses.

interpretation of rich and classic texts, which is so crucial for text-based religions such as Judaism and Christianity. This textual metaphor is expanded into a full-blown philosophical view that is suggestive and congenial for the challenges facing contemporary theology.

Another important point of contact is that, as a Christian himself, Ricoeur has made striking ventures into the areas of theology and biblical studies, revealing a level of expertise rare to philosophers. Although primarily a philosopher, he has made original contributions not so much to theology but to exegesis and biblical hermeneutics.

Before developing the specific ways in which Ricoeur's hermeneutical philosophy and theology can fruitfully be engaged, in this introduction I examine more closely the broader contemporary context from which his work arises and the resultant ferment in theology, indicating in a preliminary fashion some of the ways in which Ricoeur's work can contribute. This is followed by an overview of Ricoeur's life and work, which sets the stage for the closer examination to follow.

A Time of Troubles

Before theology had fully caught up to modernity, modernity began to collapse, in many respects taking theology with it. Langdon Gilkey, borrowing the language of Arnold Toynbee, has referred to it as "a time of troubles."[3] Clark Pinnock called the situation for theology a "maze."[4] While recognizing that Christianity has faced numerous other cultural shifts, Stanley Grenz and John Franke commented recently that this one "bears the distinctive mark of fragmentation. We've been in the midst of a widespread fragmentation and perhaps even disintegration," they say, "that appears to be affecting all dimensions of Western culture, including the theological enterprise."[5] Lonnie Kliever, speaking of a "shattered spectrum" in 1981, captured the situation well:

3. Gilkey has developed this idea in several places, most fully in Langdon Gilkey, *Reaping the Whirlwind: A Christian Interpretation of History* (New York: Crossroad, 1976), especially part 1. The reference to "a time of troubles" is to Arnold Toynbee, *A Study of History* (Oxford: Oxford University Press, 1945), 53.

4. For the idea of a maze, see Clark H. Pinnock, *Tracking the Maze: Finding Our Way through Modern Theology from an Evangelical Perspective* (San Francisco: HarperCollins, 1990).

5. Stanley J. Grenz and John R. Franke, *Beyond Foundationalism: Shaping Theology in a Postmodern Context* (Louisville, Ky.: Westminster John Knox Press, 2001). For an interesting analysis of Christianity's history in terms of six paradigm shifts, but with significant agreement concerning the nature of the current shift, see Hans Küng, *Christianity: Essence, History, and Future,* trans. John Bowden (New York: Continuum, 1998).

> The last twenty-five years of Christian thought have been a period of intense experimentation if not chaotic change. The revered traditions and towering giants of the theological past have been supplanted by a bewildering variety of theological programs and pundits. Theologies of secularity, process, liberation, hope, play, and story have emerged like the overlapping bursts of a fireworks display. First one and then another of these new interpretations of the Christian faith has captured the center of attention only to be succeeded by yet another explosion of theological energy and illumination. As a consequence, an unprecedented pluralism of belief-systems and life-styles is available today under the heading of "Christian faith."[6]

The powerful options at the beginning of the twentieth century that involved turning to the authority of some aspect of the modern worldview or to the Bible, so obvious to their adherents, are rarely viewed today with such sanguinity. As a result, defenders of reason and evidence have to argue shrilly for positions that were long taken for granted. Others attempt to forgo tradition altogether and grope for radical new beginnings. Others in despair lapse into relativism. Few desire to rebuild on the old foundations.

Any reconstruction must be cognizant of the lay of the land, since it is a new and challenging landscape that presents itself to contemporary theologizing. I therefore explore central features of the contemporary terrain under the headings of postmodernism, pluralism, and praxis.[7]

Postmodernism

One of the most imposing features generally goes under the label "postmodernism." Postmodernism is a many-splendored thing, so much so that adherents and discreditors alike are bedazzled by its polyvalence. Even its definition is much debated; nevertheless, I believe it is possible to discern enough similarity among the various versions of postmodernism to iden-

6. Lonnie D. Kliever, *The Shattered Spectrum: A Survey of Contemporary Theology* (Atlanta: John Knox Press, 1981).

7. Rebecca S. Chopp and Mark Lewis Taylor propose five similar features in Mark Lewis Taylor and Rebecca S. Chopp, eds., *Reconstructing Christian Theology* (Minneapolis: Fortress Press, 1994), 3–11. I see three of their categories, however, as falling under the broad heading of pluralism. Roger Badham, editor of a work representing the spectrum of current theology, identifies three categories characterizing the present situation that are also very similar to the three I am using. See Roger A. Badham, ed., *Introduction to Christian Theology: Contemporary North American Perspectives* (Louisville, Ky.: Westminster John Knox Press, 1998), 3–8.

tify a significant paradigm change in the West.[8] The commonality is especially one, as is often the case, in terms of critique of the traditional paradigm rather than reconstruction, but the outline of a distinctive paradigm of a positive nature can also be partially discerned.

Rather than seeing postmodernism in narrow terms, as the province of a few French thinkers, I see it as a broad movement. It includes among those who have been explicitly identified as postmodern the French poststructuralists, such as Jacques Derrida, Michel Foucault, and Jean-François Lyotard; the hermeneutical philosophies of Hans-Georg Gadamer and Paul Ricoeur; the thought of the later Ludwig Wittgenstein; and the American neopragmatists, such as Richard Rorty, Jeffrey Stout, and Cornel West. In theology, the major movement seen as postmodern is the Yale postliberal theology, inspired especially by Hans Frei and George Lindbeck. Other theological claimants are process theologians such as David Griffin and evangelicals such as Thomas Oden. As we see below, liberation theology also represents a major onslaught against the modern paradigm of theology.

Characteristics of Modernity

Beginning with the place where there is the greatest agreement, namely, critique, postmodernists almost universally reject the Western tradition's demand for absolute foundations, clarity, and certainty, paired with its assumption of a dualistic intellectualism. These are actually all deeply intertwined. *Foundationalism* refers to the way in which knowledge has commonly been pictured like a building, where one starts with a firm base and then builds upon it systematically, brick by brick. Such a "noetic structure" clearly implies that the starting point is all important. The necessity of a careful plan or method for building upon the foundation is also implied, which implies further the necessity of a *rigorous method.*

The point is that we have thought we must get things right at the start, which usually involves finding some particular philosophical basis and proceeding in a methodologically rigorous manner. Richard Bernstein terms this approach *objectivism*:

8. For fuller treatment, see Dan R. Stiver, "Much Ado about Athens and Jerusalem: The Implications of Postmodernism for Faith," *Review and Expositor* 91 (Winter 1994): 87–90; Dan R. Stiver, "The Uneasy Alliance between Evangelicalism and Postmodernism: A Reply to Anthony Thiselton," in *The Challenge of Postmodernism: An Evangelical Engagement,* ed. David Dockery (Wheaton, Ill.: BridgePoint, 1995).

> By "objectivism," I mean the basic conviction that there is or must be some permanent, ahistorical matrix or framework to which we can ultimately appeal in determining the nature of rationality, knowledge, truth, reality, goodness, or rightness. An objectivist claims that there is (or must be) such a matrix and that the primary task of the philosopher is to discover what it is and to support his or her claims to have discovered such a matrix with the strongest possible reasons. Objectivism is closely related to foundationalism and the search for an Archimedean point. The objectivist maintains that unless we can ground philosophy, knowledge, or language in a rigorous manner we cannot avoid radical skepticism.[9]

Objectivism thus includes the need for both a rock-solid foundation and a rigorous methodology.

The implication for theology has been an inordinate emphasis on the philosophical underpinning, which must be established and worked out before anything else can be done. This has led in the modern period to a preoccupation with methodology, or theological prolegomena, with a concomitantly heavy dependence on philosophical grounding. This is so much the case that some lament theologians never get around to theology proper. As William Placher ruefully remarks:

> A good many people—myself included—have urged contemporary theologians to abandon their preoccupation with methodology and get on with the business of really doing theology. I therefore confess embarrassment at being the author of a sort of extended preface to contemporary discussions about theological method. Prologomena [*sic*] to prologomena [*sic*]! Worse and worse![10]

Inherent to the foundationalist or objectivist noetic structure is the craving for *certainty*. Alvin Plantinga more precisely calls the approach that we have just considered "classical foundationalism," which calls for the basic beliefs in the foundation to be indubitable.[11] It was not until recently that philosophers noticed that the marked differences between empiricists and rationalists concealed a deeper likeness. An empiricist appeals to indubitable sense experiences while a rationalist appeals to indubitable propositions. Either way, they secure the foundation with unchallengeable "properly basic beliefs."

9. Richard J. Bernstein, *Beyond Objectivism and Relativism: Science, Hermeneutics, and Praxis* (Philadelphia: University of Pennsylvania Press, 1985), 8.

10. William C. Placher, *Unapologetic Theology: A Christian Voice in a Pluralistic Conversation* (Louisville, Ky.: Westminster/John Knox Press, 1989), 7.

11. Plantinga's important essay is Alvin Plantinga, "Reason and Belief in God," in *Faith and Rationality: Reason and Belief in God,* ed. Alvin Plantinga and Nicholas Wolterstorff (Notre Dame, Ind.: University of Notre Dame Press, 1983).

René Descartes famously identified the criterion for foundational beliefs as being "clear and distinct."[12] *Clarity* is thus also a requirement for knowledge. Jacques Derrida sums up this tradition as a "metaphysics of presence" and as "logocentrism," which expresses the need for both the clarity that comes from direct sight and the capacity to express such sight in words.[13] Going back to the philosophical foundations of Western thought, Plato's famous allegory of the cave depicts the philosopher as the one who has emerged from seeing the shadows of the cave into the clarity of seeing things in the bright light of the sun, exhibiting a deep longing for clarity that removes all doubt and ambiguity. It was also thought that knowledge must be expressible in clear language, or it could not be counted as knowledge. Descartes's similar emphasis on a precise methodology became allied with the growing hegemony of scientific methodology, likewise calling for objectivity and rigor in determining what counts as knowledge.

All together, these forces placed tremendous pressure on theology to measure up—and it has tried. Nancey Murphy points out how the conservative wing of theology attempted to find certain foundations in an inerrant theory of scripture and how the liberal wing sought such indubitable foundations in human experience.[14] Such an attempt has driven theology for several centuries. We live, however, in the ruins of the attempt, when it has become clear that theology cannot move comfortably in such confines.

In the end, nothing has been found that can live up to such high standards, leaving epistemology and even philosophy of science in general disarray, not to mention other disciplines such as theology. As Bernstein suggests, the temptation is quickly to succumb to fears of relativism, or what he terms "Cartesian anxiety."[15] When the standards of knowledge are ratcheted so extremely high, relativism and nihilism lie close at the door. This *polar oscillation between objectivism and relativism* is a striking feature of the modern paradigm.

Sometimes postmodernism itself is seen as deeply relativist, but my analysis suggests that the quick concern for relativism when the parameters

12. See René Descartes, "Discourse on Method," in *Descartes, Spinoza,* trans. Elizabeth S. Haldane and G. R. T. Ross, Great Books of the Western World 31 (Chicago: Encyclopaedia Britannica, 1952), 52.

13. See, for example, Jacques Derrida, *Of Grammatology* (1967), trans. Gayatri Chakravorty Spivak (Baltimore: Johns Hopkins University Press, 1974).

14. Nancey C. Murphy, *Beyond Liberalism and Fundamentalism: How Modern and Postmodern Philosophy Set the Theological Agenda,* Rockwell Lecture Series (Valley Forge, Pa.: Trinity Press International, 1996), 1–35.

15. Bernstein, *Beyond Objectivism and Relativism,* 16.

of knowledge are loosened is itself a modernist, not postmodernist, reaction. As Susan Hekman says, "Postmodernism does not espouse 'relativism' as its critics claim. Rather, it calls for a redefinition of knowledge that displaces the relative/absolute dichotomy and identifies all knowledge as hermeneutic."[16] Insofar as thinkers are deemed relativists, they would therefore be, in the words of David Griffin, "ultramodern" or perhaps "most-modern."[17] In terms of genuinely offering a new paradigm, postmodernism attempts to go "beyond objectivism and relativism," as in the title of Bernstein's book.

Descartes is also emblematic of *intellectualist dualism*. He sharply separated thought as a distinctive mental substance over against the body and the natural world, which he saw as extended substance. The problem was that, once shattered, Humpty-Dumpty could not be put back together again. In other words, once the split was so wide, it was difficult to see how mind and body could interact. For the last few centuries, philosophers have been preoccupied with this task. In the empirical tradition, this split also led to skepticism about knowledge of the external world. We may be aware of our immediate sensations, but how can we ever get outside ourselves to see if and how sensations connect up with the world?

Moreover, the way in which this view pits the intellect against the emotions and the body is a conflict that runs deep in the Western tradition. Plato at times saw the body as a "tomb" or "prison," from which the soul should long to escape.[18] His image of the charioteer, who represents reason, having to fight the unruly horse, which represents the passions, made this point in a picturesque way.[19] The Stoic virtue of apathy exemplified a common Greek desire to control the emotions by the reason. Numerous authors have commented on the modern "disembedded and disembod-

16. Susan J. Hekman, *Gender and Knowledge: Elements of a Postmodern Feminism,* Northeastern Series in Feminist Theory (Boston: Northeastern University Press, 1990), 135. While there are differences of emphasis, a fellow feminist in the philosophy of science, Sandra Harding, agrees that the debate between modernist objectivism and relativism is a "fruitless and depressing choice." See Sandra Harding, *Whose Science? Whose Knowledge? Thinking from Women's Lives* (Ithaca, N.Y.: Cornell University Press, 1991), 142.

17. See David Ray Griffin, *God and Religion in the Postmodern World: Essays in Postmodern Theology,* SUNY Series in Constructive Postmodern Thought (Albany: State University of New York Press, 1989), 8; Hans Küng, *Global Responsibility: In Search of a New World Ethic* (New York: Crossroad, 1991), 23–24; Thomas C. Oden, *After Modernity . . . What? Agenda for Theology* (Grand Rapids: Zondervan Publishing House, Academie Books, 1990), 77.

18. Plato, *The Dialogues of Plato,* vol. 7, *Phaedrus,* trans. Benjamin Jowett, Great Books of the Western World (Chicago: Encyclopaedia Britannica, 1952), 156.

19. Ibid., 124–25, 128.

ied" self who also seeks to be free of the body, emotions, and the world in order to be rational.[20]

A striking feature that emerges from citing both modern and ancient sources of these characteristics is that all the features we have identified characterize premodernity as well as modernity. This underscores the radicality of a postmodern shift. The entire Western theological Christian tradition has largely functioned within one broad cognitive paradigm, which is now being undermined. Every epoch has had its own novelty, of course, but we should not underestimate the challenge of thinking through the Christian faith in the context of an entirely new epistemological paradigm.

To increase the challenge, modernity added its own distinctive emphases to what it shares with premodernity. Modernity especially brought a new *turn to the subject* that has been manifested as an *atomistic, autonomous individualism,* more and more concerned with this world rather than with the world beyond and increasingly preoccupied with its own self-fulfillment, if not with hedonistic pleasure.[21] Again, Descartes's consideration of the self as an ego that might be stripped of God, its world, and its body captured an important new feature of modernity.

Another significant aspect of modernity exemplified in Descartes's tortured doubting was also to *strip the self of tradition* and to start all over for oneself. Whereas the medieval world had placed authority in tradition, modernity placed it in reason and has been antagonistic to tradition. It was not the views of faith and reason that changed so much as their estimation.[22] As Jeffrey Stout depicts it:

> The unifying historical theme is this: that modern thought was born in a crisis of authority, took shape in flight from authority, and aspired from the start to autonomy from all traditional influence whatsoever; that the quest for autonomy was also an attempt to deny the historical reality of

20. This phrase comes from Seyla Benhabib, *Situating the Self: Gender, Community, and Postmodernism in Contemporary Ethics* (New York: Routledge, 1992), 152. See also Susan Bordo, *The Flight to Objectivity: Essays on Cartesianism and Culture,* SUNY Series in Philosophy, ed. Robert C. Neville (Albany: State University of New York Press, 1987); and Robin May Schott, *Cognition and Eros: A Critique of the Kantian Paradigm* (University Park, Pa.: Pennsylvania State University Press, 1993).

21. For this point, especially see Oden, *After Modernity.*

22. Nicholas Wolterstorff, "The Migration of the Theistic Arguments: From Natural Theology to Evidentialist Apologetics," in *Rationality, Religious Belief, and Moral Commitment: New Essays in the Philosophy of Religion,* ed. Robert Audi and William J. Wainwright (Ithaca, N.Y.: Cornell University Press, 1986), 38–81.

having been influenced by tradition; and that this quest therefore could not but fail.[23]

Empiricists tended to reduce the self even further. They viewed experience as composed of atomistic experiences that finally, in the skepticism of David Hume, undermined even Descartes's assumption of a substantial thinking self. The political self in the liberal tradition is also often seen as an isolated individual who then must, grudgingly, accede to some constraints in order to live together with others.[24] As Alasdair MacIntyre points out, "The self thus conceived, utterly distinct on the one hand from its social embodiments and lacking on the other any rational history of its own, may seem to have a certain abstract and ghostly character."[25] Liberal economic theory then takes up these abstract individuals who act in their self-interest as the basis of economic theory, seeing the sum total of these individual atoms functioning as an invisible hand guiding the economy. Such radical individualism runs deep in the currents of modernity.

Postmodernists do not reject all aspects of the modern turn to the self; for example, pleasure is perhaps the chief value enunciated by Michel Foucault.[26] They do reject the atomistic self, however, in favor of a socially constructed and connected self. They usually also see the self holistically and as essentially embodied. Knowledge is not set over against the passions and external influence but is integrally immersed in the body and in the world. This may be seen negatively, as a self essentially dominated by larger power structures; Foucault famously proclaimed the death of the self.[27] Or it may be seen positively, as an intersubjective self enabled by tradition and empowered by bodily knowledge.

Characteristics of Postmodernity

The consistent rejection by postmodernists of the modern features just described is remarkable in any broad-based movement. Finding such unanimity in their constructive alternatives is much more difficult. Neverthe-

23. Jeffrey Stout, *The Flight from Authority: Religion, Morality, and the Quest for Autonomy* (Notre Dame, Ind.: University of Notre Dame Press, 1981), 2–3.

24. See, for example, Benhabib, *Situating the Self,* 149–58; and Bordo, *Flight to Objectivity.*

25. Alasdair C. MacIntyre, *After Virtue: A Study in Moral Theory,* 2d ed. (Notre Dame, Ind.: University of Notre Dame Press, 1984), 33.

26. This applies more to his later thought. For example, see the biography by James Miller, *The Passion of Michel Foucault* (New York: Simon & Schuster, 1993), chaps. 7–8; see also Foucault's multivolume work *The History of Sexuality,* trans. Robert Hurley, ed. James Miller (New York: Vintage Books, 1978–86).

27. Michel Foucault, *The Order of Things: An Archaeology of the Human Sciences* (New York: Vintage Books, 1973), 386–87.

less, what they reject implies something about what they would accept. A *nonfoundationalist epistemology,* attempting to avoid both objectivism and relativism and rejecting rigid requirements of certainty and clarity, is not totally amorphous. When these philosophies also turn away from intellectual dualism and individualism in order to make way for a *more embodied and holistic conception of the self in the world,* the outlines of a new paradigm begin to emerge. In some cases, the features have been fleshed out in some detail.

Jerry Gill points out that a different paradigm can be seen in three areas: experience, knowledge, and language.[28] Rather than experience being seen as primarily rational and dualistic, it is seen, as just mentioned, as integrally embodied and social. Experience also is not so atomistic and passive as empiricists suggest but arises when the active, embodied subject engages the world with all of the senses. The world, however, is not experienced initially as bits of raw sense data but in terms of meaningful wholes. We experience a tree, for example, not patches of color and sensations of smell that we only later construct into a whole. Meaning comes with the experience, not as an "add-on."

Similarly, with regard to knowledge, most postmodern perspectives can be described as advocating *epistemological holism,* where words and propositions do not stand in atomistic discontinuity from the larger stream of life or "form of life" in which they are embedded.[29] This emphasis on the way in which concepts are embedded in practices and tradition can be traced to the later Wittgenstein, to the "intertextuality" of the poststructuralists, and to Gadamer's "historical-effective consciousness." The Yale postliberal theology appropriates themes both from the later Wittgenstein and from the cultural anthropologist Clifford Geertz to stress the need for a "thick description" of a form of life; that is, a particular faith or theology or confessional stance is rooted in a rich backdrop of practices, history, and language that together constitute it.[30] Willard Quine refers to this epistemological structure as a web of belief rather than a foundation. In

28. Jerry Gill, *On Knowing God: New Directions for the Future of Theology* (Philadelphia: Westminster Press, 1981).

29. See Hubert L. Dreyfus, "Holism and Hermeneutics," in *Hermeneutics and Praxis,* ed. Robert Hollinger (Notre Dame, Ind.: University of Notre Dame Press, 1985), 227–47. The reference to the idea of concepts being embedded in the stream of life or form of life can be seen in Ludwig Wittgenstein, *Philosophical Investigations,* trans. G. E. M. Anscombe, 3d ed. (New York: Macmillan Co., 1958), ¶19, 23, 241.

30. See Clifford Geertz, *The Interpretation of Cultures: Selected Essays* (New York: Basic Books, 1973), 3–30. For the connection to the church, see Hans W. Frei, "An Afterword: Eberhard Busch's Biography of Karl Barth," in *Karl Barth in Review: Posthumous Works Reviewed and Assessed,* ed. H. Martin Rumscheidt (Pittsburgh: Pickwick Press, 1981), 111–12.

this sense, bundles of beliefs are tested all at once. No absolute distinction can be made between facts at the "edges" and the theories at the "center." To doubt one thing, others must be held fast; nothing is demonstrable in any strict sense.[31] In fact, in this perspective, beliefs are always underdetermined by the evidence, and the evidence is always in part shaped by the questions and assumptions brought to it. This shift has been called the *interpretive or hermeneutical turn*, meaning that all knowledge is rooted in hermeneutical acts of judgment that cannot conclusively be proven or demonstrated.[32]

The striking preoccupation with language of the postmoderns, all of whom have made the *linguistic turn,* ties in here. The realization that knowledge is always mediated through language opens up several new aspects of epistemology. One shift is to understand speech as itself a certain kind of act with several facets. Generally, philosophers have committed, in John Austin's term, the *descriptive fallacy,* taking language primarily as referring.[33] Actually, however, people do many other things with words besides describing, or even in describing. Another major shift is that philosophers have turned their attention to the way in which figurative language, such as metaphor and narrative, is not merely ornamental to language but is fundamentally cognitive. In fact, in some cases understanding is primarily conveyed through analogical language and need not be reduced to univocal language.[34] Lyotard argues that *all* understanding is embedded in narratives but that the characteristic of postmodernism is "incredulity towards metanarratives."[35] Instead, he appeals to the "little narrative" (*petit recit*).[36]

With the three areas delineated by Gill in mind—experience, knowledge, and language—argumentation looks very different from the requirement of proof in modernity. Since hard-and-fast foundations are not available, *argumentation proceeds in a dialogical manner.* One must determine, as with Aristotle's "practical wisdom" (*phronesis*), in each and every

31. W. V. O. Quine and J. S. Ullian, *The Web of Belief* (New York: Random House, 1970).

32. David R. Hiley, James F. Bohman, and Richard Shusterman, eds., *The Interpretive Turn: Philosophy, Science, Culture* (Ithaca, N.Y.: Cornell University Press, 1991).

33. John L. Austin, *How to Do Things with Words,* ed. J. O. Urmson and Marina Sbisà, 2d ed. (Cambridge, Mass.: Harvard University Press, 1975), 1.

34. A succinct account of how univocal language has been preferred as cognitive versus metaphorical language is in Mark Johnson's introductory essay to a book he edited: Mark Johnson, "Introduction: Metaphor in the Philosophical Tradition," in *Philosophical Perspectives on Metaphor,* ed. Mark Johnson (Minneapolis: University of Minnesota Press, 1981), 3–47.

35. Jean-François Lyotard, *The Postmodern Condition: A Report on Knowledge,* trans. Geoff Bennington and Frian Massumi, Theory and History of Literature 10 (Minneapolis: University of Minnesota Press, 1984), xxiv.

36. Ibid., 60.

case what will or will not bring conviction. As Richard Rorty suggests, a postmodern approach is more like building causeways between islands than like attempting to bring everyone to the same island. He adds that we do not need a skyhook that would raise us above human history so much as toeholds within history.[37] Similarly, Jeffrey Stout appropriates the idea of *bricolage* as a model, where a handyperson makes do with whatever is available.[38] Basil Mitchell indicates that argument in this context is less like the links of a chain than like the legs of a chair, as a cumulative case.[39] The Yale postliberal thinkers thus speak of ad hoc apologetics, which means that points of contact may be found but cannot be specified ahead of time and may vary from case to case.[40] Stephen Toulmin refers to this approach to knowledge as being a return to the tradition of rhetoric in philosophy.[41]Knowledge, therefore, is always local and timely; it is never absolutely certain but always has warrant and backing. Consensus is worked out by dialogue and conversation, not by knockdown arguments.

Such knowledge may seem too uncertain and too imprecise, but the argument of a Wittgenstein, for example, is that it is an illusion to think we can do better. Such knowledge is nevertheless adequate, allowing for its own kind of practical certainty. Kevin Vanhoozer expresses the problem with modernism's tendency to slide into skepticism at the first sign of epistemological trouble: "Skepticism, insofar as it dissents from this [more chastened] view in its all-or-nothing insistence on knowledge, resembles an epistemological tantrum that refuses to accept the human condition."[42] Gill, appealing explicitly to the later Wittgenstein, terms this turn to practical certainty "the principle of sufficient precision."[43] Whereas postmodernists are often accused of relativism because they reject a "God's-eye point of view," they would maintain that argument and evidence are still important. It is not true that just anything goes. In fact, as neopragmatists such as Stout and Rorty would maintain, we get along quite well even though we have never managed to find the absolute foundation or surefire

37. Richard Rorty, *Objectivity, Relativism, and Truth,* Philosophical Papers 1 (Cambridge and New York: Cambridge University Press, 1991), 14, 38, 216, 221.

38. The idea is from Claude Lévi-Strauss. See Jeffrey Stout, *Ethics after Babel: The Languages of Morals and Their Discontents* (Boston: Beacon Press, 1988), 74–77, 218, 240, 292.

39. Basil Mitchell, *The Justification of Religious Beliefs* (Oxford and New York: Oxford University Press, 1981), chap. 3.

40. See William Werpehowski, "Ad Hoc Apologetics," *Journal of Religion* 66 (July 1986): 282–301; Ronald F. Thiemann, *Revelation and Theology: The Gospel as Narrated Promise* (Notre Dame, Ind.: University of Notre Dame Press, 1985), 74–75.

41. Stephen Toulmin, *Cosmopolis: The Hidden Agenda of Modernity* (New York: Free Press, 1990).

42. Kevin Vanhoozer, *Is There a Meaning in This Text? The Bible, the Reader, and the Morality of Literary Knowledge* (Grand Rapids: Zondervan Publishing House, 1998), 300.

43. Gill, *On Knowing God,* 83–86.

method that we supposedly must have in order truly to know.[44] They point us back to the rough-and-ready ways in which we already prove and disprove, and they contend that we have enough agreement in many cases to distinguish between what we will and will not accept. The large disagreements are not so much to be lamented as to be seen as sources of new insight and creative new directions.

I offer this account as a self-consciously interpretive reading of postmodernism, which I suppose is appropriate for a perspective affirming that everything is an interpretation. I maintain, however, that this rough picture of a *situated reason that nevertheless allows for argument and critique* is one that is well grounded in the texts of the major postmodern figures. Understanding postmodernism in this more positive way, rather than as a radically relativistic movement, means that it does not just challenge theology but also beckons it. It offers the possibility of a level playing field that may yet turn out to be more hospitable than modernity. In any case, any viable contemporary theology must include a substantial response to this postmodern shift.

What has happened, ironically, is that reason has moved closer to faith. The hermeneutical texture that has long been recognized in theology—involving multiple interpretations, personal judgment, conviction, passion, argument but not proof—is now seen from a postmodern perspective as characterizing knowledge in general. Instead of theology being marginalized and suspect as an intellectual discipline, it belongs in the game. Rather than retreating into a fideism that avoids defense and warrant, theology has an open door into the public forum that has nearly been closed during the modern period. At the same time, it is not an entry into the public forum in an objectivist, rationalistic mode. Theology is instead called upon to enter in all of its particularity and vulnerability. It engages the conflict of interpretations with the realization that others, too, have plausible points of view that cannot be easily dismissed. The challenge for theology is to find a way to affirm a balance, for which Ricoeur has striven, between conviction and critique.[45]

In general, Ricoeur's philosophical approach meshes with the postmodern change. The magnitude of the postmodern shift calls for rethinking many areas and doing so in a coherent way. One of the great

44. Stout, *Flight from Authority,* 162; Richard Rorty, *Consequences of Pragmatism: Essays, 1972–1980* (Minneapolis: University of Minnesota Press, 1982), 12–13.

45. See the title of a recent account of interviews with Ricoeur: Paul Ricoeur, *Critique and Conviction: Conversations with François Azouvi and Marc de Launay,* trans. Kathleen Blamey, European Perspectives: A Series in Social Thought and Cultural Criticism, ed. Lawrence D. Kritzman (New York: Columbia University Press, 1998).

advantages of looking to Ricoeur is that he has already wrestled deeply for many years with the issues of postmodernism and has emerged with a comprehensive philosophical view that is also deeply integrated with a religious perspective. In all three areas highlighted by Gill—experience, knowledge, and language—Ricoeur has developed an elaborate postmodern view.

Pluralism

Another major challenge to contemporary theology is the growing pluralism of the world, which also impacts dramatically on culture, religion, and theology. Hans Küng makes an oft-seen connection between pluralism and postmodernity in speaking of a world that is post-Eurocentric, postcolonial, postimperialist, postcapitalist, postsocialist, postpatriarchal, postideological, and postconfessional.[46] Economically, the world is becoming transnationalistic. It simultaneously faces great new sources of economic power and also instability from a multitude of directions, such as the Middle East, the Balkans, and Africa.

The increasing interconnectedness of the world presents an ambivalent picture. On the one hand, some lament that the world is becoming more and more one world because of increased communication and interactive influence. This looks like an increasing homogenization that appears suspiciously Western, even more specifically North American. This is especially apparent when the most popular restaurant in Moscow is a McDonald's.

On the other hand, this increased interaction intensifies exposure to differences. In many cases, the Other is not around the world, off in a distant place, but down the street and working at the next desk, perhaps performing one's surgery. The ruins of the cold war have certainly not led to a bare homogenization but to the proliferation of suppressed differences that have sometimes exploded in destructive ways. Missionary organizations increasingly focus on "people groups," who represent a multitude of dizzying differences that cross national boundaries. It may depend on one's perspective, but amid a world that is increasingly one world due to ease of travel and communication, exposure to difference has greatly increased.

Rebecca Chopp and Mark Lewis Taylor point out that in the United States, the traditional image of a "melting pot" has become tarnished, seen as a way of reducing other cultures to a particular, dominant WASP

46. Küng, *Global Responsibility*, 19–20. The book was completed in May 1990, just before the fall of the Berlin Wall and the crumbling of the Soviet empire, which simply underscores these movements.

culture. They argue that the United States looks more and more like a collage.[47] For example, in Texas, the fastest-growing and second largest state, the expectations are that Caucasians will soon become a minority. Of three hundred thousand new residents each year, one-half come from outside the United States.[48] In general, the growth of denominations is often due to influx of minorities rather than to expansion of the traditional base. It is generally recognized that the energy and strength of Christianity has left the First World and has become a dynamic force in the Two-thirds World countries. Major Western theologians such as Jürgen Moltmann now urge Western theologians to listen to and to learn from what used to be mission churches.[49]

Related to this pluralism of cultures is the increasing interaction between world religions. The imperialism of a Westernized Christianity that only speaks and does not listen is out of favor even among conservative bodies. The rise in phenomenology of religion in this century has helped theologians understand religions on their own terms before evaluation on Christian terms. As John Hick, probably more than any other, has insistently emphasized, Christians must come to grips with the value and impressiveness of other religions, as well as the fact that people tend to adopt the religion into which they were born.[50] As long as the others were far away on the mission field, we could avoid dealing with difficult theological questions, giving easy answers, for example, in terms of election. Now that the other religions are next door, so to speak, and may have representatives who exhibit spiritual virtues that we can see with our own eyes, the easy answers are gone along with the easy questions.

The implication for theology is that one can no longer write from a monolithic standpoint, nor can Western theologians assume a privileged position. In the past, the Eurocentric perspective was that white European males wrote theology, but women and minorities wrote theologies from a particular point of view: feminist, Latin American, African, Korean, and so on. This is no longer the case. With the help of the postmodern critique of a universal point of view and the liberation theologies, it is increasingly recognized that everyone writes from a point of view. Douglas John Hall,

47. Chopp and Taylor, *Reconstructing Christian Theology,* 4–5.

48. Jerald McBride, "The Church in the New Millennium," *Window* 2 (Fall 1999): 2.

49. Moltmann was urging this as long ago as 1975: see Jürgen Moltmann, *The Church in the Power of the Spirit,* trans. Margaret Kohl (New York: Harper & Row, 1977), xvi, 7–8.

50. Among numerous works, his most complete statement is John Hick, *An Interpretation of Religion: Human Responses to the Transcendent* (London: Macmillan Publishers, 1989), based on his Gifford Lectures in 1986–1987. For a concise statement, see John Hick, "The Theological Challenge of Religious Pluralism," in *Introduction to Christian Theology,* ed. Badham, 24–36.

for example, self-consciously writes a "North American theology" from the perspective of a white male in a particular socioeconomic class.[51] Any contemporary theology must address this challenge of pluralism.

The best theologies will not nostalgically seek to avoid and suppress pluralism; neither will they succumb to sectarian, privatistic spheres, with no attempt to communicate to others. Traditional theologies have suppressed their particularity, but it is possible to celebrate pluralism so much that one falls into the opposite ditch of privatism and fideism. Modern theology has oscillated between these poles, just as has modern philosophy. As Murphy has pointed out, the influence of Kant's dualism of spheres between knowledge and morality has often led to the privatization of religion.[52] In liberalism, religion often had to do with a private sphere of morality or experience; in neo-orthodoxy it was often a private sphere of faith, or *Heilsgeschichte*. The problem is that not only could religious groups not communicate with the wider world; they could not even communicate with one another. Some have observed a so-called Wittgensteinian fideism at work in religion as well as philosophy, where every group has its own language game or form of life that cannot be addressed from outside, leaving what seems to be an impenetrable communication barrier.[53] Such are the dilemmas bequeathed to theology by the modern period.

How can one present a gospel with universal implications from a particular perspective? With the categories of modernity, it was virtually impossible. In that paradigm, an idea of a situated universality, as Seyla Benhabib has now suggested, is like speaking of a square circle.[54] The alternatives were either universality or particularity. As we saw in speaking of postmodern epistemology, however, the most genuinely postmodern approaches strive to avoid the dilemma of objectivism and relativism. New resources are therefore available that have hardly been tapped in theology.

51. Douglas John Hall, *Confessing the Faith: Christian Theology in a North American Context* (Minneapolis: Fortress Press, 1996).

52. Nancey C. Murphy, *Theology in the Age of Scientific Reasoning*, Cornell Studies in the Philosophy of Religion (Ithaca, N.Y.: Cornell University Press, 1990), 13–14. She is drawing particularly on Stout, *Flight from Authority*, chap. 7. Stout appears to distinguish Barth from a Kantian response, but I would argue that Barth's sphere of faith reflects the Kantian distinction between spheres.

53. See Kai Nielson, "Wittgensteinian Fideism," *Philosophy* 42 (July 1967): 192–93. For critical discussion, see D. Z. Phillips, *Belief, Change, and Forms of Life* (Atlantic Highlands, N.J.: Humanities Press International, 1986), chap. 1; Dan R. Stiver, *The Philosophy of Religious Language: Sign, Symbol, and Story* (Cambridge: Blackwell, 1996), 69–72.

54. Benhabib, *Situating the Self*, 3. The language she uses is an "interactive universalism" that is "contextually sensitive." She later says, "Interactive universalism is the practice of situated criticism for a global community" (228).

One of Ricoeur's early influential works was titled *The Conflict of Interpretations*, where he addressed in a number of essays how, in many spheres, no universal adjudication procedure among different points of view can be found. He stressed that we must not underestimate or overestimate difference and offered indications of how to go forward. He continued that theme through the rest of his work, where the issues of sameness and difference, the one and the other, are central. To anticipate the kind of contribution Ricoeur can make, an adequate theology needs a nuanced approach to pluralism that does justice to it but does not despair over it. It also needs to capture the multiplex ways in which pluralism is manifested, for example, through different *forms,* such as metaphor and narrative, as well as in *content.*

Praxis

The third major challenge for theology in the contemporary period is doing justice to justice, that is, to practical issues of oppression and liberation. What an ironic problem this should be for a faith rooted in the Hebrew Bible, where over and over a major prophetic theme is social justice. Amos's vision illustrates this thread that runs through all the prophets (Amos 7:7–9). He saw Israel measured by a plumb line. His clarion appeal was "Let justice roll down like waters, and righteousness like an ever-flowing stream" (Amos 5:24). As Isaiah 58:6 put it:

> Is not this the fast that I choose: to loose the bonds of injustice, to undo the thongs of the yoke, to let the oppressed go free, and to break every yoke? Is it not to share your bread with the hungry, and bring the homeless poor into your house; when you see the naked, to cover them, and not to hide yourself from your own kin? Then your light shall break forth like the dawn, and your healing shall spring up quickly.

The fact is, though, that Western theology has been privatized, individualized, and internalized. What is worse, in the North American context, an unfortunate split developed between mainline churches that emphasize social issues and conservative churches that emphasize evangelism, as if these were oil and water. Perhaps we should say, "What God hath joined together, let no one put asunder." Of course, many social reasons exist for the split, and not all of them are attractive—for example, the sustained generational necessity of Southern churches having to separate private morality from social issues in order to protect the institutions of slavery and prejudice. Whatever the rationale in the past, theology strains to overcome such divisions and to address the issues of praxis and oppression.

The greatest impetus in this task has come from liberation theology, a persistent voice that cannot be ignored. A major characteristic of liberation theology is that it begins and is written from the bottom up rather than from the top down. It originated with the oppressed and is developed unapologetically from their particular point of view. This is true of the oppressed not only in general but in particular. Thus there are Latin American, African, Korean, black, feminist, womanist, and *mujerista* liberation theologies.[55] Any oppressed group, in fact, has its own theology. Does this mean it is only local, with no universal implications? This is the tension we have already mentioned. We are still finding our way on this point, but the challenge for theology is to find a way for both the universal and the local. At the least, we increasingly recognize that all theology is, in significant ways, particular and local. What liberation theologians have helped point out is that the traditional Western theologians were self-deluded in professing to speak for everyone. Instead, they were actually in many ways representing the interests of a white male privileged class. This does not mean that everything in their theology is false; but it does mean that it has no privileged standpoint over any other and was not nearly as universal as they thought. Theologies of the past are clearly seen as time bound, written in their epoch, such as the classical theologies of Augustine, Aquinas, Luther, Calvin, Wesley, Schleiermacher, Barth, and now contemporaries such as Gilkey, Moltmann, and McGrath. Every age and context asks its own questions and addresses its own issues from the perspective of the gospel. This we have learned from the liberation theologians. And is this so different from the way in which, in scripture itself, the gospel is told from many different vantage points and historical contexts?

What is hoped is that, from a particular perspective, claims can arise that have bearing on anyone and everyone. For example, many in the First World have heard the challenge of liberation theology and have found it compelling for their theologies. The common liberation theme of the preferential option for the poor is a biblical theme, as we saw in Amos, and can hardly be ignored in any theology. Certainly, no adequate First World theology can have implications of western or white superiority. Nor can it demean the basic equality of women, for example, by suggesting that they are not fully in the image of God. Of course, these implications in our own theologies are often subconscious and hidden, so the lessons learned usually come from other theologies. Liberation theologians have

55. A general account is Alfred T. Hennelly, *Liberation Theologies: Pursuit of Justice* (Mystic, Conn.: Twenty-third Publications, 1995).

emphasized how ideologies that have little to do with the gospel impact on theology in hidden and insidious ways. For example, liberation theology began as the Two-thirds World became more aware, after World War II, of how the prosperity of the First World occurred at their expense. Such ideology critique is something they can usually do more easily than First World theologians. It is also apparent that liberation theologians have been able to draw at times on the legacy of First World theologies. Such a dialogue, where each theology helps broaden the other, does not necessarily deny particularity but makes locality consistent with "universal intent."[56] The locality thus becomes the place where a theology is applied; its intent, however, can be consistency and complementarity with other theologies.

Further aspects of liberation theology have been given by Leonardo and Clodovis Boff, as they reflected after some years on the essentials of their Latin American liberation theology. One aspect is that liberation theology arises from the situation of the poor and is thus contextual. Second is that it is rooted in suffering and liberating praxis. Third is that theology is then reflection on action, which involves critical social analysis. It also involves hermeneutical reflection that invariably turns to liberation texts in scripture, such as the exodus, the prophets, the Gospels, and Revelation. Such reflection leads, fourth, to further praxis in a hermeneutical spiral.[57] The Boffs summarize:

> Liberation theology is far from being an inconclusive theology. It starts from action and leads to action, a journey wholly impregnated by and bound up with the atmosphere of faith. From analysis of the reality of the oppressed, it passes through the word of God to arrive finally at specific action. "Back to action" is a characteristic call of this theology. It seeks to be a militant, committed, and liberating theology.[58]

Liberation theology thus stands in sharp contrast to a more traditional theological methodology that understood itself to speak from a universal, noncontextual standpoint. This traditional approach began with the biblical text rather than with concrete life and derived a theology in logical and rational fashion. Only then did it, sometimes, turn to praxis in a

56. The language of having universal intent while speaking from a particular personal perspective is in Michael Polanyi, *Personal Knowledge: Towards a Post-Critical Philosophy*, 2d ed. (Chicago: University of Chicago Press, 1962), 37–145.

57. Leonardo Boff and Clodovis Boff, *Introducing Liberation Theology*, trans. Paul Burns (Maryknoll, N.Y.: Orbis Books, 1987). They do not number the steps as I did, spreading these stages out in chapters 1 and 3.

58. Ibid., 39.

deductive way, deriving application on the basis of the theology. It also tended to eschew narratives and metaphors in favor of univocal propositions. Often the derived theologies and creeds functioned, in fact, as the primary authorities, rather than scripture. Against this, liberation theology, as Gustavo Gutierrez has said, "stands theology on its head."[59]

Liberation theologians of the Two-thirds World are usually strongly biblically based, so the issue is not one of rejecting biblical authority for the authority of contemporary experience. Rather, the issue is how the role of scripture arises. They would say that, in their approach, the Bible is more closely engaged with their lives. Reading the whole of scripture from the viewpoint of the oppressed is what they call "a new way of reading the Bible: a hermeneutics of liberation."[60] In any case, besides their strong questioning of the attempt to speak universally, they challenge theologians radically to rethink the relation of theology and praxis, being very critical of the tendency to leave praxis to last, and sometimes off altogether.

North American feminist liberation theology does not speak so clearly from a position of minority or poverty.[61] Nonwhite feminist theologies do, however, such as womanist theology, from the perspective of black women, and *mujerista* theology, from the perspective of Hispanic women. But much feminist theology is First World theology.[62] Nevertheless, feminist theology in general shares many themes with other types of liberation theologies. Feminists point out that women's experiences have not been adequately represented, since traditional theology has largely been done by men. They highlight the significant roles of women in scripture and have seen warrant for a larger role for women's leadership in the contemporary church, pointing again to the significance of theology as written from a situation and a point of view. Feminist theology also focuses on praxis against an overemphasis on theory, which feminist theologians see as typically masculine. An example is this summary statement from one type of feminist theology: "Because Hispanic Women's Liberation Theology is praxis, it demands three very clear and concrete commitments: to *do*

59. Cited in Alfred T. Hennelly, ed., *Liberation Theology: A Documentary History* (Maryknoll, N.Y.: Orbis Books, 1990), 63–64.

60. Ibid., 32.

61. See, for two important texts, Rosemary Radford Ruether, *Sexism and God-Talk: Toward a Feminist Theology* (Boston: Beacon Press, 1983); and Elizabeth A. Johnson, *She Who Is: The Mystery of God in Feminist Theological Discourse* (New York: Crossroad, 1992).

62. For womanist theology, see Emilie M. Townes, "Womanist Theology: Dancing with Twisted Hip," in *Introduction to Christian Theology*, ed. Badham, 212–24. For *mujerista* theology, see Ada María Isasi-Díaz and Yolando Tarango, *Hispanic Women, Prophetic Voice in the Church: Toward a Hispanic Women's Liberation Theology* (San Francisco: Harper & Row, 1988).

theology; to do theology from a *specific* perspective; to do theology from a *specific* perspective *as a communal process*."[63]

Similarly, another major issue of praxis for theology stems as much from the First World as from the Two-thirds World, namely, ecological theology.[64] Increasingly, theologians have seen how existentialist and neo-orthodox theologies, which were so focused on humanity, did not represent a theology of creation. With the awareness that the world itself is oppressed, as it were, particularly by the consumption of the First World, liberation concerns are high. Besides the depletion of natural resources, Ted Peters mentions several ecological dangers: the greenhouse effect, deterioration of the ozone layer, deforestation, and toxic wastes.[65] Ecological theology points not only to the way in which the First World, in particular, damages the environment but also to how we all threaten the well-being of generations to come. The postmodern emphasis on holism and embodiment chimes in with ecological concern, recognizing that one can separate humans from their environment only at their peril.

Ricoeur will be especially pertinent at this point, since he sees theology as a second-order discipline to praxis and experience and regards application as integral to any thought. He also has a major emphasis on ideology critique, as well as, more recently, a developed political philosophy. Any theology adequate to the times needs these dimensions. This is not to say, though, that a philosophy provides and says everything necessary. We will see later, for example, how Ricoeur's ideas are enlarged with the help of dialogue with liberation theologians.

Ricoeur's Life and Work

In light of the present context, it may be easier to perceive the significance of a philosophical resource for theology such as Ricoeur's that already addresses many of the issues confronting theology. Ricoeur's hermeneutical philosophy thus potentially provides a *postmodern* philosophical resource for contemporary theology that is still relatively untapped. It is a direct response to the challenge of *pluralism,* and it is focused on the primacy of *praxis* and appropriation.

63. Isasi-Díaz and Tarango, *Hispanic Women,* 2.

64. Sallie McFague ties ecology in to feminist theology in Sallie McFague, *Models of God: Theology for an Ecological, Nuclear Age* (Philadelphia: Fortress Press, 1987).

65. Ted Peters, *God—The World's Future: Systematic Theology for a New Era,* 2d ed. (Minneapolis: Fortress Press, 2000), 383–86.

His overall philosophical project must be set within the context of his life. Consideration begins with the recognition that he has been hailed as one of the greatest living philosophers; certainly, he ranks as one of the premier philosophers of the twentieth century.[66] It is difficult to think of another major twentieth-century philosopher who has comparable breadth and depth.[67] As such, he offers a provocative face to theologians: Not only have aspects of his thought been appropriated by them, but he has contributed directly to biblical and religious studies.

Despite his continual forays into the religious realm, however, there are several reasons why Ricoeur's work is yet to be fully explored. As mentioned already, few, including Ricoeur himself, have been able to integrate the manifold subjects and dimensions of his thought. Theologians and biblical scholars usually latch onto piecemeal insights but neglect vast stretches of the rest of his thought. He has followed so many byways, or in his words, taken so many "detours," that, while they have been richly rewarding in their own right, they have exasperated efforts to attain a panoramic view—until recently. With his Gifford Lectures that culminated in *Oneself as Another* in 1992—the closest to a magnum opus of all of his works—along with new collections of religious essays, biographical material, and secondary material, it is now possible to envision a unitary and comprehensive philosophy. He has dialogued with virtually all the major movements of thought in the twentieth century, representing one of the few figures who has deeply integrated French and German philosophy with Anglo-American philosophy, then again integrating his philosophy with religious reflection. In the end, he has developed what is probably best called a *hermeneutical philosophy* that has also been considered a philosophy of the will and a philosophy of the imagination. His philosophical anthropology is at the heart of his thought, but the central model of the interpretation of texts not only illuminates his anthropology but enables him to extend his work in all directions.

In many ways, Ricoeur's life as well as his philosophy has a dialogical and hermeneutical flair. While, until recently, he has been quite reticent about his experiences, saying at one point that "no one is interested in my life," it is a tortuous tale, not without significance for one of the foremost

66. See, for example, Lewis Edwin Hahn, ed., *The Philosophy of Paul Ricoeur,* The Library of Living Philosophers 22 (Chicago: Open Court, 1995), esp. the preface.

67. In this respect, he is comparable to Alfred North Whitehead and Jürgen Habermas, surpassing even them with his range. Other great philosophers of the twentieth century, such as Ludwig Wittgenstein, Edmund Husserl, Martin Heidegger, Jacques Derrida, and W. V. O. Quine, have certainly been as significant but more focused and less constructive and comprehensive in their work.

theorists on narrative.[68] Born February 27, 1913, near Lyons, France, his mother died only months after giving him birth. He poignantly remarks on the significance of experiencing motherhood for the first time with his wife's mothering of their children.[69] He also relates the poignance of his father being missing in action in World War I only two years after Paul was born, and thus of not knowing of his father's fate for many years, until 1932.[70] Perhaps the richness of his narrative reflections on identity stems in part from early questions of identity sharpened by the circumstances of his childhood.

Ricoeur was raised by his grandparents, who encouraged his education. Ironically, although he was a brilliant student, he failed the philosophy section on his first try at qualifying for going to school in Paris. The probable reason was a misreading of the question, but it indicates an early ambivalence he had toward philosophy that caused him to shy away from it, due to its seeming tension with his deep Protestant faith. (He spoke of it as an "internecine war" between faith and reason.)[71] One of his teachers, Roland Dalbiez, then challenged him to tackle directly whatever he was afraid of—and the rest is history.[72] Ricoeur became a philosopher par excellence, but we will also see that he was always careful, perhaps too careful, to keep it at some distance from religious faith.

During 1934, while studying at the Sorbonne, Ricoeur experienced the death of his sister, with whom he had been very close. In Paris he also met with Gabriel Marcel, the great French existentialist philosopher, who would be one of Ricoeur's first significant philosophical mentors. Ricoeur joined some of Marcel's famous Friday-afternoon meetings, in which participants were instructed to describe an experience freshly, without resorting to other's views.[73] This painstaking attempt to describe experience afresh is the hallmark of the phenomenological method, a consistent feature of Ricoeur's thought. Ricoeur later saw this kind of training as a great source of his own original thinking. During the last half of the 1930s, Ricoeur began publishing articles on pacifism and Christian social justice. The ironic aftermath to this effort was the outbreak of World War II, for which Ricoeur was called up to serve in the French army.

68. Charles E. Reagan, *Paul Ricoeur: His Life and His Work* (Chicago: University of Chicago Press, 1996), 1. Two other important sources for these biographical remarks are Paul Ricoeur, "Intellectual Biography," trans. Kathleen Blamey, in *The Philosophy of Paul Ricoeur,* ed. Hahn, 3–53; Ricoeur, *Critique and Conviction.*

69. Ricoeur, *Critique and Conviction,* 4. He says, "The word 'mama' was a word pronounced by my children but never by me."

70. Ibid., 3.

71. Ricoeur, "Intellectual Biography," 6.

72. Ibid., 4; Reagan, *Paul Ricoeur,* 5.

73. Reagan, *Paul Ricoeur,* 17; Ricoeur, "Intellectual Biography," 6–7.

Two dramatic experiences happened to Ricoeur during the war. One was standing next to his close friend, his captain, who was killed by a sniper bullet to the head. Ricoeur realized that it could easily have been him—near the same place where his father had been killed by a sniper in the First World War. Ever after, he said, he had a strong sense of human mortality and of not taking life for granted—significant existentialist themes. The second major experience was being captured and becoming a prisoner of war for nearly five years. He was apprehended while his wife, Simone, whom he had married in 1935, was pregnant with their third child, so he did not get to see his daughter until she was almost five years old. Amazingly, Ricoeur and other professors in the camp began a "university," offering classes, largely from memory, and exams, which were later validated by the French educational system. It was also in the camp that he had a fateful and fortunate deepening encounter with the works of Edmund Husserl. Husserl was another major philosophical figure in Ricoeur's development, who, along with Marcel, was a founder of the phenomenological movement. The influence of these two thinkers led to Ricoeur's initial notoriety as an interpreter of Husserl and as a phenomenologist. While a prisoner, he began his translation of one of Husserl's major books, which he later published.[74] Each prisoner had the right to one book a month from the Swiss Red Cross, so during this time Ricoeur was also able to make a major study of the German existentialists Karl Jaspers and Martin Heidegger. Marcel wrote to Ricoeur in the camp, and Ricoeur and others took hours, he reported, to decipher his difficult handwriting. Ricoeur also began work on his own first major book, *Freedom and Nature*.[75]

Lest one think things were easy with all this productivity, one should note how the war ended for Ricoeur. After almost losing hope that they would ever get out, the prisoners learned of the Allied successes by means of a clandestine radio. At the end, they were ordered to make a several-hundred-mile walk to another camp, beginning in January 1945. Along the way, the German guards left Ricoeur and others to fend for themselves, saying that they would be shot or, perhaps worse, captured by the coming Russians. With shelling going on all around as they took refuge in

74. The book was Edmund Husserl, *Ideas: General Introduction to Pure Phenomenology* (1913), trans. W. R. Boyce Gibson (New York: Collier Books, 1962), originally *Ideen zu einer reinen phaenomenologie und phaenomenologischen Philosophie*. Ricoeur's translation was *Idées directrice pour une phénoménologie* (Paris: Éditions Gallimard, 1950).

75. Paul Ricoeur, *Freedom and Nature: The Voluntary and the Involuntary*, trans. Erazim Kohák, Northwestern University Studies in Phenomenology & Existential Philosophy (Evanston, Ill.: Northwestern University Press, 1966).

barns, at one point they made only about four miles in eleven days. Finally, after long days of train rides—one part of which took thirty hours in a cattle car to travel about eighteen miles—multiple stays, and repatriation, Ricoeur returned to Paris on May 9, 1945, to meet his wife, then the daughter he had never met and his other children.

After the war, Ricoeur and his family settled in the site of Le Chambon, which was famous for its pacifism and aid to Jews during the war. Ricoeur began teaching again and soon published works on Jaspers and Marcel. When Ricoeur went to teach at the University of Strasbourg in 1948, he started a Marcellian tradition of having intellectual discussions with students and friends on Sunday afternoons. The fruit of what his wife recalled as the happiest time of their lives were his commentary on Husserl and *Freedom and Nature*, both of which were his doctoral dissertations.

Freedom and Nature, published in 1950, was projected as the first volume of a three-volume philosophy of the will. The success of this and other publications led to Ricoeur's achieving an appointment to the Sorbonne in Paris in 1956. His lectures in the later 1950s and early 1960s were very popular, sometimes with more than a thousand students pouring into his classes. The second volume of his philosophy of the will came out in 1960 as two important books, *Fallible Man* and *The Symbolism of Evil.*[76] The former described humans as caught in numerous ways in the tension between the finite and the infinite, leading to fallibility but not necessarily to actual fault. The latter he dealt with in *The Symbolism of Evil*, representing his conclusion that phenomenology, which dealt with essences, could not handle the basically irrational act of evil. Evil, he thought, could be expressed only indirectly, through symbol and narrative. His follow-up study of Freud, in order to deal with the interpretation of symbols, was a major book from the perspective of hermeneutics rather than psychiatric analysis and also represented a linguistic turn that occupied Ricoeur for three decades.[77]

With his three books on the will, Ricoeur had become, in Charles Reagan's words, "one of the most famous and well-known professors in France."[78] Sometimes loudspeakers had to be set up for overflow crowds. Ricoeur had also become very vocal and active as an antiwar protester against the Algerian war, saying that he did not want to be silent like some

76. Paul Ricoeur, *Fallible Man,* trans. Charles Kelbley (Chicago: Henry Regnery, 1965); Paul Ricoeur, *The Symbolism of Evil,* trans. Emerson Buchanan, Religious Perspectives 17 (New York: Harper & Row, 1967).

77. Paul Ricoeur, *Freud and Philosophy: An Essay on Interpretation,* trans. Denis Savage, Terry Lectures (New Haven, Conn.: Yale University Press, 1970).

78. Reagan, *Paul Ricoeur,* 25.

of the German professors under Hitler. At one point he was arrested, and there were times when the Ricoeurs were afraid that every car going up their street might result in a bomb being thrown over their wall.[79] His courage and conviction consequently became widely admired.

In 1968 and 1969, however, he became embroiled in the student revolts in the experimental university of Nanterre, in the suburbs of Paris, where he had gone from the Sorbonne in 1967 to teach, ironically, as part of a movement to make reforms in favor of students. In 1968, Ricoeur was elected as dean of the Faculty of Letters. In 1969, as problems heated up, he was attacked by a student in the cafeteria with a trash-can lid; the student finally just sat it on Ricoeur's head. This was a profoundly humiliating experience that led to a two-week leave of absence for Ricoeur on doctor's orders.[80] In another experience, he was charged in the hall by a student on horseback, who was in the same commune as one of Ricoeur's sons; this student tried to "lance" him with a stick.[81] As a result of these difficult experiences, Ricoeur finally resigned.

Ricoeur then was somewhat lost in the French firmament for almost two decades, as he spent time negotiating the divide between Continental and Anglo-American philosophy. He spent much of each year teaching at the University of Chicago in the United States, possessing a chair as the successor to Paul Tillich. As a result, he is one of the few philosophers who has drunk deeply of both Continental and Anglo-American philosophy, and he manifests the heady mixture of this "conflict of interpretations," the title of the collection of his essays that first came out, ironically, in 1969.[82]

Around the same time that he became well known again in France, in the 1980s, tragedy struck. He lost a son to suicide in 1986, and to him he dedicated an important part of his prestigious Gifford Lectures. Although Ricoeur has indicated that he thinks few would be interested in his life, it is clear that he has experienced the depths of sadness and the heights of success, personally experiencing the vicissitudes of the twentieth century among the French, German, and Anglo-American worlds. This dialectical flavor, along with the fact that his life, in all its particularity, has a certain universality about it, representing the saga of the European twentieth century, would have fascinated Hegel, one of Ricoeur's favorite philosophers.

79. Ibid.

80. Ibid., 35.

81. Ibid., 58–59.

82. Paul Ricoeur, *The Conflict of Interpretations,* ed. Don Ihde, Northwestern University Studies in Phenomenology & Existential Philosophy (Evanston, Ill.: Northwestern University Press, 1974).

Ricoeur's professional writing has the same dialectical quality of crossing boundaries in search of a new and larger identity. An expert on phenomenology, with its focus on thought and consciousness, he moved it in the direction of including the will and the unconscious in *Freedom and Nature*. As I mentioned, he soon traveled beyond the direct description in phenomenology itself to experiences of tragedy and hope that he thought could be captured only in indirect and symbolic expression, in *The Symbolism of Evil* and *Freud and Philosophy*.

Throughout his life, he has reflected on religion while trying to keep these reflections and his personal faith distinct from his professional life.[83] A very influential collection of his essays on religion was published as *Essays on Biblical Interpretation* in 1980.[84] A similar seminal work in the field of biblical studies was an essay of over one hundred pages on the parables of Jesus, published in 1975.[85] Ricoeur continued his work on symbolic language with further works on the philosophy of metaphor and hermeneutics in the 1970s, incorporating the major French emphasis on structuralism at that time.[86] He followed his work on metaphor with a major trilogy in the early 1980s on narrative.[87] Along the way, he offered a significant work on ideology and utopia that represents a distinctive appropriation of the Marxist tradition, *Lectures on Ideology and Utopia*.[88]

At this point, it is no wonder that scholars found Ricoeur enormously helpful in sporadic ways but frustratingly difficult to grasp in general. Even he himself confessed at one point an inability to draw the various strands of his work together into a whole. In an introduction to the essays on biblical hermeneutics in 1980, he responded to an attempt to do so by Lewis Mudge:

> Lewis S. Mudge attempts to provide the reader with a coherent overview of my writings. It is precisely this attempt which requires my heartily felt thanks, because I am unable to draw such a sketch on my own, both because I am always drawn forward by a new problem to wrestle with and because,

83. Paul Ricoeur, *Oneself as Another*, trans. Kathleen Blamey (Chicago: University of Chicago Press, 1992), 23–25. We explore in the final chapter how this effort by Ricoeur would not wholly succeed.

84. Paul Ricoeur, *Essays on Biblical Interpretation*, trans. Robert Sweeney, ed. Lewis S. Mudge (Philadelphia: Fortress Press, 1980).

85. Paul Ricoeur, "Biblical Hermeneutics," *Semeia* 4 (1975): 27–138.

86. Paul Ricoeur, *The Rule of Metaphor: Multi-Disciplinary Studies of the Creation of Meaning in Language*, trans. Robert Czerny, Kathleen McLaughlin, and John Costello (Toronto: University of Toronto Press, 1977); see also an important collection of articles, Paul Ricoeur, *Hermeneutics and the Human Sciences*, ed. and trans. John B. Thompson (Cambridge: Cambridge University Press, 1981).

87. Paul Ricoeur, *Time and Narrative*, trans. Kathleen Blamey and David Pellauer, 3 vols. (Chicago: University of Chicago Press, 1984–1988).

88. Paul Ricoeur, *Lectures on Ideology and Utopia*, ed. George H. Taylor (New York: Columbia University Press, 1986).

> when I happen to look backward to my work, I am more struck by the discontinuities of my wanderings than by the cumulative character of my work.[89]

Ricoeur finally began to pull together this "cumulative character" of his work in his Gifford Lectures, delivered in 1986, which in their spoken but not their printed version included important essays on religion. The published version, without the religious essays, *Oneself as Another*, is the closest to a one-volume presentation of his thought yet available.[90] It returns to his early focus on a philosophy of the self and of action, seen in *Freedom and Nature*, but draws on deepened reflection on narrative and ethics. He has followed up that work with a major treatment of political philosophy, titled *The Just*.[91]

Some of the religious ideas in the Gifford Lectures have now been published, along with some of the first biographical materials.[92] Taken together with continuing secondary works, such as the Library of Living Philosophers volume on Ricoeur, it is now perhaps possible for the first time to see his work as a unitary whole, involving a full range of issues such as philosophy of the self, epistemology, hermeneutics, ethics, political philosophy, and philosophy of religion.[93] All of these together imply a full metaphysical view of reality, chastened, however, by the humbler status of philosophy in a postmodern age, which Ricoeur himself emphasizes.

There are therefore several reasons that make Ricoeur an intriguing contemporary resource for theology. First, he has already contributed significantly to the theological task by his own religious writings. Second, theologians and religious scholars have appropriated key aspects of his philosophical thought. Third, due in part to the incredible range of his philosophical reflection, the larger shape of his thought has previously been something of a mystery not only to theologians but also to philosophers, with the result being a piecemeal appropriation that leaves much untouched and unintegrated. Fourth, until recently the biographical backdrop to his work has been largely unknown, but it is clearly pertinent and revealing. Fifth, and finally, the central metaphor of his philosophy is the

89. Paul Ricoeur, "Reply to Lewis S. Mudge," in *Essays on Biblical Interpretation,* 41.

90. Ricoeur, *Oneself as Another.*

91. Paul Ricoeur, *The Just* (Chicago: University of Chicago Press, 2000).

92. Paul Ricoeur, *Figuring the Sacred: Religion, Narrative, and Imagination,* trans. David Pellauer, ed. Mark I. Wallace (Minneapolis: Fortress Press, 1995). In addition to Reagan's *Paul Ricoeur,* see Ricoeur, Azouvi, and de Launay, *Critique and Conviction.*

93. See Hahn, ed., *Philosophy of Paul Ricoeur.*

interpretation of rich texts, offering notable affinity with theologians, whose focus is the interpretation of sacred scripture.

An apt comparison with another approach is with George Lindbeck's *The Nature of Doctrine,* which is one of the most influential theological works of the last two decades of the twentieth century.[94] Lindbeck drew particularly on the thought of the later Ludwig Wittgenstein and the social anthropologist Clifford Geertz in order to propose a significant new paradigm for theology. Called variously "postliberal theology" and "the Yale school," it has been perhaps the liveliest "research program" in theology in the United States since its appearance.[95] It represents an attempt to do "theology after Wittgenstein," the title of the book by Fergus Kerr that prompted this work on Ricoeur.[96]

While Ricoeur's work was seen initially by Lindbeck as incompatible with his own approach, it is now clear that in several ways it offers some of the same advantages.[97] Ricoeur's thought is distinctly postmodern in pointing away from a pristine, universal source of theology apart from interpretation and interpretive communities, and in emphasizing the significance of the scriptural world over against its eclipse in the context of modernity.[98] As is well known, Lindbeck did not envisage philosophy or other disciplines as foundations for theology, but he occasionally drew on them in an ad hoc fashion, as a rich resource. Similarly, Ricoeur's approach does not see philosophy as the foundation or dictator to theology; it points to both philosophy and theology as secondary to the fundamental experiences and texts of faith.

Moreover, Ricoeur's model offers several distinct advantages to Lindbeck's. While doing justice to the centrality and authority of scripture, it provides a more coherent and workable model that acknowledges the role of the horizon of the interpreter, as well as a more realistic (as opposed to Lindbeck's idealistic) view of the plurality of the Christian communities.

94. George Lindbeck, *The Nature of Doctrine: Religion and Theology in a Postliberal Age* (Philadelphia: Westminster Press, 1984).

95. The phrase "research program" is taken especially from Nancey Murphy's appropriation of it from the philosopher of science Imre Lakatos. She develops the idea in several works, but a prime example is Murphy, *Theology in the Age of Scientific Reasoning.*

96. Fergus Kerr, *Theology after Wittgenstein* (Oxford: Basil Blackwell, 1986).

97. See, for example, Placher, *Unapologetic Theology,* chap. 5; William Placher, "Paul Ricoeur and Postliberal Theology: A Conflict of Interpretations," *Modern Theology* 4 (1987), 35–52. Two other works that bring them closer together are Wallace, *Second Naiveté*; and Charles J. Scalise, *Hermeneutics as Theological Prolegomena: A Canonical Approach,* Studies in American Biblical Hermeneutics 8 (Macon, Ga.: Mercer University Press, 1994).

98. This language comes from the seminal work by Hans W. Frei, *The Eclipse of Biblical Narrative: A Study in Eighteenth and Nineteenth Century Hermeneutics* (New Haven, Conn.: Yale University Press, 1974).

It develops a clearer role for critique while allowing for a postcritical naïveté. It has a more robust view of truth and reference that avoids the reputed fideism of Lindbeck's approach while also rejecting modern foundationalism. In addition, Ricoeur has elaborated a much more extensive analysis of hermeneutical issues, relating them to interpretation of the Bible, to general epistemology, and to current issues relating to the self and ethics. As we have seen, Ricoeur has major works on biblical interpretation, on hermeneutics in Freud, on metaphor, on narrative, on the self, and on ideology critique—all of which supply a rich panoply of resources for theological reflection. Ricoeur also deals in a much more wide-ranging way than Lindbeck with the issues of the conflict of interpretation, ideology critique, and pluralism.

This is not to say that Ricoeur's work rules out the contributions of Wittgenstein to the Yale school or contributions of other postmodern philosophies. In postmodern fashion, theology does not look to any one foundational support. What is interesting is the fact that Ricoeur's work has great promise for theology but is still largely unexplored. Even in terms of his own thought, we saw how only with the aid of more recent publications is it possible to integrate his work adequately. Given the complexity of his thought, it is also true that any appropriation will be a distinct and creative interpretation, thus allowing for various directions in interpretation. What this study offers, therefore, is a particular integration of Ricoeur's work that, in turn, provides a distinctive postmodern resource for theological reflection.

We begin in chapter 1 by taking a closer look at the broad background to the hermeneutical direction of Ricoeur's thought. Chapter 1 particularly points to the tradition of hermeneutical philosophy in general in drawing out the central significance of the paradigm of the text. The second chapter develops this hermeneutical focus further in elaborating Ricoeur's threefold hermeneutical arc and in dealing with the challenge of connecting it with his later threefold narrative arc. The third chapter treats a number of Ricoeur's distinctive hermeneutical issues, such as the surplus of meaning and the distancing of writers from their texts. Chapter 4 turns to Ricoeur's specific development of a philosophy of metaphor and of narrative. The fifth chapter deals with the issue of the conflict of interpretation, developing it with reference to Ricoeur's "hermeneutic of suspicion" and his dialogue with the tradition of ideology critique.

The last two chapters and the conclusion focus on the significance of Ricoeur's hermeneutically based philosophy for different major aspects of philosophy and theology. Chapter 6 explicates his anthropology and chapter 7 his epistemology. In each case, a number of critical issues in Ricoeur's own work and in other approaches are treated. Finally, the implications of his work for the work of the theologian "after Ricoeur" are spelled out in the conclusion. Along the way, I relate Ricoeur's ideas to theological concerns, but the conclusion summarizes and develops major areas of connection, among them being the relationship of faith and reason and then of philosophy and theology in general. By that time, it should be clear what promise Ricoeur's work holds for theology, and also in what particular ways I have shaped it. In other words, in accord with Ricoeur's hermeneutics, my presentation of his philosophy is one among several possible interpretations and appropriations. What I hope to show is that this interpretation makes Ricoeur's thought available in a new and fruitful way.

CHAPTER ONE

The Paradigm of the Text

A striking affinity between hermeneutical philosophy and Christian theology lies in the preoccupation of both disciplines with texts. Scripture is the hermeneutical center around which Christian theology revolves. For hermeneutical philosophy, the experience of reading a text also provides the central heuristic focus. Ricoeur, for example, says, "For us, the world is the ensemble of references opened up by the texts."[1] Even beyond this, in his philosophical approach the dynamic of interpretation or hermeneutics becomes the paradigm for all understanding. Human beings are understood, then, as hermeneutical beings. Our way of being-in-the-world is seen as irreducibly hermeneutical.

At the outset, therefore, one might suspect fruitful dialogue between Christian theology and hermeneutical philosophy. The stimulus of this work, and of this chapter in particular, is that cross-fertilization between theology and hermeneutical philosophy goes a step beyond a few significant insights to deep structural support.

An advantage for hermeneutical philosophy in beginning with such a common experience as intepreting a text is that it provides an experiential foothold for exploring issues that continue to perplex philosophers, such as the nature of the self, of knowledge, and of reality. Because these issues are complex and because philosophical reflection tends to encumber them with yet more complexity, it is invaluable to have firm footing at the outset. As hermeneutical philosophy has developed, it has spun out a distinctive perspective from that central metaphor that is surprisingly postmodern—surprising because hermeneutical philosophy, as indicated in the introduction, has been long in the making, emerging before

1. Paul Ricoeur, "The Model of the Text: Meaningful Action Considered as a Text," in *Hermeneutics and the Human Sciences: Essays on Language, Action, and Interpretation*, ed. John B. Thompson (Cambridge: Cambridge University Press, 1981), 202.

postmodernity hit the scene. I begin in this chapter to unpack some of those striking implications that will be the basis of elaboration in further chapters.

In sketching out the historical development of hermeneutical philosophy, I take my cue from Ricoeur in seeing a movement from regional hermeneutics to general hermeneutics to ontological hermeneutics, culminating in the work of Hans-Georg Gadamer and Ricoeur.[2] In the process, I indicate prominent themes relating to the model of the text that are significant for theology.

From Regional to General Hermeneutics

Until the modern period, as Ricoeur notes, hermeneutical practice was regionalized, that is, shaped by particular types of literature. The interpretation of scripture, of course, was the focal center in the medieval and Reformation periods. The practice of law and the interpretation of classical literature, growing out of the Renaissance, were also important.

While other methods of interpretation were sometimes applied to scripture, such as Calvin's drawing on humanistic learning,[3] by and large the Bible was seen as a special case. The view of its divine inspiration precluded its being interpreted along the same lines as other literature. Since God was seen as inspiring the whole of the Bible, somewhat unique hermeneutical principles developed rather early. One was to interpret scripture by scripture. Another such canonical principle was to interpret the obscure by the clear.[4] Such canonical strategies often meant interpreting a work from one author in light of a completely different one, separated by centuries, context, and even genre and purpose. This interrelating of texts is a quite different process from interpreting, for example, a Greek drama by one author. An early principle that was devised to deal with this canonical complexity was to interpret scripture, especially allegorizing methods, by "the rule of faith." This referred to the distilled nature of the gospel, enshrined in creeds and oral tradition, especially rooted in the bishops of the major Christian centers of Rome, Constantinople, Jerusalem, and Alexandria. This ecclesial approach, with its canonical

2. I am especially following Ricoeur, *Hermeneutics and the Human Sciences,* 43–62.

3. For example, see Timothy George, *Theology of the Reformers* (Nashville: Broadman Press, 1988), 170–71.

4. Karlfried Froehlich, ed. and trans., *Biblical Interpretation in the Early Church: Sources of Early Christian Thought* (Philadelphia: Fortress Press, 1984).

emphasis and utilization of an external standard, had little parallel in the interpretation of classical literature, further intimating that hermeneutics was regionalized and did not allow for a general theory.

Friedrich Schleiermacher, who is commonly known as the father of modern theology, could also be considered the father of modern hermeneutics. He desired to move in the direction of a general theory of interpretation.[5] As a classical scholar and a Christian theologian, he is largely responsible for the shift from regional hermeneutics to general hermeneutics. By emphasizing that scripture should be interpreted like any other text, he looked for principles of interpretation that any kind of interpretation shared. For example, a principle that Schleiermacher enunciated was the hermeneutical circle, that is, one interprets the whole in terms of the parts and the parts in terms of the whole. He related it not to the canon as a whole, however, but to individual books, the way one would apply it to texts in general.

Schleiermacher is especially known for his emphasis in hermeneutics on "the whole internal process of an author's way of combining thoughts" in order to ascertain meaning, which is a view largely rejected by later hermeneutical philosophers.[6] This aspect of his approach was related to the emphasis on genius in the Romantic movement and thus to re-creating the creative act in interpretation. Schleiermacher's approach, however, was more complex. He actually posited a twofold act of interpretation that utilized interpretation of the text in order to understand authorial intent, involving a "grammatical" as well as a "divinatory" dimension. The grammatical side involved analysis of a text whereas the divinatory referred to the process of intuiting the mind of the author. While Gadamer and Ricoeur emphasize that the focus should be on the meaning of the text and not on re-creating the author's consciousness, they still draw on Schleiermacher's grammatical emphasis.[7]

5. A reason Schleiermacher is not always given as much credit in hermeneutics as in theology is that a full edition of Schleiermacher's notes on hermeneutics and an English translation of any of them were not available until midway through the twentieth century. See Friedrich D. E. Schleiermacher, *Hermeneutics: The Handwritten Manuscripts*, trans. James Duke and Jack Fortsman, American Academy of Religion Texts and Translation Series, ed. Heinz Kimmerle, vol. 1 (Atlanta: Scholars Press, 1986). Additionally, his views on hermeneutics were mediated largely through Wilhelm Dilthey's account, which does not do justice to the development and balance of his views. See Heinz Kimmerle, "Editor's Introduction," in Schleiermacher, *Hermeneutics,* 21–40. Cf. Ricoeur, *Hermeneutics and the Human Sciences*, 45–48.

6. Schleiermacher, *Hermeneutics*, 188.

7. As Ricoeur points out, Schleiermacher's earlier emphasis was not so psychological. He distinguished between the grammatical and the "technical" aspects. Later he emphasized more the psychological act of divining but still insisted that it be tested by comparison and contrast. See Ricoeur, *Hermeneutics and the Human Sciences*, 47.

Another important figure in the nineteenth century is Schleiermacher's biographer, Wilhelm Dilthey. Dilthey wanted to defend the intellectual respectability of the human sciences (*Geisteswissenschaften*), especially the developing discipline of history, over against the growing positivism of the natural sciences (*Naturwissenschaften*). In so doing, he made the fateful move of distinguishing the mode of knowing of each type of discipline. He saw that the natural sciences attempted to "explain" (*erklären*), which is an external, objective approach, whereas the human sciences attempted to "understand" (*verstehen*), which is an intersubjective, empathetic approach. In this way, he appropriated Schleiermacher's emphasis on divining the meaning of the author, although he attempted to find some external basis for this by seeing internal life as objectively expressed in symbols.

Despite these efforts to defend the scientific status of the human sciences, Dilthey was not successful. He intended to prevent the reductionist collapse of the humanities into the methods of the natural sciences but ended up in many ways contributing to their marginalization. With the growing hegemony of the natural sciences, his approach could be seen as an admission of defeat, in essence conceding that the human sciences could not live up to the rationality of the natural sciences. Theology in the modern period has constantly been faced with the similar dilemma of choosing between measuring up to the natural sciences or conceding its seeming irrationality and consequently lapsing into fideism. Dilthey's enormous influence unwittingly continued and contributed to this enervating dualism. One of Ricoeur's projects has been to overcome this gap.

From General to Ontological Hermeneutics

The young Martin Heidegger landed on the philosophical scene in the early twentieth century much as the young Karl Barth did on the theological scene—like a bombshell.[8] Gadamer and others describe seminars with Heidegger in almost mystical terms. In retrospect, while Heidegger is generally regarded as one of the most influential philosophers of the century, his work is qualified by being marked with incompleteness,

8. See the exclamation about Barth by Karl Adam: "[The second edition of his commentary on Romans] fell like a bomb on the playground of the theologians." Cited in David L. Mueller, *Karl Barth*, Makers of the Modern Theological Mind, ed. Bob E. Patterson (Waco, Tex.: Word Books, 1972), 23. For a sense of the impact of the young Heidegger, see Hans-Georg Gadamer, "Martin Heidegger and Marburg Theology (1964)," in *Philosophical Hermeneutics*, ed. David E. Linge (Berkeley: University of California Press, 1976), 198–212.

obscurity, and flirtation with the Nazi movement in the 1930s. His work, like that of his similarly influential contemporary, Ludwig Wittgenstein, has been more provocative than finished. For our purposes, he was the creative spirit who provided the impetus to hermeneutical philosophy.

For one thing, he was the designated heir to the original phenomenological movement begun by his mentor Edmund Husserl. Although Husserl kept revising his understanding of phenomenology, writing at least four different major "introductions," his work consistently focused on the intentional nature of perception and knowledge.[9] Generally speaking, Husserl envisaged phenomenology as the accurate and neutral description of the essence of our experience as it appears to us. In a fresh way, he attended to experience by bracketing "reality," or what might actually be the case, in order to capture conscious experience. This phenomenological "reduction," as he termed it, was supposed to allow a presuppositionless and certain account of experience. In applying his method of description in this way, he and his disciples, one of whom was Heidegger, made several discoveries. One was that they discerned the intentional nature of consciousness. Consciousness is not passive, as in the British empiricist tradition, but is active and directive. A second finding was the holistic nature of consciousness (similar to the emphasis of Gestalt psychology that was developing at the time), which they also opposed to the atomistic and reductionist approach of the dominant empiricist tradition. A third was the importance of background, or the horizon, as well as foreground. This opened the door to consider the role of history, tradition, and presuppositions in shaping the nature of what we experience.

In Husserl's idealist—and modern—temperament, he hoped that these careful descriptions of consciousness could provide the objective foundation for all the sciences and even that they could represent the most basic reality. At one point, he suggested, Cartesian-like, that the ego is the prime reality grounding all other reality, obviously running against the grain of the more positivistically and externally oriented natural sciences.

In carrying forward Husserl's phenomenological approach, Heidegger moved beyond the description of knowledge to the application of phenomenology to human existence, which is usually known by the German term he used, *Dasein.*[10] In the process, his conclusions, at least in Husserl's

9. For a concise account of Husserl and Heidegger, see Dan R. Stiver, "Edmund Husserl," in *Great Thinkers of the Western World*, ed. Ian P. McGreal (New York: HarperCollins, 1992), 424–27; Dan R. Stiver, "Martin Heidegger," in *Great Thinkers of the Western World*, ed. McGreal, 519–23.

10. Martin Heidegger, *Being and Time*, trans. John Macquarrie and Edward Robinson (New York: Harper & Row, 1962), 183, 193.

eyes, burst phenomenology apart.[11] From our later vantage point, we realize that Heidegger's interests were much more metaphysical than Husserl's at the outset; Heidegger was interested in Being, not beings.[12] Nevertheless, Heidegger's preparatory phenomenological work in *Being and Time*, which was hastily published under pressure and never finished, is surely one of the most creative and important philosophical works of the twentieth century. For our story, one of the major moves he made in this book was to see human beings or *Dasein* as irreducibly or ontologically "hermeneutical."[13] In this way, he shifted hermeneutics from being the theory of interpretation in general, à la Schleiermacher, to being the hermeneutical key, if you will, to understanding human beings. It was this provocative insight that Heidegger's student Gadamer took far beyond the suggestive ideas of Heidegger.

Heidegger rejected Husserl's idealism and the Cartesian legacy of modernity in arguing that human beings are inextricably beings-in-the-world who precede the subject-object split. Thus any idea of separating the human ego or mind from its body or the world is an impossibility.[14] He thus set aside the modern philosophical preoccupation with the attempt to put the two together, which had been the legacy of Descartes's division of mind and body into two entirely separate substances. In Heidegger's perspective, they cannot be pulled so far apart in the first place. He also challenged the empiricist tendency to see perception as the experience of atomistic bits of sense data that are later organized into wholes. Heidegger pointed out that such reductionism is an abstraction from what is actually our primordial experience of perceiving the world in terms of meaningful wholes. As he picturesquely makes the point:

11. Husserl's later work, *The Crisis of European Sciences*, made a similar move and has had enormous influence, for example, on Maurice Merleau-Ponty and Edward Schutz. There is controversy over influence. Was Husserl influenced by Heidegger, despite his protestations to the contrary, since *Being and Time* came several years before *Crisis?* See Edmund Husserl, *The Crisis of European Sciences and Transcendental Phenomenology: An Introduction to Transcendental Phenomenology*, trans. David Carr, Northwestern University Studies in Phenomenology and Existential Philosophy (Evanston, Ill.: Northwestern University Press, 1970).

12. For example, in *Being and Time* itself, which is focused on Dasein, he says, "An analytic of Dasein must remain our first requirement in the question of Being" (37), indicating that his monumental existential analysis of human being was nevertheless only a step along his way to his primary concern, Being (Heidegger, *Being and Time*).

13. See especially ibid., 188–95. Heidegger sees "understanding" as a structure, or *existentiale,* of *Dasein* (182), which is realized in (hermeneutical) "interpretation": "As understanding, Dasein projects its Being upon possibilities. . . . The projecting of the understanding has its own possibility—that of developing itself. This development of the understanding we call 'interpretation.' . . . In interpretation, understanding does not become something different. It becomes itself" (188).

14. Ibid., 86–87.

> What we "first" hear is never noises or complexes of sounds, but the creaking waggon, the motor-cycle. We hear the column on the march, the north wind, the woodpecker tapping, the fire crackling. It requires a very artificial and complicated frame of mind to "hear" a "pure noise."[15]

At the beginning, we interpret the world in terms of meanings. Only later, by abstraction, do we break it up into its parts. Maurice Merleau-Ponty expressed this point well in reaction to Jean-Paul Sartre's well-known statement "We are condemned to freedom" by observing, in contrast, "We are *condemned to meaning*."[16] We could also say, we are *condemned to interpretation.*

Husserl was never particularly interested in history, whereas Heidegger saw that part of our horizon is our temporal and historical horizon. This understanding spelled the doom of Husserl's hope of phenomenology being a rigorous science. We always experience the present influenced by our memories of the past and our projections into the future. We experience the world in terms of *retentions* and *protentions,* as part of our *intentions.* This drive to lay a cloak of meaning on the world at the outset means that we experience the world not directly but "as" something. These interpretive conclusions are fallible; they may or may not be corrected in light of further experience. This assumption is radically distinct from the empiricist assumption that our basic perceptions are incorrigible. Even for Husserl, the idea that we can bracket our presuppositions and their influence was thus ironically undermined by careful phenomenological description of knowing. As Merleau-Ponty comments, "The most important lesson which the reduction teaches us is the impossibility of a complete reduction."[17]

Further, we ourselves are a kind of project or story that is being written through time, and we are continually writing and revising that story in the light of experience. This is not a wholly conscious and intentional project, since we are initially "thrown" into existence, into a particular situation, and into a particular tradition. At the dawn of consciousness, we find ourselves already with a story and an interpretation.[18] Our conscious attempts

15. Ibid., 207. Maurice Merleau-Ponty takes up this aspect of Heidegger in light of the later work of Husserl most thoroughly in Maurice Merleau-Ponty, *Phenomenology of Perception*, trans. Colin Smith, International Library of Philosophy and Scientific Method (New York: Humanities Press, 1962).

16. Merleau-Ponty, *Phenomenology of Perception*, xix. The full sentence is: "Because we are in the world, we are *condemned to meaning*, and we cannot do or say anything without its acquiring a name in history."

17. Ibid., xiv.

18. Heidegger, *Being and Time*, 174, 219–24.

to interpret ourselves are not free creations but rewriting of a story that already contains many chapters. In so many ways, our experience is inherently and unavoidably hermeneutical. Gadamer summarizes Heidegger's achievement on this point:

> Heidegger's temporal analytics of Dasein has, I think, shown convincingly that understanding is not just one of the various possible behaviors of the subject but the mode of being of Dasein itself. It is in this sense that the term 'hermeneutics' has been used here.[19]

As the one often considered to be the father of twentieth-century existentialism, Heidegger sees this engagement with the world that we must continually interpret as one of "care."[20] Our primary experience is thus not the detached scientific or philosophical perspective but one of existential and practical engagement. This philosophical shift connects with the way philosophy of science has seen science's strict methodology as secondary to a more hermeneutical kind of knowing. Given the heavy emphasis of an idealized, impersonal scientific methodology upon theology, such a reorientation of epistemology is fraught with implications. This shift makes it possible for theology to avoid the tempting project of mimicking positivistic science. In turn, it allows one to affirm theological "knowing" as more self-involved and existential without thereby marginalizing it in relation to other kinds of knowing.

Heidegger soon made his controversial turn toward Being and largely left these ideas relatively undeveloped, but Gadamer more than anyone else took up the hermeneutical mantle from him. Gadamer steers the trajectory of hermeneutics from a regional emphasis to the ontological nature of the self and moves it toward a full-blown epistemology. Ricoeur is thus able to presume and build upon Gadamer's efforts.

Gadamer's Philosophical Hermeneutics

Gadamer and Ricoeur represent the intersection where hermeneutics and phenomenology meet. This intersection can be further specified as the point where hermeneutics that has become ontological meets a phenom-

19. Hans-Georg Gadamer, *Truth and Method,* trans. Joel Weinsheimer and Donald G. Marshall, rev. ed. (New York: Crossroad, 1991), xxx.
20. Heidegger, *Being and Time,* 225ff.

enology that has become hermeneutical.[21] The result is a substantial hermeneutical philosophy, which I hope to demonstrate in these pages.

As a classicist, whose works on Plato and Aristotle are of great significance in their own right, Gadamer was well-prepared to take up Heidegger's hermeneutical cues. He took the basic paradigm of interpreting a text and extended it into the "universality of hermeneutics," which is crucial for understanding Ricoeur.[22]

Truth in Art and History

In *Truth and Method,* Gadamer was keenly interested in defending the sense of truth in art and in history as fully defensible against the mania for objectivity in the sciences.[23] In this sense, he seemed to be furthering Dilthey's project. In the process, however, he completely undermined the Diltheyan distinction between two spheres of knowledge, as he explicitly stated in the foreword to the second edition.[24] Gadamer was reacting against the tendency to privatize and subjectivize the humanities in contrast to the hegemony of science in the arena of knowledge. Since the sciences are seen as the paradigm for knowing, and their approach is so obviously inadequate as a way of explaining art, art came to be seen as a matter of private taste, with no connection to reality. Gadamer traces the way in which Kant's aesthetic theory, which sees art as taste, played into the hands of this drive toward subjectivity.

Conversely, Gadamer also traces the tendency of the discipline of history, or historiography, to strive to live up to the model of the natural sciences, thus seeing a historical event as an objective instance of some general or "covering" law. In this light, Dilthey's insight into the human dimension of history and also the uniqueness of historical events becomes obscured, if not lost. Theology has played out both tendencies in its movements toward an incontestable subjectivity or a more public objectivity. It is therefore evident that an approach that can avoid the horns of this dilemma is of great significance for theology.

21. One might add that phenomenology passed through an existential phase on the way to hermeneutics. Ricoeur appropriated the classical and existential dimensions through Heidegger, Gabriel Marcel, Jean-Paul Sartre, and Merleau-Ponty.

22. For specific discussion of the universality of hermeneutics, see Hans-Georg Gadamer, "The Hermeneutical Universality of the Hermeneutical Problem," in *Philosophical Hermeneutics,* ed. David E. Linge (Berkeley: University of California Press, 1976), 3–17.

23. Gadamer, *Truth and Method,* Parts 1–2.

24. Ibid., xxix–xxx.

Practical Wisdom (*Phronesis*)

Against the oversubjectification of art and the overobjectification of history, Gadamer proposes a third way "beyond objectivism and relativism." He argues that art and historiography disclose reality, but in a way not reducible to the "methodism" of the sciences. In effect, he turns Aristotle on his head. Aristotle saw science and knowledge in the strict sense as certain and demonstrable. Anything that was changeable, such as ethics or politics, could, *ipso facto,* not count as knowledge in this strong sense. At the same time, he was realistic enough to see that politics and ethics are not simply subjective or reducible to universal laws. He suggested a practical wisdom, *phronesis,* that represents the critical judgment of a wise person to evaluate the good in a certain situation. Since every situation is different, no general rule or law could suffice to determine a specific moral decision. In other words, the law and the facts underdetermine a sound judgment without the aid of practical wisdom.[25]

Gadamer makes the dramatic proposal that knowledge in general is based on such "phronetic" judgments, which cannot be fully justified by a method, however rigorous. Neither are these judgments whimsical or capricious. They are "considered judgments" that are not necessarily convincing to everyone.

Initially, Gadamer was staking out turf for the human sciences, much like Dilthey, but he ended up arguing that even the natural sciences in their presuppositions and other kinds of judgment involve such practical wisdom. All knowledge is rooted in practical, phronetic judgment. The more exact sciences are exact only because they are pockets of knowledge artificially protected by holding fast certain assumptions that themselves can be considered suspect.[26]

As the philosophy of science has developed, from Michael Polanyi and Thomas Kuhn to Stephen Toulmin and Imre Lakatos, it has confirmed Gadamer's judgment. Ian Barbour, a major figure in relating science and religion, portrays a common understanding of how science and religion had been viewed:

25. Aristotle, *Nichomachean Ethics,* trans. W. D. Ross, in *The Works of Aristotle,* ed. Robert Maynard Hutchins, Great Books of the Western World 9 (Chicago: Encyclopaedia Britannica, 1952).

26. Jean-Francois Lyotard, *The Postmodern Condition: A Report on Knowledge,* trans. Geoff Bennington and Frian Massumi, Theory and History of Literature 10 (Minneapolis: University of Minneapolis Press, 1984), xxiv. "There are many different language games—a heterogeneity of elements. They only give rise to institutions in patches—local determinism."

> Science alone is objective, open-minded, universal, cumulative, and progressive. Religious traditions, by contrast, are said to be subjective, closed-minded, parochial, uncritical, and resistant to change. . . . historians and philosophers of science have questioned this idealized portrayal of science, but many scientists accept it and think it undermines the credibility of religious beliefs.[27]

Mary Hesse, a philosopher of science, points out that a major philosopher such as Jürgen Habermas could, in the 1960s, still indicate features of science in contrast to the humanities, as Barbour describes.[28] By the 1970s, such a change had occurred that Habermas's description of the humanities had come to fit the understanding of science by philosophers of science. As she observes:

> What is immediately striking about it [the column describing natural science] to readers versed in recent literature in philosophy of science is that almost every point about the human sciences has recently been made about the natural sciences, and that the . . . points made about the natural sciences presuppose a traditional empiricist view of natural science that is almost universally discredited.[29]

We are still adjusting to such a change in what we have regarded as the paradigm of knowledge, namely, the natural sciences. Gadamer's work from the perspective of a hermeneutical philosophy represents one of the first major portrayals of an alternative paradigm.

On another front, in the rationalist tradition, mathematics had long been privileged as the epitome of knowledge. Its exactitude and certainty were prized as the best examples of knowledge. Kurt Gödel's revolutionary mathematical proof in the twentieth century, however, showed that no system can ground itself or be complete in itself. Mathematics, too, must in terms of its assumptions rely on considered judgments that themselves cannot be conclusively demonstrated in order to proceed.[30] In the end, all knowledge is finally based on practical wisdom. As Gadamer intimated, this turns Aristotle topsy-turvy. The upshot is that highly precise and certain types of knowledge are parasitic upon judgments of practical wisdom, and not vice versa.

27. Ian G. Barbour, *Religion and Science: Historical and Contemporary Issues*, rev. ed. (San Francisco: HarperSanFrancisco, 1997), 78–79.

28. She refers to Jürgen Habermas, *Knowledge and Human Interest* (London: William Heinemann, 1968).

29. Mary Hesse, *Revolutions and Reconstructions in the Philosophy of Science* (Bloomington: Indiana University Press, 1980), 171–72.

30. For example, see John Polkinghorne, *Reason and Reality: The Relationship between Science and Reality* (Philadelphia: Trinity Press International, 1991), 6, 51.

This reversal is fundamentally what makes Gadamer a postmodern philosopher, since he rejects the certainty, clarity, and objectivity requisite for knowledge in the modern sense and calls for a paradigmatic change with regard to knowledge. Richard Bernstein as well as several others have identified Gadamer's philosophy particularly as one that transcends the poles of objectivism and relativism that constrain modernity.[31]

It is not difficult to see how such a shift represents a sea change with regard to theology. It is plain that practical wisdom (*phronesis*) is the type of knowledge characteristic of all theological judgment, and Gadamer has shown how such knowledge is neither subjective nor fideistic but at the center of any claim to knowledge. Rather than being marginalized or banned altogether, the types of claims that are common in theology are situated firmly in the province of knowledge. Theology in this sense is not the same as science; disciplines do differ. The difference, however, is relative and not absolute, as it tended to be viewed in modernity. Theology in effect moves from being an inherently private and sectarian activity to a public one, that is, if it is willing to enter the public arena. Theologians are only just now beginning to move about more freely, loosed from the cramped quarters of modernity. But currently there is more challenge than there is accomplishment. Gadamer points to the need for a radical reframing of traditional approaches to knowledge, in theology as well as in all other areas. The point, however, is that, in principle, no philosophical stumbling block looms ahead, as was the case in modernity.

The Phenomenology of Play

In developing an approach to truth not dependent on method, Gadamer made several important observations that characterize a hermeneutical epistemology. Here is where the fundamental experience of reading a text comes into play. It is a common experience in interpreting a text for people to differ in their interpretations; yet their views are not considered purely subjective. They can offer reasons and evidence—even the text itself—but they usually underdetermine the conclusions. Presuppositions from one's training and tradition are easily seen as contributing to the difference, but these do not necessarily preclude discussion. Gadamer teased out these dynamics in a fruitful way.

31. See Richard J. Bernstein, *Beyond Objectivism and Relativism: Science, Hermeneutics, and Praxis* (Philadelphia: University of Pennsylvania Press, 1985), part 3. Others are Susan J. Hekman, *Hermeneutics and the Sociology of Knowledge* (Notre Dame: University of Notre Dame Press, 1986); Georgia Warnke, *Gadamer: Hermeneutics, Tradition, and Reason* (Stanford, Calif.: Stanford University Press, 1987).

First, he saw that the interpretation of art is not something we can observe at a distance, as scientists until the late twentieth century have seen themselves as able to do with regard to the physical world. Rather, there is interaction between the text and the interpreter. Gadamer illuminated this point by a phenomenology of game playing.[32]

In a game, it is not so much that a player is consciously in control as that the player is caught up in the game. This does not preclude skillful performance. In fact, skill depends on being engaged in the game. Rather than us playing the game, Gadamer suggests, the game "plays" us.

The game thus transcends the players. In terms of the "hermeneutical game," this means that the "matter" (*Sache*) of the text is not something wholly within the interpreter's control.[33] We often are first seized or grasped by a text before we turn it into an object. Critical control always comes too late. This also means that the focus on authorial intent is misguided, since the game is larger than any one player. As Gadamer says, "Not just occasionally but always, the meaning of a text goes beyond its author. That is why understanding is not merely a reproductive but always a productive activity as well."[34]

A Fusion of Horizons

Gadamer emphasizes that interpretation is therefore always a creative rendering of the text. This involves his famous image of a "fusion of horizons."[35] Since, in understanding, we are always connecting our horizon of assumptions, culture, and traditions to the horizon of the text, it always involves a creative synthesis. "It is enough," Gadamer says, "to say that we understand in a different way, if we understand at all."[36] At this point, Gadamer shifts from the image of a game to the image of a theatrical performance.[37] Each performance is a new event, although it presents the meaning of the original. In terms of a philosophy of education, this means that learning is always active. Learning does not occur when the teacher has conveyed the material, nor when the learner can parrot the material, but only when the learner has been able to relate it to his or her own "horizon."

32. Gadamer, *Truth and Method*, 101–10.
33. Ibid., 267.
34. Ibid., 296.
35. Ibid., 306.
36. Ibid., 297.
37. Ibid., 110.

This does not mean, as it has sometimes been interpreted to mean, that we always come up with a hybrid, evenly matched between the ancient and the modern horizon.[38] Nor does it mean that the current horizon swamps the text's horizon.[39] Both of these approaches result in a substantial revision of the original meaning. To the contrary, the point is that the original meaning is accessible in no other way than through a fusion of horizons. Gadamer is making here a frontal assault on the traditional notion that we can first access what the text "meant," which involves exegesis, and later question what it "means," which is the task of hermeneutics.[40] Rather, access to the "meant" of the text involves creative interplay at the first moment with what it "means." Gadamer actually insists that the dimension of application, which is usually seen as added after the second stage of hermeneutics, is also already at work in the first stage of discerning the text.[41]

In a sense, Gadamer is saying that we cannot bracket ourselves from interpretation, only bringing in ourselves and our assumptions at a later stage. We come with all of our presuppositions at the beginning. The idea of presuppositionless understanding was the Enlightenment dream and continues to live on to some extent in the scientific method, namely, to remove the self so that knowledge can be objective and thus true. Gadamer provocatively terms this the Enlightenment "prejudice against prejudice itself."[42] Gadamer is not alone in perceiving the self-deception involved in such a claim to objectivity. Alasdair MacIntyre argued that the

38. This seems to be Hans Frei's understanding of Gadamer, which appears to be the result of assimilating Gadamer to David Tracy's notion of a "revisionist theology." See Hans W. Frei, "The 'Literal Reading' of Biblical Narrative in the Christian Tradition: Does It Stretch or Will It Break?" in *The Bible and the Narrative Tradition,* ed. Frank McConnell (New York: Oxford University Press, 1986), 60.

39. This is especially a common opinion of Gadamer among evangelicals. For example, see Walter C. Kaiser and Moses J. Silva, *An Introduction to Biblical Hermeneutics: The Search for Meaning* (Grand Rapids: Zodervan Publishing House, 1988), 29, 33; John P. Newport, "Contemporary Philosophical, Literary, and Sociological Hermeneutics," in *Biblical Hermeneutics: A Comprehensive Guide to Interpreting Scripture,* ed. Bruce Corley, Steve Lemke, and Grant Lovejoy (Nashville, Broadman and Holman, 1996), 138, 142; Grant Osborne, *The Hermeneutical Spiral: A Comprehensive Introduction to Biblical Interpretation* (Downers Grove, Ill.: InterVarsity Press, 1991), 371. Evangelicals appear to be heavily influenced by the notable but misguided criticism of Gadamer by E. D. Hirsch Jr. Hirsch criticizes Gadamer for having the position of radical historicism, which does not allow the interpreter to escape the current horizon, and the position of textual indeterminacy, which may be true of Jacques Derrida but not of Gadamer. The irony is that Gadamer goes to some lengths to reject both of these positions. See E. D. Hirsch Jr., "Gadamer's Theory of Interpretation," in *Validity in Interpretation* (New Haven, Conn.: Yale University Press, 1967), 246, 249.

40. Krister Stendahl, "Biblical Theology, Contemporary, 1," in *Interpreter's Dictionary of the Bible* (Nashville: Abingdon Press, 1962), 419–20.

41. Gadamer, *Truth and Method*, 307–11.

42. Ibid., 270.

Enlightenment was a narrative that eschewed narrative. Instead of attaining a cherished "God's-eye point of view," the result was blindness to assumptions that continued to exert their influence, whether acknowledged or not.[43]

It is clear from Gadamer's wider thought that he is making a fundamental claim about the necessary interplay of horizons and not a claim about the predominance of one horizon over the other. In fact, the image might better be conveyed as an expanding horizon, since one might infer from the image that one can isolate the two horizons and then bring them together, which is precisely what Gadamer is concerned to reject. His work implies that our horizon is expanded in the encounter with another so that we understand the other horizon *through* ours. This dynamic process is open to a variety of results. We may reject the claims of a text; still, our horizon has been enlarged when we understand it enough to reject it. We may accept the claims of a text, which results in a refiguration of our horizon. Or we may appropriate the claims of the text in a creatively new way, much as Aquinas drew on Aristotle but substantially modified Aristotle's thought in the process. In each case, a fusion of horizons is involved.

Gadamer's emphasis on the fusion of horizons, as I indicated, is sometimes seen as allowing the modern world to absorb the biblical world (in the language of the Yale school). This is a misunderstanding of his thought. Rather than seeing us imprisoned within our language game, as some have claimed of Wittgensteinian fideism, Gadamer is filled with wonder that we understand across horizons. In fact, he is probably closer to the opposite charge, that he gives too much weight to the ancient horizon and thus is too "conservative." Ironically, he is closer to the insistence of the Yale school that we allow the biblical world to dominate the modern world. Gadamer's paradigm is sounder, however, because while he allows for privileging the ancient text, such as scripture, we cannot simply repeat the biblical message. To be grasped by it, a synthesis is always involved. In the end, his model is neutral with respect to the judgment of truth or falsity that we might make about another text. He is concerned with what precedes and makes such a judgment possible, that is, with understanding the text.

43. Alasdair C. MacIntyre, *Three Rival Versions of Moral Enquiry: Encyclopaedia, Genealogy, and Tradition,* Gifford Lectures (Notre Dame, Ind.: University of Notre Dame Press, 1990). The reference to a "God's-eye point of view" draws particularly from Hilary Putnam's characterization of the problem of the modern quest for objectivity. See Hilary Putnam, *Reason, Truth, and History* (New York: Cambridge University Press, 1981), 49.

One might wonder if Gadamer's model allows for any distinction at all between the ancient horizon and the modern. If the two are fused, and appropriation is involved at the beginning, then can we distinguish at all between the meaning of the text and our appropriation of it? It seems that such a distinction is necessary, but in Gadamer's terms, it can only be a relative distinction. Even with Gadamer's model, one can make a relative distinction between what a text meant and what it might mean today; in Gadamer's own studies of Plato and Aristotle, he constantly does so. Like other interpreters, he speaks of what Aristotle understood and meant and what we might do with it. His creative appropriation of Aristotle's notion of practical wisdom is a case in point. What Gadamer would insist on, however, is that the very understanding of Aristotle already involves an idea of how his work might be applied today. We gain access to Aristotle's horizon by means of our own, but we do not thereby collapse Aristotle's horizon into our own. What we have is an expanded horizon that allows us to understand, to some extent, Aristotle's world and also to differentiate it from our own world. It would be nonsense to say that we cannot distinguish between Aristotle's more limited and ambiguous notion of practical wisdom and Gadamer's expanded notion of it. Yet the understanding of Aristotle's notion occurs in part because we have an idea of how it might be appropriated today. Gadamer similarly draws upon Plato's emphasis on dialogue to indicate that our understanding is always dialogical, involving a to-and-fro movement between two horizons that are never absolutely distinguishable, only relatively so. Gary Madison made this distinction in an essay in the early 1970s, defending Gadamer against the objectivist hermeneutic of E. D. Hirsch Jr., who stressed the absolute distinction between the meaning of a text and its significance for us:

> There is a difference between the discernment of meaning (interpretation) and the application of meaning (criticism). However, the meaning of a text as determined by interpretation is not for all that immutable and self-subsistent; it arises and exists only in and through acts of interpretation and is related essentially to them. While interpretation and criticism are two somewhat different kinds of activity and have two somewhat different kinds of roles to play, it is, nonetheless, impossible to separate them radically, in Hirsch's fashion.[44]

44. Gary Madison, "A Critique of Hirsch's Validity," in *The Hermeneutics of Postmodernity: Figures and Themes,* Studies in Phenomenology and Existential Philosophy (Bloomington: Indiana University Press, 1988), 20.

The Rehabilitation of Tradition

Gadamer unpacks the hermeneutical dynamic further by relating it to history and tradition. Rather than pursuing the continual modern attempt to bracket the past, which is another way of expressing the attempt to bracket the self's presuppositions and start anew, Gadamer argues that we are formed by tradition and cannot escape it. Instead, tradition gives us presuppositions that enable us to understand. Tradition offers us questions to ask and then a foothold to grasp new ideas. It is indeed the case that presuppositions can become deformed into prejudices, but the answer is not to engage in another form of self-deception by supposing that we can rid ourselves of our past and our presuppositions. Rather, our presuppositions *enable* our understanding, as well as sometimes *disable* it. The one thing we cannot do is escape them. Dealing critically with a text is nevertheless possible, but it includes rather than precludes our presuppositions. Gadamer explains:

> A hermeneutically trained consciousness must be, from the start, sensitive to the text's alterity. But this kind of sensitivity involves neither "neutrality" with respect to content nor the extinction of one's self, but the foregrounding and appropriation of one's own fore-meanings and prejudices. The important thing is to be aware of one's own bias, so that the text can present itself in all its otherness and thus assert its own truth against one's own fore-meanings.[45]

Gadamer thus sees us as historical beings who have become conscious that we are effectuated by history (a creative rendering of his *wirkungsgeschichtliches Bewußtsein*).[46] As Habermas has charged, this emphasis on tradition may make Gadamer seem a traditionalist and a conservative and incapable, consequently, of ideology critique. But this is again to misunderstand him.[47] He is not saying that we should always favor the tradition or be uncritical of it; he is making the ontological point that we cannot avoid its influence, nor should we strive, as the Enlightenment did, to free ourselves from it altogether. For one thing, such an effort is doomed to failure and leads to its own kind of deceptive ideology. For another, recognition of the effects of history, Gadamer argued in response to Habermas,

45. Gadamer, *Truth and Method,* 269.

46. Ibid., 300–307. Weinsheimer and Marshall translate the phrase as "historically effected consciousness," and in the first edition of *Truth and Method* it was translated as "effective-historical consciousness." See the translator's discussion in Gadamer, *Truth and Method,* xv.

47. We take up this issue in more detail in chapter 5, which concerns ideology critique.

is what enables one critically to engage history.[48] Gadamer did not, in fact, provide the detail for critique that one might want, but he maintained that his purpose is more general. Later we will see how Ricoeur mediates the Gadamer-Habermas debate by providing more specificity. At this point, it is important only to see that Gadamer's approach is not antagonistic to critique but rather allows for it. On Gadamerian terms, one could favor the past or the present. His point is that tradition enables both.

The Linguistic Turn

One final textual dimension of Gadamer's hermeneutic is his affirmation of the linguistic nature of understanding. Gadamer thus makes the linguistic turn that is characteristic of virtually every twentieth-century philosophical movement. The modern turn to epistemology in the seventeenth century saw that before one can consider what is real, one has to consider how one knows the real. Thus followed the ups and downs of attempts to secure the foundations of knowledge. With the twentieth century came the realization that knowledge comes in linguistic form and cannot be considered apart from language. Opposing the traditional view, Gadamer says, "It is not that the understanding is subsequently put into words; rather, the way understanding occurs—whether in the case of a text or a dialogue with another person who raises an issue with us—is the coming-into-language of the thing itself."[49] Some philosophers then virtually reduced philosophy to philosophy of language and gave up the return route to epistemology and metaphysics. Gadamer is not so restrictive, but he agrees that understanding inevitably involves language. As he puts it, "Being that can be understood is language."[50] This is another way of saying that human beings and philosophy are irreducibly hermeneutical. It implies, of course, that theological reflection is also unavoidably hermeneutical.

Gadamer and the Yale School

As I have already indicated, I believe that Gadamer's metaphor of a fusion of horizons has advantages over the Yale school's metaphor of allowing the biblical world to absorb the modern world. It may be helpful to develop the contrast between fusion and absorption a little further at this point,

48. Hans-Georg Gadamer, "On the Scope and Function of Hermeneutical Reflection (1967)," in *Philosophical Hermeneutics*, ed. Linge, 18–43.
49. Gadamer, *Truth and Method*, 378.
50. Ibid., 474.

keeping in mind the proper understanding of Gadamer's metaphor. Gadamer's model does not mean at the outset privileging either the modern or the ancient world; nor does it mean that the final outcome is always a revisionist compromise, a halfway house between the modern and ancient world. It means that the ancient world cannot be understood except as it is related to our horizon. In other words, we cannot jump out of our skin. Our horizon has to be enlarged in order to understand another. The "miracle of understanding" for Gadamer is that humans are capable of this feat.[51]

The fundamental problem for the Yale school metaphor of absorption is that it does not include a critical way of distinguishing between what can and cannot be absorbed, or between what should and should not. On the surface, it is preposterous that Frei and Lindbeck are suggesting that we emulate cultural details of the ancient world, such as giving up cars and TVs in favor of donkeys and scrolls. Obviously, they mean something different—but what? In the end, total absorption is an impossibility, which means that something more like a creative fusion occurs, which is Gadamer's point. The assumption that there is a single "biblical" world that has been appropriated in a monolithic way in Christianity until the modern period also bears an enormous burden of proof. As Terrence Tilley says, the Christian tradition "is intrinsically plural in that it has always had a multiplicity of canons and texts in which textual interpretation takes place."[52] Ignoring these hermeneutical issues diminishes the place for the hard work of critical interpretation. For example, how do we treat the "holy war" idea in the Old Testament, the failure to reject slavery outright in the New Testament, or the role of women throughout both Testaments? The imagery of simply letting the biblical world absorb our world conceals a multitude of critical issues, whereas the imagery of fusion points precisely to the need for critical judgment about what is changed and what is not.

The Yale school model is heavily influenced by the thought of the later Wittgenstein and partakes of a liability that is often drawn from it. Wittgenstein focused on the way words have meaning in the stream of life. He is commonly recognized as brilliant in showing how words do not have universal meanings but must first be understood in the rich texture of their situation, in his words, their "form of life" or "language game." As

51. Ibid., 292.

52. Terrence W. Tilley, "Narrative Theology *post Morten Dei?* Paul Ricoeur's *Time and Narrative,* III, and Postmodern Theologies," in *Paul Ricoeur and Narrative: Context and Contestation,* ed. Morny Joy (Calgary: University of Calgary Press, 1997), 185. Tilley is criticizing here the weakness of Lindbeck's metaphor over against Ricoeur's notion of refiguration (akin to Gadamer's fusion of horizons).

such, he is making a point not dissimilar to Gadamer's that we understand in terms of our tradition and situation. One difference seems to be that Wittgenstein was entranced by the challenge of comprehending how we understand *within* a form of life, whereas Gadamer was fascinated more by how we understand *across* forms of life. As a result, Wittgenstein has often been interpreted as limiting understanding between horizons, whereas Gadamer emphasizes that we can understand across horizons.

Wittgenstein and Gadamer nevertheless share many similarities. As we have seen, Gadamer rejects any simplistic conception of understanding another horizon without regard to our own. Wittgenstein defenders argue that Wittgenstein's thought is just as capable of dealing with encounter with ancient traditions as Gadamer's, perhaps more so.[53] Nevertheless, the Yale school's appropriation reveals this common understanding of Wittgenstein: They tend to think in terms of being either in one form of life or another, that is, of one horizon's absorbing the other. They also tend to minimize issues of universal truth, emphasizing that truth is so conditioned by a particular form of life that adjudication between claims is something one can hardly consider. Gadamer certainly complicates issues of truth in his rejection of the Enlightenment paradigm, but he is still concerned with the question of truth that arises through dialogical encounter with other traditions. He expresses the import of his approach in this way:

> Such a conception of understanding breaks right through the circle drawn by romantic hermeneutics. Since we are now concerned not with individuality and what it thinks but with the truth of what is said, a text is not understood as a mere expression of life but is taken seriously in its claim to truth.[54]

What makes Gadamer distinctive as a postmodern philosopher, in fact, is that he does not give up on the truth question but considers it to be raised in a more appropriate and human way with the rejection of the unwieldy aims of modernity. In the end, his approach is rich in significance for a theology attempting to understand itself after the demise of modernity, a theology that is rarely content with avoiding or rejecting the question of truth.

The strength of the Yale school model, it seems to me, comes at the second stage, after accepting the beginning point of Gadamer's model. Realizing that a fusion of horizons must occur, the Yale image indicates that in

53. For example, see Patrick Neil Rogers Horn, "The Unity of Language and Religious Belief: Gadamer and Wittgenstein" (Ph. D. diss., Claremont Graduate University, 1999).

54. Gadamer, *Truth and Method*, 297.

the Christian context, the ancient text of scripture has a privileged place. The biblical story stands as a constant challenge to our story and calls for a creative modification of our story in the direction of the biblical story. At this point, both approaches have to work out what that means. As we shall see, Ricoeur gives some direction in this effort in his biblical studies and also in his more detailed model of a hermeneutical arc.

Paul Ricoeur and the Text

By following the rise of hermeneutical philosophy through Gadamer, we can see how the dynamics of interpreting a text became progressively broadened to become a full-fledged philosophy, or at least the scaffolding of one. The philosophy that emerges is also a radical challenge to modern and premodern conceptions and thus clearly falls within the postmodern camp. It emphasizes that the basis of all knowledge is irreducibly hermeneutical, involving interpretive judgments flowing from one's situatedness in history and one's presuppositions. Contrary to the relativistic tendencies of some postmodern philosophies, however, it still allows for considered judgments based on evidence and reasons that claim to be true. What makes it postmodern is that it considers these judgments in the final analysis to be underdetermined by such evidence and reasons. Reasonable people, even experts, may disagree, which is a common phenomenon that this style of postmodernism explains and does not consider an embarrassment. The influences of traditions and presuppositions are considered as the necessary grounds for understanding rather than as inevitable impediments. Critical judgment arises not from a superhuman attempt to extricate oneself from the human situation in order to be totally objective but from the traditions themselves that set horizons in critical dialogue with one another. As Ricoeur says against Habermas, "Critique is itself a tradition."[55]

Ricoeur follows this basic Gadamerian lead. He began with phenomenology but saw its limitations, soon making the hermeneutic turn with an attention to detail far surpassing Gadamer. From the beginning, he rejected a foundationalist approach and argued that we can never start from scratch but always too late, so to speak, in and with our presuppositions. This is no reason to lament, however, because our precritical, naïve experience funds our thought. Borrowing from Kant, he has made a

55. Paul Ricoeur, "Hermeneutics and the Critique of Ideology," in *Hermeneutics and the Human Sciences*, ed. Thompson, 99.

central theme of his work the idea that "the symbol gives rise to thought."[56] Our prereflective and first-order language is filled with symbolic and figurative language. This moves us to critical reflection, but unlike the modernist impulse, we never leave such first-order language behind; rather, we continue to return to it and to test our reflections by it. In a theological context, leaving primary language behind would be like replacing scripture with one's theology. In Ricoeur's view, theology is always a second-order discipline that cannot in principle take the place of the primary language of scripture, prayer, worship, confession, and so on. Ricoeur originally understood hermeneutics, as an interpretive discipline, to concern double-meaning expressions that we find in symbol and metaphor. He later broadened his understanding to include narratives and the wider issue of interpretation in general. In the background to this more general understanding of hermeneutics was his concern for the ontological turn in hermeneutics found in Heidegger and Gadamer, which concerns not only the meaning but the very being of humanity.[57]

Another important extension of hermeneutics for Ricoeur is where, in an important 1971 essay, he explicitly makes the model of the text the paradigm for interpreting action and events as well.[58] We flesh out his argument in more detail later, but for now, it suffices to point out that actions become a kind of text that is left for others to interpret. The hermeneutical dynamic means that they then are susceptible to multiple interpretations, influenced by the various traditions and presuppositions of the interpreters. A fusion of horizons is inherently involved in any such interpretation.

With this article, Ricoeur moves even hermeneutics per se (quite apart from ontological hermeneutics) from the province of texts alone to history and human life. He later develops in more detail the way in which narrative dynamics of plot and character are crucial in understanding ourselves and history, far beyond the confines of fiction. As one can see, such a broadening of hermeneutics is fraught with implications for an understanding of how the Yale school calls for the biblical story to become our story. It does so in a way, however, that deals with how we must engage the biblical story with our story at the outset. We cannot leap out of his-

56. Paul Ricoeur, *The Symbolism of Evil,* trans. Emerson Buchanan, Religious Perspectives 17 (New York: Harper & Row, 1967), conclusion.

57. An exceptionally clear statement of these shifts occurs in Paul Ricoeur, "On Interpretation," trans. Kathleen Blamey and John B. Thompson, in *Front Text to Action: Essays in Hermeneutics, II,* Northwestern University Studies in Phemenology and Existential Philosophy (Evanston, Ill.: Northwestern University Press, 1991), 16–19.

58. Ricoeur, "Model of the Text."

tory into the past but must allow for a fusion of horizons. All of Ricoeur's work develops the way in which this is possible in a postmodern context that does justice to both horizons.

The fundamental model of textual interpretation that undergirds the hermeneutical tradition behind Ricoeur's work came, as we saw, primarily from scriptural interpretation. It is perhaps easier to see the reason for the claim that there is a fundamental affinity, at least in principle, between this philosophical approach and theology, which has as its center in most traditions the interpretation of scripture as an authoritative text. Succeeding chapters continue to explicate this affinity as we elaborate the themes in Ricoeur's thought briefly sketched here.

CHAPTER TWO

A Hermeneutical Arc

With the fundamental paradigm of the interpretation of a text at the center of Ricoeur's hermeneutical philosophy, it is not surprising that his development of a "hermeneutical arc" functions like a backbone to the body of his thought. It is also to be expected that his hermeneutical arc is directly relevant in many ways to the theological enterprise so keyed to interpretation.

Ricoeur first elaborated his threefold hermeneutical arc in the 1970s, in connection with his intensive reflection on the significance of metaphor.[1] In the early 1980s, he further developed a threefold "narrative arc" in *Time and Narrative*.[2] It is easy to assume a one-to-one correspondence between Ricoeur's earlier hermeneutical arc and his later narrative arc. On the one hand, Ricoeur encourages this assumption by the fact that the third stage of each he sometimes calls "appropriation." On the other hand, despite their initial similarity, they cannot simply be overlaid, as we shall see. Ricoeur, however, does little to disentangle them. In fact, several ambiguities are contained in each taken by itself, which are only accentuated when they are uncritically assimilated. It is moreover striking that, given the importance and use of these conceptions, little comment about their ambiguity has appeared.[3] Mario Valdés is one of the few to try

1. See, for example, Paul Ricoeur, "The Model of the Text: Meaningful Action Considered as a Text," in *Hermeneutics and the Human Sciences: Essays on Language, Action, and Interpretation,* ed. John B. Thompson (Cambridge: Cambridge University Press, 1981), 131–44; Paul Ricoeur, *Interpretation Theory: Discourse and the Surplus of Meaning* (Fort Worth: Texas Christian University Press, 1976), 71–88.

2. See especially Paul Ricoeur, *Time and Narrative,* vol. 1, trans. Kathleen McLaughlin and David Pellauer (Chicago: University of Chicago Press, 1984), chap. 3.

3. An example of a major interpreter who confusedly parallels the two is Mark I. Wallace in *The Second Naiveté: Barth, Ricoeur, and the New Yale Theology,* Studies in American Biblical Hermeneutics, no. 6 (Macon, Ga.: Mercer University Press, 1990), 56. I have great appreciation for Wallace's inter-

to synthesize them but implies that the latter arc is a rather smooth development of the earlier arc; thus he does not deal with the tensions between them.[4] This means that the elaboration of Ricoeur's hermeneutical arc must be a critical and constructive one, clarifying and modifying it in ways that Ricoeur himself has not. In the end, such a "re-figured" arc, I believe, does not undermine the fruitfulness of his ideas but allows them to be further extended.

In this chapter we therefore explore this significant aspect of Ricoeur's work by explicating his hermeneutical arc in its original context in the 1970s, examining its relationship to the later threefold narrative arc in the 1980s, and then dealing with some unresolved questions concerning the understanding of the two arcs. Finally, we look at their implications for theological reflection.

A Hermeneutical Arc

In a series of articles in the 1970s, Ricoeur elaborated a hermeneutical arc that consisted of a first, rather innocent act of understanding; a second moment of explanation; and a third moment that he variously characterized as a second immediacy, a postcritical naïveté, appropriation, and application.[5] (See Figure 1.) As he intimates at one point, the figure might better be called a hermeneutical spiral since one may return again and again to a text.[6] While there appear to be three temporal stages, a great deal of overlap occurs, so the three stages are sharply distinguished more in analysis than in reality.

---

pretation of Ricoeur, but in this instance he describes the two threefold arcs fairly accurately as different, then goes on as if they were the same. As we shall see, putting the two together requires at a minimum four aspects, not three, but Wallace continues to speak of three moments. See also the lack of attention to this issue in Lewis Edwin Hahn, ed., *The Philosophy of Paul Ricoeur,* The Library of Living Philosophers (Chicago: Open Court, 1995).

4. See Mario J. Valdés, "Introduction: Paul Ricoeur's Post-Structuralist Hermeneutics," in *A Ricoeur Reader: Reflection and Imagination,* ed. Mario J. Valdés (Toronto: University of Toronto Press, 1991), 3–40. To show, however, that the development is not so simple, Valdés ends up actually with four dimensions of the first arc that he then relates as critical dimensions of two of the aspects of Ricoeur's later arc, namely, configuration and refiguration (27–28). It is not at all clear how the move is made from Ricoeur's arcs to his, although, as I will show, I similarly relate the critical aspect to both configuration and refiguration.

5. The idea of a "second naïveté" that is a second immediacy and postcritical is found earlier in Paul Ricoeur, *The Symbolism of Evil,* trans. Emerson Buchanan, Religious Perspectives 17 (New York: Harper & Row, 1967), 352.

6. Paul Ricoeur, "Metaphor and the Central Problem of Hermeneutics," in *Hermeneutics and the Human Sciences,* ed. Thompson, 171.

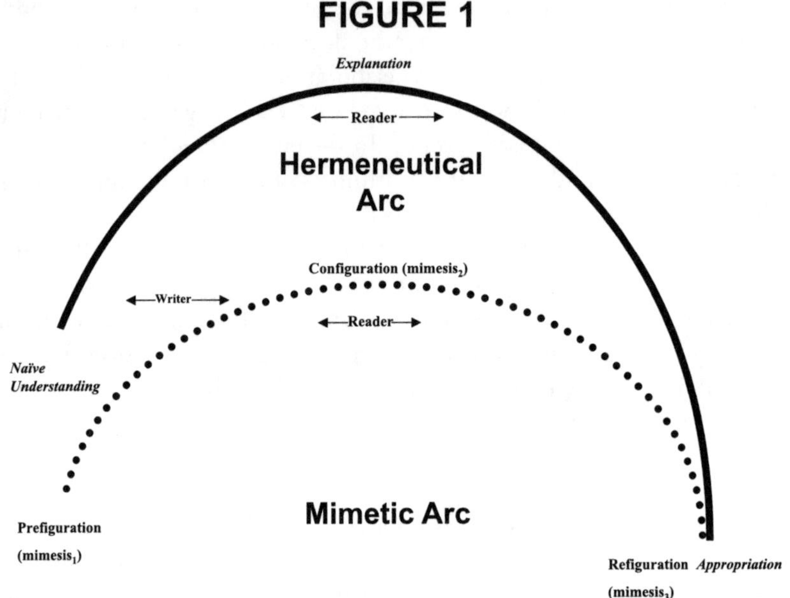

The First Understanding

In the background of the first moment of understanding in the arc are Continental debates about the Diltheyan dichotomy that we described in the previous chapter between the *Geisteswissenschaften* (the humanities or social sciences), which relied on understanding, and the *Naturwissenschaften* (the natural sciences), which relied on explanation.[7] Ricoeur characteristically desires to integrate the two, while giving priority to the more holistic "understanding." As he sees it, thinking particularly of a work of fiction, a first reading yields an holistic grasp of the meaning and its import. Drawing on the work of E. D. Hirsch Jr., Ricoeur sees this as amounting to a first "guess" or a first "wager" about the meaning.[8]

It is surprising that Ricoeur appeals to Hirsch at this point, given Hirsch's opposition to Gadamer and to anything but an author-centered understanding of interpretation. What Ricoeur seems to derive from Hirsch, however, is the idea of a dynamic, imaginative conception of meaning that can be tested, as opposed to a carefully worked-out notion that is at the outset founded strictly on the evidence.

7. Ricoeur, "Model of the Text," 209.
8. Ibid., 211; Ricoeur, "Metaphor," 175.

Interestingly, a hermeneutic that was tied strictly to facts was prominent in nineteenth-century conservative theology and represented the way in which Baconian induction was refracted through Scottish Common Sense Realism. As George Marsden says in his major study of this subject, *Fundamentalism and American Culture: The Shaping of Twentieth-Century Evangelicalism 1870–1925*:

> When it came to identifying their philosophical stance, until after the Civil War American evangelicals overwhelmingly preferred the method of Francis Bacon to "metaphysical speculations." Common Sense philosophy affirmed their ability to know "the facts" directly. With the Scriptures at hand as a compendium of facts, there was no need to go further. They needed only to classify the facts, and follow wherever they might lead.[9]

In this way, this evangelical tradition developed the Reformation sense of the "perspicuity of scripture" into an idea of a transparent object, involving little interpretation.[10]

In contrast, Ricoeur's view is similar to Gadamer's insistence that in interpretation we are not initially in control; rather, we are first seized by meaning rather than being the ones doing the seizing. To draw on Gadamer's analogy, we find ourselves being played by the game rather than dominating the action. This attitude approaches scripture, for example, as a powerful text fraught with meaning and full of potential, certainly not as a pedestrian assortment of facts that we must manipulate, classify, and comprehend clearly.

We are thinking in terms of the reading of texts at this point; but the arc applies to our reaction to other things as well, such as film, experiences of actions, and larger historical events, all of which at times similarly cry out for interpretation. For example, throughout Ricoeur's work, he stresses the gift of a "primary affirmation" of the meaning of existence, akin to the idea of the reaffirmation of a "basic trust" found in the theological works of Schubert Ogden, David Tracy, and Hans Küng.[11] In an early article, Ricoeur emphasizes that primary affirmation "seems quite fitting to

9. George M. Marsden, *Fundamentalism and American Culture: The Shaping of Twentieth-Century Evangelicalism 1870–1925* (Oxford: Oxford University Press, 1980), 56.

10. On the Reformation view of the perspecuity of scripture, see Robert M. Grant, *A Short History of the Interpretation of the Bible* (New York: Macmillan Co., 1963), 128–33. For later developments, see Marsden, *Fundamentalism and American Culture,* 16, 110–11.

11. Schubert Miles Ogden, *The Reality of God, and Other Essays* (New York: Harper & Row, 1977), 34; David Tracy, *Blessed Rage for Order: The New Pluralism in Theology,* The Seabury Library of Contemporary Theology (New York: Seabury Press, 1979), 135; Hans Küng, *Does God Exist? An Answer for Today,* trans. Edward Quinn (Garden City, NY: Doubleday, 1980), 442–77. Ricoeur acknowledges his debt for this idea to Jean Nabert, a fellow French philosopher.

designate the intense passion for existence which anguish puts into question and pursues from level to level in an uncertain battle."[12] Such fundamental experiences of meaning, like some texts, catch us up and pitch us into a hermeneutical battle of interpretation. Such experiences also have obvious relevance for understanding religious encounters.

Explanation

It is distinctive of Ricoeur to press beyond our initially "naïve" understandings associated with such experiences or reading. Although we may remain with an original, untested interpretation, he sees that there is much, especially in modern, critical societies, that disallows such contentment. In fact, Ricoeur sees virtue in testing our insightful understandings by critical methodologies at a second, explanatory stage. In Dilthey's terms, this is a shift from understanding to explanation. Unlike Dilthey, however, Ricoeur sees a place for the more analytical and critical mode of thought, even in the interpretation of texts. As he put it in later work, "To explain more is to understand better."[13]

At the same time, Ricoeur looks for a kind of objectivity that is appropriate to texts and not necessarily to the objects of natural science. Since Ricoeur is not seeking to "divine" the mental intentions of the author, as were Schleiermacher and Hirsch, he can see a text or an action as an interpretive object that allows for methods of explanation. As he has said, "To understand a text is not to rejoin the author."[14] This allows for a critical focus on construing the meaning of a text that is before the interpreter, rather than on the elusive sense of what the author might have experienced in producing the text.

Despite this sense of the objectivity of the text, Ricoeur terms the initial understanding as a guess, but he looks for methods to validate guesses. A text needs such critical reflection because it involves a holistic grasp that includes the hermeneutical circle of relating the whole to the parts and the parts to the whole. A text is complicated and allows for different readings and different perspectives, the significance of which we explore further in the next chapter.[15] For the moment, Ricoeur explains at length:

12. Paul Ricoeur, "True and False Anguish," trans. Charles A. Kelbley, in *History and Truth,* Northwestern University Studies in Phenomenology and Existential Philosophy (Evanston, Ill: Northwestern University Press, 1965), 288.

13. Ricoeur, *Time and Narrative,* vol. 1, 5.

14. Ricoeur, "Model of the Text," 210.

15. Ibid.

> For all these reasons there is a problem of interpretation not so much because of the incommunicability of the psychic experience of the author, but because of the very nature of the verbal intention of the text. This intention is something other than the sum of the individual meanings of the individual sentences. A text is more than a linear succession of sentences. It is a cumulative, holistic process. This specific structure of the text cannot be derived from that of the sentence. Therefore the kind of plurivocity which belongs to texts as texts is something more than the polysemy of individual words in ordinary language and the ambiguity of individual sentences. This plurivocity is typical of the text considered as a whole, open to several readings and to several constructions.[16]

Ricoeur concedes that the validation of which he speaks with respect to texts is "closer to a logic of probability than to a logic of empirical verification."[17] He exhibits an exaggerated opposition between the natural sciences and the humanities here, but the point he is making is still pertinent. As he explains:

> To show that an interpretation is more probable in the light of what is known is something other than showing that a conclusion is true. In this sense, validation is not verification. Validation is an argumentative discipline comparable to the juridical procedures of legal interpretation. It is a logic of uncertainty and of qualitative probability. . . . The method of conveyance of indices, typical of the logic of subjective probability, gives a firm basis for a science of the individual deserving the name of science.[18]

While his sharp distinction between verification and validation no longer holds, his emphasis on the legitimate objective character of interpretation is very important—and very postmodern. In other words, objectivity no longer has the meaning of verification but can have a postmodern sense that involves arguments, evidence, and conclusions that are probable but not proofs.

At the time of his development of the hermeneutical arc in the 1970s, the critical methodology that Ricoeur stressed was structuralism.[19] Structuralism had been in vogue in France, and Ricoeur was obligated, as it were, to respond to it. He characteristically appropriated structuralism, at the same time limiting it. Structuralism as a general approach to literature looks for the deeper codes that "structure" a text behind the surface

16. Ibid., 212.
17. Ibid.
18. Ibid.
19. For example, see Ricoeur, "Model of the Text," 216; Paul Ricoeur, "What is a Text? Explanation and Understanding," in *Hermeneutics and the Human Sciences*, ed. Thompson, 153.

meaning. In fact, part of the significance for structuralists is not only in discerning the codes used in a particular text but in designating the codes that underlie many texts, even to the deep structure of an entire culture. A favorite example is the basic binary opposition between good and evil or clean and unclean behind native folktales. Structuralism was initially seen as a rigorous, scientific approach to texts and to culture that rivaled the certainty and precision of science. In this sense it was a last gasp of modernity. It also became popular in biblical studies in the United States for a season. Soon, however, it fell to "poststructuralism" (a form of what we have described as postmodernism).[20]

Ricoeur wants to make a place for structural analysis while not ceding the whole interpretive enterprise to it. He sees that it provides a certain rigor and objectivity to textual analysis, but it also is limited to the deep structures rather than surface structures. Speaking of the structural approach of Claude Lévi-Strauss, Ricoeur protests, "As a matter of fact, nobody stops with a conception of myths and of narratives as formal as this algebra of constitutive units."[21] Ricoeur points out that mythical analysis can hardly work without drawing on the existential world external to the text: "Structural analysis merely represses this function. But it cannot suppress it."[22] Ricoeur thus claims, concerning the way structuralism implicitly points beyond itself to an understanding of the world, "I really believe that if such were not the function of structural analysis, it would be reduced to a sterile game, a divisive algebra, and even the myth would be bereaved of the function which Lévi-Strauss himself assigns to it."[23] In the end, Ricoeur criticizes the way in which structuralism cannot move beyond *structures* to *meaning,* from the *text* to the *world.* Structural analysis thus could be a "moment" along the way, but no more than that.

Because of his focus on structuralism at the time, Ricoeur himself did not clearly point to other critical methodologies; it appears, however, to be an obvious implication of his conception that they would fit in at this point. For example, at this time he was preparing his important book on ideology critique, to which he could have appealed.[24] One could integrate

20. For a concise account of both and the transition from one to the other, see "Structuralism and Poststructuralism," in Dan R. Stiver, *The Philosophy of Religious Language: Sign, Symbol, and Story* (Cambridge: Blackwell, 1996), chap. 7.

21. Ricoeur, "Model of the Text," 217.

22. Ibid.

23. Ibid., 217–18.

24. Paul Ricoeur, *Lectures on Ideology and Utopia,* ed. George H. Taylor (New York: Columbia University Press, 1986).

here also Ricoeur's fruitful notion, developed earlier in his reflections on Freud, of a hermeneutics of suspicion.[25] In the religious field, this would be the place for traditional historical methods—for example, textual criticism, tradition criticism, form criticism, redaction criticism, and social criticism.[26] At one point, Ricoeur calls for "adding a theory of *structural reading* to the method of historical criticism," by which he meant "biblical criticism."[27]

For our purposes, the most significant critical addition would be systematic theology. Systematic theology could function here as "explanation," as second-order language, offering clarification and criticism to first-order language. It is clear that Ricoeur understands systematic theology (and also philosophy) as involving such a second-level, critical response to more originary language. Theology does not replace first-order language but serves to deepen and extend our understanding of it. Its purpose is then to enhance what Ricoeur calls a postcritical return to the original text.

The Postcritical Understanding

Ricoeur sees the third aspect of the arc as dealing with the claim of a text to describe, or better, redescribe, reality. He typically depicts this as the place where one moves beyond the world of the text per se to consider the import of a work for imaginatively opening up a new world in which we might live "in front of the text."[28] He explains, "What we want to understand is not something hidden behind the text, but something disclosed

25. Paul Ricoeur, *Freud and Philosophy: An Essay on Interpretation,* trans. Denis Savage, Terry Lectures (New Haven, Conn.: Yale University Press, 1970), 32–36.

26. Ricoeur himself does not delineate these critical methodologies that are at home in biblical studies, but he uses them in his religious work, e.g., *Symbolism of Evil.*

27. Paul Ricoeur, *Essays on Biblical Interpretation,* trans. Robert Sweeney, ed. Lewis S. Mudge (Philadelphia: Fortress Press, 1980), 44. See also, for a similar point, Charles J. Scalise, *Hermeneutics as Theological Prolegomena: A Canonical Approach,* Studies in American Biblical Hermeneutics 8 (Macon, Ga.: Mercer University Press, 1994), 70, who is critiquing Brevard Childs's misunderstanding that Ricoeur does not deal with the historical element. See Brevard S. Childs, *Introduction to the Old Testament as Scripture* (Philadelphia: Fortress Press, 1979), 77.

28. Ricoeur is not always clear about this distinction. In one article in the 1970s, he seemed to equate the world of the text with the world in front of the text. By contrast, it seems clear in his later *Time and Narrative* that he distinguishes between the world of the text, as referring to the immanent "narrated world" of the text, and the fused horizons of the world in front of the text. For the earlier equation, see Paul Ricoeur, "The Hermeneutical Function of Distanciation," in *Hermeneutics and the Human Sciences,* ed. Thompson, 141–42; for the later distinction, see Ricoeur, *Time and Narrative,* vol. 1, 77–81; Paul Ricoeur, *Time and Narrative,* vol. 3, trans. Kathleen Blamey and David Pellauer (Chicago: University of Chicago Press, 1988), chap. 7.

in front of it."[29] Ricoeur's point is intended as a critique of traditional historical-critical approaches that have focused on the world behind the text, which, as in Hans Frei's terms, eclipse the text itself.

Ricoeur typically uses the language of "application" or "appropriation" for this stage. Like Gadamer, he considers appropriation not as an ancillary or optional aspect of interpretation but as integral to it. In other words, the work of interpretation and understanding the text is not complete until one grasps what it might mean for life. Against the structuralist and New Critical tendencies to restrict meaning to the confines of the text, Ricoeur is passionate about what he once termed, in connection with metaphor, the "ontological vehemence" of language. He says:

> The spirituality of discourse manifests itself through writing, which frees us from the visibility and limitation of situations by opening up a world for us, that is, new dimensions of our being-in-the-world.
>
> In this sense, Heidegger rightly says—in his analysis of *verstehen* in *Being and Time*—that what we understand first in a discourse is not another person, but a project, that is, the outline of a new being-in-the-world. Only writing, in freeing itself, not only from its author, but from the narrowness of the dialogical situation, reveals this destination of discourse as projecting a world.[30]

He adds, "If you suppress this referential function, only an absurd game of errant signifiers remains."[31]

In terms of his early book, *The Symbolism of Evil,* he offers the highly influential suggestion that one moves from the "first naïveté" of the initial understanding to a "second naïveté." With the help of his hermeneutical arc, one more clearly sees how this is a move from a first understanding, through critical explanation, to a second, postcritical understanding. The holistic nature of understanding over against the analytic and decompositional modes of criticism is necessarily re-engaged in order fully to understand.

Ricoeur is well aware that the modern world has not often attained the third moment. As he puts it, it has languished in an analytical "desert of criticism."[32] While Ricoeur hopes to provide a pathway out of the life-sapping critical desert, he does not offer a shortcut. He calls for a *postcritical* naïveté, not simply naïveté. It is as much a mistake to evade criticism by being reactionary or iconoclastic as it is to be stuck in criticism. He says:

29. Ricoeur, "Model of the Text," 218.
30. Ibid., 202.
31. Ibid.
32. Ricoeur, *Symbolism of Evil,* 349.

> The same epoch holds in reserve both the possibility of emptying language by radically formalizing it and the possibility of filling it anew by reminding itself of the fullest meanings, the most pregnant ones, the ones which are most bound by the presence of the sacred to man.
>
> It is not regret for the sunken Atlantides that animates us, but hope for a recreation of language. Beyond the desert of criticism, we wish to be called again.[33]

In addition to drawing on structuralism, Ricoeur relates this hermeneutical arc to the philosophical distinction that Gottlob Frege made between sense and reference: sense paralleling explanation and reference paralleling appropriation. For Ricoeur, this means that sense relates to the structure of the text, whereas reference relates to how the text depicts reality, or "the world in front of the text." For the latter, Ricoeur draws on Gadamer's notion of a "fusion of horizons."[34] In yet another terminology, sense relates to a semiotic analysis, whereas reference relates to semantic analysis.

As one can see, Ricoeur has synthesized a motley collection of academic apparatuses into his hermeneutical arc, some of which do not fit comfortably together. For example, it is not clear that structural analysis rises to the level of establishing an actual world of the text. It can establish deep structures and even semiotic relationships of words, but it does not necessarily yield a narrative world. If it does, there is some tension with seeing Ricoeur's middle moment as explanatory and analytical. Is the kind of holistic understanding involved in construing a literary world of the text possible in the more analytical, critical mode? Ricoeur says, "To explain is to bring out the structure, that is, the internal relations of dependence which constitute the statics of the text; to interpret is to follow the path of thought opened up by the text, to place oneself *en route* towards the *orient* of the text."[35] Is not the construction of a narrative world more than "constituting the statics of the text"? At one point, Ricoeur says that structural analysis as a "surface semantics" points beyond itself to a "depth semantics," by which he seems to equate depth to the meaning of the world in front of the text.[36] His characterization of a structuralist surface semantics does not sound at all like a construal of the literary world of a text, so where does such a construal belong? It cannot belong to the third moment, because that is where Ricoeur placed the imagination of an appropriated world in front of the text. It cannot simply be placed in the

33. Ibid.

34. Hans-Georg Gadamer, *Truth and Method,* trans. Joel Weinsheimer and Donald G. Marshall, rev. ed. (New York: Crossroad, 1991), 306.

35. Ricoeur, "What Is a Text?" 161f.

36. Ibid., 217.

first moment, because this would allow no place for a critical and reflective rendering of the world of the text in the second moment. It appears to be homeless. It is interesting that in Ricoeur's later narrative arc, which I explain next, this narrative construal is highlighted as the second moment—but at the cost of speaking of a second explanatory moment. In other words, the moment of "explanation" that is central to his earlier hermeneutical arc appears to be homeless in his later mimetic arc.

Moreover, is there not a need for a postcritical construction of the world of the text similar to Ricoeur's postcritical construction of the world in front of the text? In other words, reading with a postcritical naïveté does not only come in at the point of appropriation of the text. It is necessary even to understand the narrative world of the text. Concomitantly, in terms of Gadamer's thought, does not a fusion of horizons occur even in understanding the world of the text, and not just in appropriating a world in front of the text? In fact, the implication of Gadamer's work is that a fusion of horizons must occur at every stage of the arc in order for any understanding to occur at all, not just at the last stage, thus calling into question the adequacy of Ricoeur's appropriation of Gadamer. We explore this enlarged role of the fusion of horizons further after examining Ricoeur's narrative arc.

A Narrative Arc

In his three-volume *Time and Narrative,* published in French in the early 1980s, Ricoeur proposed a framework of a threefold process of "mimesis" or "figuration," which I term a "narrative" or "mimetic" arc, divided into prefiguration (mimesis_1), configuration (mimesis_2), and refiguration (mimesis_3).[37] (See Figure 1.)

Prefiguration

Prefiguration refers to the preunderstanding that one brings to writing or reading a text. It is akin to Gadamer's "prejudices" (*Vorurteil*) that shape our approach to a text.[38] Ricoeur portrays configuration, then, as mediating between prefiguration and refiguration. In a general way, he says, "[i]t

37. See particularly Ricoeur, *Time and Narrative,* vol. 1, 52–87; Paul Ricoeur, *Time and Narrative,* vol. 2, trans. Kathleen McLaughlin and David Pellauer (Chicago: University of Chicago Press, 1985), 157–79.

38. Gadamer, *Truth and Method,* 235–74.

is the task of hermeneutics . . . to reconstruct the entire set of operations by which a work lifts itself above the opaque depths of living, acting, and suffering, to be given by an author to readers who receive it and thereby change their acting."[39] Prefiguration refers to that opaque world on which an author draws to write and on which a reader draws to interpret. Ricoeur's understanding of the self is that all of us construe an ongoing narrative, or at least a protonarrative, of our lives, so the prefigured world in which we act as agents, while not written as a text, already contains a protoplot. As Ricoeur says, "If, in fact, human action can be narrated, it is because it is always already articulated by signs, rules, and norms. It is always already symbolically mediated."[40] This tacit narrative activity does not imply a wholly coherent outcome. Ricoeur brings out the tensions of our attempts to narrate our lives by probing the paradoxes or aporias that concerned Augustine in his meditations on lived time at the end of his *Confessions.* Ricoeur sets these tensions over against Aristotle's *Poetics,* with its emphasis on the way narratives evade the aporias of time through their ordering and arranging. Ricoeur's particular interest in *Time and Narrative* is how narrative helps us mediate, without eliminating, the tensions of time. Our lives are thus not full-blown narratives, but they are the basis of, and in turn draw on, such narratives.[41]

Ricoeur can be seen here as focusing Gadamer's emphasis on the way in which we are constituted and shaped by tradition, which is itself a kind of story. In fact, *Time and Narrative* explores more deeply his earlier conviction that "the world is the ensemble of references opened up by the texts."[42] Ricoeur summarizes this theme in *Time and Narrative:* "Yet despite the break it institutes, literature would be incomprehensible if it did not give a configuration to what was already a figure in human action."[43] The prefiguration implicit in our lives is a nascent story that points toward and in turn is shaped by configuration.

39. Ricoeur, *Time and Narrative,* vol. 1, 53.

40. Ibid., 57.

41. Ricoeur is careful about speaking of a "prenarrative" structure of experience in the way that many narrativists do. This is due to his conclusions about the aporetic tensions that are finally irresolvable in our experience of time, which he insistently develops throughout the entire three volumes of *Time and Narrative.* At best, these tensions can be mediated by fiction and historiography. David Carr is a noted narrativist and scholar of the later Husserl who disagrees with Ricoeur, arguing that our lived experience is already strongly narratively shaped. See David Carr, "Discussion: Ricoeur on Narrative," in *On Paul Ricoeur: Narrative and Interpretation,* ed. David Wood, Warwick Studies in Philosophy and Literature (New York: Routledge, 1991), 160. Hank Stam and Lori Egger argue that Carr and Ricoeur are actually not that different; see Hendrikus J. Stam and Lori Egger, "Narration and Life: On the Possibilities of a Narrative Psychology," in *Paul Ricoeur and Narrative: Context and Contestation,* ed. Morny Joy (Calgary: University of Calgary Press, 1997), 69–85.

42. Ricoeur, "Model of the Text," 202.

43. Ricoeur, *Time and Narrative,* vol. 1, 64.

Configuration

Drawing on this prefigured world, *configuration* refers on the one hand to an author's imaginative construction of a text, particularly the emplotment, and on the other to the reader's construal of a narrative world of the text. Ricoeur argues that such configuration as the work of the productive imagination is as true of historiography as it is of fiction per se, thus the term *configuration* rather than *fiction.* The author and the reader at this point have to take the more chaotic prefigured time and artfully order it into a synthetic whole. Ricoeur says, "In short, the act of narrating, reflected in the act of following a story, makes productive the paradoxes that disquieted Augustine to the point of reducing him to silence."[44] Ricoeur desires to move beyond an Augustinian silence, but he also believes that any equilibrium is a fragile one and that no final resolution of the tension is possible.

It is significant that any narrative reading involves a holistic act of judgment that is in part creative. As already indicated, Ricoeur taps the Kantian tradition of the productive imagination that enables such judgment, which Kant develops both in his *Critique of Pure Reason* and in his *Critique of Judgment.*[45] Such imagination, as in Kant, may be rather ordinary in the case of traditional forms or genres such as myths and folktales, or it may be radically creative as in much modern fiction.[46] In any case, it appears that what is involved is something like the act of holistic understanding in the first and third moments of his earlier hermeneutical arc, as opposed to the middle moment of critique or explanation. Although configuration is the middle moment of his narrative arc, Ricoeur seems to go beyond the analytical, critical middle moment of explanation in the hermeneutical arc. This tension raises the question of where such critical explanation fits in his narrative arc.

Refiguration

Finally, *refiguration* replaces the term *reference,* which Ricoeur now thinks is too foreign a category for his use, but it parallels his earlier language of

44. Ibid., 68.
45. Ibid.
46. Ibid., 69–70.

appropriation and application. (See Figure 1.)[47] Ricoeur draws on reader-response theory in this connection for the way in which a fusion of horizons occurs between the text and an appropriated world in front of the text. As indicated above, he searches for a middle ground between a view that sees the writer or text as wholly in control and a view that sees the reader as wholly in control. In short, he would argue that a good text avoids tyranny and anarchy. This means that a text, in a sense, does not have meaning until it is read. As he says, "However well-articulated the 'schematic views' proposed for our execution may be, the text resembles a musical score lending itself to different realizations."[48] This accounts for the way in which most texts, not least the text of scripture, have a surplus of meaning that is virtually inexhaustible, while nevertheless offering constraints for reading. We explore Ricoeur's idea of a surplus of meaning further in the next chapter.

Ricoeur is basically following Gadamer at this point, rejecting the idea that application is simply an external addition to the text, after exegesis and hermeneutics. This point of his mimetic arc parallels his emphasis in the hermeneutical arc on the fact that one cannot stop at critical explanation but must move to a postcritical naïveté. Similarly, one cannot stop at the configured world of the text but must move to a refigured or appropriated world in front of the text, which "offers a possible world in which one might live," to use Ricoeur's earlier language. This does not mean that one has to accept or actually live out the proffered world, but it means that one grasps to some extent what it might mean so to live. And then one can accept, reject, or accept with modifications.

Appropriation relates to historiography and fiction. *Time and Narrative* is a study of both, suggesting an intimate interweaving of the two. Appropriation in fiction, Ricoeur suggests, parallels "standing-for" or "taking-the-place-of" in historiography. By the latter he means the way in which historiography involves a debt to the past but cannot simply re-create the past or tell history "as it actually happened." In other words, he maintains that historiography itself involves a "fictive" or figurative element that nevertheless attempts to represent or "stand for" the past. This figurative element is obviously more explicit in fiction; but even fiction, he argues, has a certain indirect connection with reality. In its own way, as Aristotle

47. This is why, in Figure 1, I drew the arcs as coming together at the third point on the arc. For his change of mind using the language of reference, see Ricoeur, *Time and Narrative,* vol. 3, 157–58. For example: "the point where, in order to signify something like a productive reference in the sense in which, following Kant, we speak of a productive imagination, the problematic of refiguration must free itself, once and for all, from the vocabulary of reference" (158).

48. Ibid., 167.

realized, fiction offers truth and is not locked up inside an unreal world. It is worth quoting Ricoeur at length on this point, where he is comparing his criticism of a naïve conception of reality "as it really is" in historiography with fiction:

> This critique of the naïve concept of "reality" applied to the pastness of the past calls for a systematic critique of the no less naïve concept of "unreality" applied to the projections of fiction. The function of standing-for or of taking-the-place-of is paralleled in fiction by the function it possesses, with respect to everyday practice, of being undividedly revealing and transforming. Revealing, in the sense that it brings features to light that were concealed and yet already sketched out at the heart of our experience, our praxis. Transforming, in the sense that a life examined in this way is a changed life, another life.[49]

It is not difficult to imagine that such a nuanced view of the similarities yet differences of historiography and fiction might be fruitful in reflecting on the ambiguous and contentious role of history in scripture, a point we explore in chapter 4.

Between the Arcs

With this background, it is tempting to lay the later mimetic arc over the early hermeneutical arc, as some have assumed. Just a little reflection, however, reveals an uneven fit. They are strikingly similar in some ways: for example, the third moment of both arcs is appropriation. They are dissimilar, however, in both of the first two moments. The later, narrative arc also represents refinement of Ricoeur's thinking, such as the abandonment of the sense and reference model. The result is in many ways a positive development of his thought. At the same time, several questions arise in terms of how the two arcs are to be related. This is especially true since neither Ricoeur nor other commentators have particularly dealt with their relationship.

One question relates to the tension between the writer and the reader. The hermeneutical arc appears to imply only readers, whereas the mimetic arc includes both. The mimetic arc begins with a writer and reader in prefiguration, then with a writer and reader in configuration, and seems to end with a reader in refiguration. (Cf. Figure 1.)

A second tension lies between the first understanding and prefiguration. Prefiguration is a category that precedes a first reading and thus a

49. Ibid., 158.

first understanding of a text, so these seem to be discrete moments, yielding at least four points if one considers a synthesized arc, namely, prefiguration, first understanding, explanation, and postcritical understanding (refiguration).

A third tension lies between the analytical mode of explanation and the synthesizing mode of configuration. As indicated above, the analytical, semiotic mode of explanation does not appear to allow for a configured narrative world of the text. The configuration of a fictive world is an act of the synthetic imagination. The critical analysis of such a world into its parts is quite a different process. Thus there seems to be a distinction between a configurative moment and an explanatory moment. If we stop at this juncture, we now seem to have at least five points on a synthesized hermeneutical-mimetic arc. In other words, we have preunderstanding, first understanding, explanation, configuration, and refiguration.

A fourth tension is one that may afflict both arcs. Ricoeur recognizes the significance of placing a work in its historical context, but he does not seem to note the ambiguity between thinking of the refigured world in front of the text at the time of the text and a contemporary refiguration of the world in front of the text. This is especially important in the case of fiction. What was the intended and actual appropriation of, say, *The Adventures of Huckleberry Finn* roughly in the time in which it appeared? The words and concepts can hardly be understood without understanding their original context, taken in a broad sense. This does not mean that the original reception of the meaning has absolute priority, but it does mean that it must be taken into account even in order to offer a revisionist meaning. At the very least, one can make a relative distinction between the earlier reception and one's own critical reception. One would, of course, have to add the history of reception, bringing to mind Gadamer's "historical-effective consciousness."[50] Does one not have to consider the history of the reception of the Gospels in one's own, contemporary appropriation?

Moreover, regarding a fifth tension, do we not have to consider also a fusion of horizons at the point of the reader's configuration of the world of the text? To take up a point we made earlier, Ricoeur does not always clearly distinguish between the fictional world of the text in the sense, say, of a novel set in the nineteenth century, or the narrative world of the book of Jonah, and the world in front of the text in the sense of what our world would look like if we appropriated a nineteenth-century novel or the book of Jonah. It is apparent that a *configuring* reader response is needed to

50. For Gadamer's notion of *wirkungsgeschichtliches Bewußtsein,* translated as "historically effected consciousness," see ibid., 301–2.

construe the book of Jonah that would, in turn, lead to a *refiguring* reader response in terms of application. In effect, Ricoeur's placement of a fusion of horizons only at the point of refiguration conceals the actual Gadamerian point that a fusion of horizons already occurs at the point of configuration.[51] Further, going back to Ricoeur's earlier hermeneutical arc, there must already be at least a tacit sense of appropriation at the first guess, at the precritical understanding, for Gadamer contends that one cannot separate appropriation from any of the other moments of hermeneutics.[52] In other words, appropriation already affects the configuration of the world of the text, as well as, more explicitly, the world in front of the text. As James DiCenso remarks, "The differentiations of threefold mimesis cannot be such as to segregate these modes into watertight compartments."[53] Bringing in these issues that intensify the role of the productive imagination at the level of configuration is certainly not foreign to Ricoeur's approach, but it adds complexity to an arc that has already been complicated quite beyond his original three points. In fact, it is now beginning to look more like a pincushion than a simple three-point arc.

A final tension is the ambiguity between possibilities for judgment and one's actual judgment. This arises in terms of both configuration and refiguration. For example, there are usually several possible refigurations of a text, such as possible meanings of a Shakespeare play or of one of the Gospels. Even one interpreter may be pulled in a variety of directions. One can distinguish between the possibilities one is considering and the

51. Ironically, the emphasis in Wolfgang Iser's reader-response theory is on the role of the reader in configuring the text and not on refiguration. In other words, there is no immanent world of the text apart from the configuring construal of a reader. See Wolfgang Iser, *The Implied Reader: Patterns of Communication in Prose Fiction from Bunyan to Beckett* (Baltimore: Johns Hopkins University Press, 1974). While Ricoeur seems to recognize at times that reader-response theory concerns the reading of the world of the text, he consistently aligns reader response with refiguring a world in front of the text and neglects its role in terms of a fusion of horizons already in terms of configuration. Cf. Ricoeur, *Time and Narrative,* vol. 3, 164, 178–79.

52. See Gadamer, *Truth and Method,* 274–75: "In the course of our reflections we have come to see that understanding always involves something like the application of the text to be understood to the present situation of the interpreter. Thus we are forced to go, as it were, one stage beyond romantic hermeneutics, by regarding not only understanding and interpretation, but also application as comprising one unified process. This is not to return to the traditional distinction of the separate 'subtleties' of which pietism spoke. For, on the contrary, we consider application to be as integral a part of the hermeneutical act as are understanding and interpretation." An interesting example of this difference between Gadamer and Ricoeur is illustrated by Mario J. Valdés's analysis of Ricoeur, "Paul Ricoeur and Literary Theory," in *Philosophy of Paul Ricoeur,* ed. Hahn, 259–80. Valdés identifies the hermeneutical dimension of interpretation only with the very last moment of appropriation. Gadamer sees it as coming in at the first understanding as well as in explanation. I agree with Gadamer at this point. Valdés edited an important recent collection of Ricoeur's writings: *A Ricoeur Reader: Reflection and Imagination* (Toronto: University of Toronto Press, 1991).

53. James DiCenso, *Hermeneutics and the Disclosure of Truth: A Study in the Work of Heidegger, Gadamer, and Ricoeur* (Charlottesville: University Press of Virginia, 1990), 126.

final appropriation, where a reader judges among the possibilities. If one takes the ending of the Gospel of Mark, for example, several possible configurations and refigurations notoriously arise. A reader may become convinced of the cogency of one of them, but this does not mean that a refiguring activity has not occurred several times in order to grasp the various options. In general, Ricoeur does not clearly differentiate between these different dimensions and sometimes slides from one to another unknowingly.

A Refigured Arc

With these tensions and ambiguities in mind, is it possible, so to speak, to "refigure" Ricoeur's arcs in terms of a helpful and simpler synthesis, creating a more adequate hermeneutical arc? I suggest six conclusions in light of the previous discussion. (1) To focus on the standpoint of the reader may simplify matters. This does not negate the value of Ricoeur's reflections on the author at the level of prefiguration and configuration, but these are not as important for our purposes. (2) It is helpful to distinguish between a semiotic analysis and a narrative configuration, in order to differentiate critical analysis and synthetic, imaginative configuration. (3) Another distinction is that between the original and historical world of the text and world in front of the text, on the one hand, and a contemporary rendition of both, on the other. (4) Following Gadamer, a fusion of horizons must occur at every point but is more thematic and pronounced at the last stage. (5) Prefiguration can be collapsed into the idea of a first reading or figuration. In other words, a first reading already implies that we bring our prefigurative assumptions to a first figuration. (6) We can distinguish between possible configurations and refigurations and the issue of appropriating one of these possibilities as one's considered judgment.

How, then, do we relate the arcs? My initial impulse was to see the later mimetic arc as superseding the earlier. But on reflection, I think the basic structure of Ricoeur's first hermeneutical arc, which includes the distinction of a naïve, critical, and postcritical approach, is more helpful. Thus, I propose a revised arc consisting of a movement from a first, more naïve reading, through a critical and explanatory reading, and then to a third, postcritical reading (which can itself be subdivided into postcritical readings of possibilities and a postcritical actualized appropriation). The mimetic arc cannot be left behind, however, because its distinction between configuration and refiguration is crucial, especially for fiction.

The problem is that each "reading"—precritical, critical, and postcritical—implies both a configurative and a refigurative dimension.[54] What I suggest, therefore, is to "fold" the later arc into the earlier, resulting in one threefold arc in which each moment of the hermeneutical arc includes a mimetic arc. The resulting picture can be seen in Figure 2. Since each reading involves holistic synthesis, one could substitute "understanding" for "reading," thus having a naïve understanding, a critical understanding, and a postcritical understanding.

The initial understanding thus includes the prefiguration and an initial construal of both the world of the text and the world in front of the text. At this point, an initial judgment or "guess" has probably already been made about the nature of both but could well involve a more or less tacit sense that other possibilities exist.

The next moment is the critical stage of analysis, which includes the use of any and every critical tool. This applies most easily to an analytical breakdown of the text into its components but can also apply to a critical analysis of the possible configurations of the world of the text and possible implications of the text, that is, possible refigurations. In other words, a possible world in front of the text needs ideological critique as much as the literary world of the text. This critical stage would also especially include an effort to grasp the "effective history" of the text, that is, its original and later receptions.

A very important related advantage is that this revised arc brings in holistic "understanding," even in the middle momentum of explanation. It retains Ricoeur's emphasis on critique, but it recognizes that critical evaluation of the configured and refigured world of the text demands synthetic imagination. It thus represents a further step in Ricoeur's desired goal of overcoming the Continental split between explanation and understanding.

Note especially that this is the point where systematic theology represents a critical perspective on the text, raising questions, for example, about a text's implications for the nature of God, Christ, or salvation. This "doctrinal" perspective in fact is a part of the "effective history" of the text

54. Valdés does something similar in relating several critical aspects to both configuration and refiguration. The problem with his view, even though it is a helpful model, is that it is confusing with respect to Ricoeur's arcs. Valdés divides the earlier hermeneutical arc into four critical dimensions—formal, historical, phenomenological, and hermeneutical—leaving the "first understanding" out altogether. See Valdés, "Introduction," 27–28. A further problem is that Valdés connects the hermeneutical dimension of interpretation only with the very last moment of appropriation. In my own correction of Ricoeur by means of Gadamer, I see a degree of appropriation, the hermeneutical moment, as involved at every stage. See also Valdés, "Paul Ricoeur and Literary Theory," 259–80.

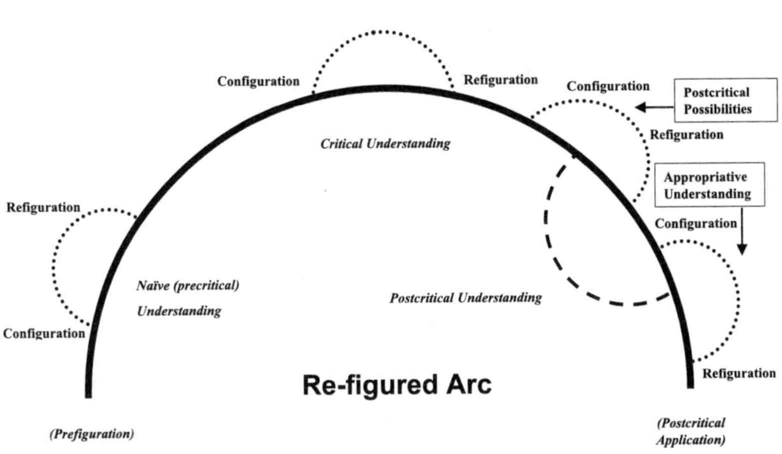

and puts questions back to the text just as the text raises questions, or "gives rise to thought," about traditional doctrine. For example, the "Christology" in Philippians 2 raises the issue of what is said in the text and also what it implies about a fully formulated Christology. The history of interpretation of this important text, especially with the later use of it as the paradigmatic case of a kenotic Christology, inevitably influences our understanding. Interpretation of the text usually involves dialogue with its theological appropriation, even if the dominant kenotic view is rejected.[55] The hermeneutical circle in the larger sense is clearly in play, where the more highly developed Christologies that came centuries after Paul shape interpretation. Sometimes they may help and sometimes they may hinder; what cannot be avoided is their role in interpretation. With Ricoeur's hermeneutical arc as a framework, we can affirm this interrelationship while keeping the main focus on the scriptural text. We have therefore a nuanced and inseparable interweaving of the configuration and refiguration of the text that nevertheless allows us to make a relative distinction between the text and our interpretation of it.

55. For example, see James McClendon's reinterpretation in James Wm. McClendon Jr., *Doctrine: Systematic Theology* (Nashville: Abingdon Press, 1994), 267: "Is it possible to see the Godlike image attributed to Jesus (*morphe,* v. 6) *not* as the characteristic of his heavenly pre-existence (for which, after all 'God*like*ness' seems far too weak, far too 'Arian') but of his human circumstances as he set out to make his career? Paul the proud Pharisee, Jesus the gifted young leader? Then we would read of Jesus' refusal to grasp equality with God not as a Miltonian tale of a heavenly God who refused to rebel, but as a reference to the human Jesus' earthly temptations."

The final judgment about which of these configurations and refigurations is best occurs in the postcritical moment. This third stage includes a reading of the text in a holistic, receptive way, yet with all of the critical analysis in the background, rather like hearing a piece of music for enjoyment or listening to a sermon for edification, after studying it, rather than attending to all the critical questions while engaging in the activity. This holistic and receptive reading applies to both configuration and refiguration. For example, in the case of the Philippians text, this would involve the judgment of its meaning in Philippians but also its significance for a developed Christology. This last stage would also involve a postcritical consideration of the various possibilities for interpretation, but a postcritical decision among these possibilities belongs especially to this moment, yielding in a sense two "sub-arcs" (see Figure 2), one for possibilities and another for an actualized appropriation. Thus, appropriation of the text in terms of its truth for *me,* its application, especially coalesces in this postcritical phase, yielding the world in front of the text in which I try, at least, to live.

As Ricoeur says, such distinct moments exist more in analysis than in reality, and therefore the last, postcritical phase would typically lead to further critical reflection and then to further postcritical appropriation, in a hermeneutical spiral rather than an arc.

Theological Implications

It is now time to take up some of the clues we have noted along the way and elaborate implications of this refigured arc for theology. First, Ricoeur's and Gadamer's understanding of how a text plays us as much as we play the text is a significant move away from an Enlightenment notion of a sovereign self, transparent to itself and in firm control of the factual world external to itself. As I mentioned, this conception of a sovereign self was ironically embedded in conservative North American theology in the nineteenth century, which in many ways represented mainstream theology in the United States. As Marsden stresses, the Bible as a text was modeled after a Baconian–Scottish Common Sense Realist conception of science. Rather than being antagonistic to science, at this time conservatives were eager to claim the prestige of such an objectivist, factual model for their biblical hermeneutic. The latter, they claimed, was "scientific." Of course, as science moved away from their conception in both content—the Scopes "Monkey Trial" of 1925—and form—the Kuhnian revolution in the 1960s—this marriage led to a bitter divorce and the marginalization of conservatives. The emergence of the evangelicals after World War II has gradually led to a search for a more adequate hermeneutic, one that does not equate science and faith, nor, in effect, place the reader above the text, nor drain the text of a surplus of meaning. Ricoeur's model offers aid in all these areas.

His model also starts with the text and the way in which it speaks to us in a first naïveté, but then it allows for further critical examination instead of staying within a noncritical, fideistic mode. In addition, the value of Ricoeur's third hermeneutical moment is that it points back to the text rather than leaving the text behind as a result of distilling a transparent proposition that is then detached from the text. As we shall see in the next chapter, Ricoeur's emphasis on the surplus of meaning, which calls for repeated spiraling back to the text, places greater emphasis on the text, not less.

On the less conservative side, Ricoeur's model offers a way of avoiding the tendency to eclipse the biblical narrative, in Frei's words, by a theological or metaphysical substitute. It emphasizes the necessity of the critical moment but also presses beyond it. The critical dimension allows for philosophical engagement without making scripture and theology subservient to a foundational philosophical view. On the other side of things, it especially aids in moving the historical-critical method, which is so important to understanding the biblical text, beyond its preoccupation with the world behind the text such that it never engages the text as we have it.

This revised Ricoeurian model provides an expansive framework that allows for traditional historical-critical methods, such as form and redaction criticism, along with newer emphases on canonicity, narrativity, and the social context. Systematic theology plays an important role at the point of critical reflection, but as second-order rather than first-order language. It thus has a significant supportive and clarifying role but not a dominating and substitutive role. In addition, the emphasis on appropriation as an inherent aspect of hermeneutics brings out the important liberal emphasis on praxis in a way that does not minimize the role of either scripture or theology.

In short, in several ways, Ricoeur offers a postmodern model that helps theology move past the impasse of the modern two-party system of conservatives and liberals that Nancey Murphy has described.[56] More

56. Nancey C. Murphy, *Beyond Liberalism and Fundamentalism: How Modern and Postmodern Philosophy Set the Theological Agenda,* Rockwell Lecture Series (Valley Forge, Pa.: Trinity Press International, 1996).

important, it offers the possibility of reframing, or "refiguring," traditional theological disputes that have been stuck in the polar opposition between these two camps, which is one of the more hopeful aspects of the post-modern turn. We will be delineating more of how this can occur in subsequent chapters. We consider first, however, how both groups can appropriate the affirmation of a surplus of meaning of texts.

CHAPTER THREE

The Surplus of Meaning

The promise of hermeneutical philosophy for theology is built on a root experience in both areas, namely, the phenomenology of reading and interpreting texts. The central aspect of the interpretation of texts, especially of rich texts, is their fecundity of meaning. In other words, such texts contain a reservoir of meaning that can be tapped again and again. People find themselves returning to a text to locate, sometimes surprisingly, new understanding and new insights.

This common experience is not always reflected in hermeneutical theory, however, and has a checkered past. The modern emphasis on clear and objective meaning moves in quite a different direction. Paul Ricoeur nevertheless makes an essential component of his hermeneutical theory the idea of a "surplus of meaning" and offers complex, albeit controversial, support for it. In the process, he deals with one of the most contested aspects of interpretation, that is, the issue of authorial intent.

In this chapter, we first consider the historical background of the current shift away from authorial intent and literal meaning toward the meaning of the text and its plurivocity. Then I unfold the specific way in which Ricoeur understands the surplus of meaning.

Historical Background

The history of biblical interpretation is wide and varied, but to understand the contemporary situation, we can trace a few limited patterns. In some ways, postmodern exegesis can be seen as a return to premodern exergesis. It is not a simple return, however, and to attend to the differences, we need to outline the contours of premodern and modern hermeneutics.

Premodern Hermeneutics

Medieval hermeneutics is noted for its luxurious surplus of meaning that developed in a particular way based on the allegorical method.[1] Each text of scripture was thought potentially to contain four levels of meaning. The classic example was Jerusalem, which *literally* referred to the earthly city, *allegorically* to the Christian church, morally or *tropologically* to the soul, and eschatologically or *anagogically* to the future heavenly city of God. This approach had its roots in Alexandria, with its heavy Greek influence. Origen (d. ca. 250) was a precursor of this approach, advocating a threefold sense based on a tripartite anthropology in which humans consisted of body, soul, and spirit. Often, though, the contrast was simply between "the letter and the spirit," as in 2 Corinthians 3:6.

The church's allegorical method was not completely unfettered. First, in reaction to the Gnostics, who favored the method but who took it in unorthodox directions, early Christian leaders such as Irenaeus (d. ca. 202) and Tertullian (d. ca. 222–225) pointed to the bishops who stood in the line of the apostles as determinative interpreters. Second, these leaders looked to what they called the "rule of faith" *(regula fides),* the basic beliefs of the churches, as providing hermeneutical control.[2] Thus, the play of allegory had fences around it. These responses reveal that the church leaders as well as the Gnostics saw the complexity of interpretation. They realized that meaning was not simply lying plainly on the page, and that what one brings to the text shapes the interpretation of the text.

Such an approach nevertheless led to a profusion of meanings, sometimes wild and fanciful. There was a surplus of meaning, to be sure, that might even be orthodox, but sometimes the surplus far exceeded any legitimate meaning. At the time, the Alexandrian school was countered by the Antiochian school, with leaders such as Theodore of Mopsuestia. The Antiochian school appealed to the literal, historical sense and were critical of how the allegorical method got lost "in a world of symbols and shadows."[3] The allegorical excesses led finally to a reaction in the Reformation toward a literal sense that since has dominated conservative theology, sometimes with consequences just as misleading.

1. See, for helpful accounts, Karlfried Froehlich, ed. and trans., *Biblical Interpretation in the Early Church,* Sources of Early Christian Thought (Philadelphia: Fortress Press, 1984); Robert M. Grant, *A Short History of the Interpretation of the Bible* (New York: Macmillan Co., 1963); Werner Jeanrond, *Theological Hermeneutics: Development and Significance* (New York: Crossroad, 1991), chap. 2.

2. Grant, *Short History of the Interpretation of the Bible,* chap. 8.

3. Ibid., 66.

Conservative Hermeneutics

The Reformers sharply rejected the allegorical approach in favor of the plain or literal sense. Martin Luther expressed their viewpoint well:

> No violence is to be done to the words of God, whether by man or angel; but they are to be retained in their simplest meaning wherever possible, and to be understood in their grammatical and literal sense unless the context plainly forbids, lest we give our adversaries occasion to make a mockery of all the Scriptures. Thus Origen was repudiated, in olden times, because he despised the grammatical sense and turned the trees, and all else written concerning Paradise, into allegories; for it might therefrom be concluded that God did not create trees.[4]

Part of the background for the Reformers was the issue of authority. With the need for the *sola scriptura* principle over against the authority of the pope and Roman Catholic hierarchy, the Reformers' concern for clarity of meaning is understandable.

Their emphasis on the perspicuity of scripture led to the idea that not only did scripture have a plain sense but also a plain person could interpret it—at least in its basic message. The Reformers themselves nevertheless had a sense of the profundity of scripture that mitigated their appeal to clarity.[5] Luther stressed testimony to Jesus Christ and to the grace of God as critical hermeneutical principles, accounting for his notorious discomfort with the book of James. Both Luther and Calvin stressed the importance of the Holy Spirit in interpreting scripture. Calvin referred to arguments for the inspiration of scripture but in the end based conviction of the divine authority of scripture on "the inward testimony of the Spirit."[6] Moreover, he argued that God's majesty and transcendence were such that God had to "accommodate" to human capacities, so the height of human expression is akin to God lisping to us the way a nurse would speak to infants.[7]

As we have seen, these nuances were largely lost among conservatives by the nineteenth century, under the influence of modern science and a common reliance on Baconian induction and Scottish Common Sense

4. Martin Luther, *The Babylonian Captivity of the Church,* Works of Martin Luther 2 (Grand Rapids: Baker Book House, 1982), 189f.

5. See Timothy George, *Theology of the Reformers* (Nashville: Broadman Press, 1988), for helpful discussions of these issues among the major Reformers.

6. John Calvin, *Calvin: Institutes of the Christian Religion,* trans. Ford Lewis Battles, ed. John T. McNeill, The Library of Christian Classics 20 (Philadelphia: Westminster Press, 1960), 1.7.4.

7. Ibid., 1.13.1.

Realism. The upshot was an emphasis on the "facts" of scripture, which are basically clear and uninterpreted, similar to the empirical facts of science. This was long before the contemporary view in philosophy of science that all facts are "theory-laden." Rather, facts were seen as the obvious and trustworthy data on which theories are built, the theories not being as reliable as the facts. The fascinating shift in this story is the way in which the Bible came to be seen as comparable to science, being scientific and factual in its own way, thus trading on the growing prestige of science. George Marsden observes, "Common Sense philosophy affirmed their ability to know 'the facts' directly. With the Scriptures at hand as a compendium of facts, there was no need to go further. They needed only to classify the facts, and follow wherever they might lead."[8] This focus on the facts also developed in the midst of a budding interest in dispensational millennialism, with its attempt to decipher the "facts" of prophecy. "It was vital to the dispensationalists that their information be not only absolutely reliable but also precise."[9] The new term *inerrant* was suited to convey this requirement. The corresponding apologetic was one captured in the title of a popular evangelical work, *Evidence That Demands a Verdict.*[10] There is so little room for conflict in interpretation that the evidence is supposed to work like coercive scientific facts, not realizing that even science is not nowadays so understood.

The understanding of scripture as composed of sciencelike facts accentuated the idea of the perspicuity of scripture. There was no surplus of meaning here. If so little interpretation is involved, however, these conservatives struggled to explain why opinions varied so widely, even among professional theologians. At one point, the president of an evangelical col-

8. George M. Marsden, *Fundamentalism and American Culture: The Shaping of Twentieth-Century Evangelicalism 1870–1925* (Oxford: Oxford University Press, 1980), 56. Kevin Vanhoozer expresses the same point in terms of the way in which evangelicals focus on basic propositions in scripture: "The task of theology thus becomes the systematization of the information conveyed through biblical propositions." See Kevin J. Vanhoozer, "The Voice and the Actor: A Dramatic Proposal about the Ministry and the Minstrelsy of Theology," in *Evangelical Futures: A Conversation on Theological Method,* ed. John G. Stackhouse Jr. (Grand Rapids: Baker Book House, 2000), 70. Stan Grenz and John Franke similarly note, in terms of what they call a rationalist approach, "The rationalist approach that typifies evangelical theology is characterized by a commitment to the Bible as the source book of information for systematic theology. As such, it is viewed as a rather loose and disorganized collection of factual, propositional statements. The task of theology in turn becomes that of collecting and arranging these varied statements in such a way as to bring their underlying unity into relief and reveal the eternal system of timeless truths to which they point." See Stanley J. Grenz and John R. Franke, *Beyond Foundationalism: Shaping Theology in a Postmodern Context* (Louisville, Ky.: Westminster John Knox Press, 2001), 13f.

9. Marsden, *Fundamentalism and American Culture,* 57.

10. Josh McDowell, *Evidence That Demands a Verdict* (San Bernardino, Calif.: Campus Crusade for Christ, 1972).

lege surmised that the reason for diverse interpretation must be chalked up to "high pay and extended vacations."[11]

In response to this frustration, conservative theologians have often retreated into a fideistic appeal to revelation inaccessible to unbelievers. Sometimes appealing to Karl Barth, whom Jeffrey Stout charges with advocating a positivism of faith, they eschew apologetics. Stout argues that Barth represents the strategy of escape into a private zone that is invulnerable to criticism but also incapable of communication to the rest of the world.[12] The irony is that such a strategy does not address at all the conflict of interpretations *within* the Christian community of faith, which is virtually as sharp as the differences with non-Christians.

Nancey Murphy confirms this problem in claiming that conservatives have, in general, adopted a foundationalist approach to the text. Calling it an "outside-in" approach, she maintains that they presuppose an external text that is unchallengeable and that sharply constrains interpretation.[13] The "inerrant" text is like a Cartesian indubitable foundation, surprisingly, for many who have long explicitly criticized modernity, revealing the tacit influence of a modern epistemological structure. The Scottish Common Sense Realist legacy along with the need for a reliable foundation pushed conservatives to make the text as clear as possible and to downplay the surplus of meaning, much less the conflict of interpretations. What good is the scripture as a foundation if it is not clear and perspicuous? *The challenge for conservative theology on the contemporary scene is thus to find a nonfoundationalist hermeneutical approach that can deal with diversity and richness of meaning while avoiding the anarchy and privatism of fideism.*

Liberal Hermeneutics

One would expect less-conservative theologians to have another trajectory that lands in neither inerrancy nor fideism, but the story is not a simple

11. Marsden, *Fundamentalism and American Culture,* 220. The president was Charles Blanchard, president of Wheaton College from 1877 to 1925.

12. Jeffrey Stout, *The Flight from Authority: Religion, Morality, and the Quest for Autonomy* (Notre Dame: University of Notre Dame Press, 1981), 141–48. Of course, this is just one reading of Barth, albeit a common one. Probably a more balanced approach is to see the more radical, fideistic perspective as applying to the earlier Barth, in conflict with Brunner on general revelation. The later Barth is thus often seen as much more open to general revelation and a "point of contact." For example, see Garrett Green, *Imagining God: Theology and the Religious Imagination* (San Francisco: Harper & Row, 1989), 3.

13. Nancey C. Murphy, *Beyond Liberalism and Fundamentalism: How Modern and Postmodern Philosophy Set the Theological Agenda,* Rockwell Lecture Series (Valley Forge, Pa.: Trinity Press International, 1996), 15–19, 32–35. Grenz and Franke make a similar point, like Murphy charging both conservative and liberal hermeneutics with foundationalism. See Grenz and Franke, *Beyond Foundationalism,* 32–37.

one.[14] With the rise of biblical criticism, the straightforward meaning of the biblical text was questioned. As Hans Frei has pointed out, the result was to turn to "the world behind the text" in order to convey meaning.[15] On the one hand, this resulted in an emphasis on the factual history behind the text, in its own way falling into an empiricist, factual hermeneutic. In other words, what the text is about is factual history, and this can be reconstructed by modern historical method, which may yield a history quite different from the world of the text. The result was "the eclipse of the biblical narrative," which is the title of Frei's book. Karl Barth, notably, reacted against his liberal training because of this avoidance of the meaning of the biblical text for today.[16]

On the other hand, if the factual history behind the text differs so sharply from the ostensible world of the text, the meaning must lie elsewhere, often in a philosophical worldview, such as the Kantian or the Hegelian. Albert Schweitzer pointed out how such a view can be imposed on interpretation in his devastating criticism of nineteenth-century "lives of Jesus" efforts. He pointed out that these depictions looked much more like bourgeois Germans and nineteenth-century philosophers than a first-century apocalyptic Jesus.[17] In yet another way, according to Frei, the biblical narrative itself was eclipsed.

In subtle ways, liberal theology, like conservative theology, was also urged toward direct, univocal meaning. Modern science and philosophy were exerting pressure toward clear facts on liberal theologians as well, a continuation of the earlier Cartesian model of "clarity and distinctness." Philosophers were wary of figurative language and appealed to direct discourse. At the outset of the modern period, Thomas Hobbes (1588–1679) vehemently dismissed metaphor as harmful to the cause of truth. Hobbes charged that people abuse speech "when they use words metaphorically; that is, in other sense than that they are ordained for; and

14. I am not entirely happy with the terminology of "liberal" hermeneutics, used to mean the major approaches of "less-conservative" theologies, ranging from liberal theology per se such as Schleiermacher and Harnack to theologians such as Paul Tillich. I here follow Nancey Murphy in *Beyond Liberalism and Fundamentalism,* seeing a largely two-party system in theology that can be contrasted as two different foundationalist approaches. Such an ideal model, she, too, recognizes, cannot deal perfectly with all cases.

15. Hans W. Frei, *The Eclipse of Biblical Narrative: A Study in Eighteenth and Nineteenth Century Hermeneutics* (New Haven, Conn.: Yale University Press, 1974).

16. David L. Mueller, *Karl Barth,* Makers of the Modern Theological Mind, ed. Bob E. Patterson (Waco, Tex.: Word Books, 1972), 22.

17. Albert Schweitzer, *The Quest of the Historical Jesus: A Critical Study of Its Progress from Reimarus to Wrede,* trans. W. Montgomery (New York: Macmillan Co., 1968).

thereby deceive others."[18] In the early twentieth century, the young Ludwig Wittgenstein captured this spirit in his *Tractatus Logico-Philosophicus,* which became the bible of the logical-positivist movement: "Everything that can be thought at all can be thought clearly. Everything that can be put into words can be put clearly."[19] Science came to be seen as the prime exemplar of this drive toward clear and verified truth.

The challenges of contesting the hegemony of science were probably more severe in liberal theology than in conservative because of the desire to accommodate and take seriously the finding of science. The language of religion, however, could hardly compete with science. As Ian Barbour notes, modern theology in the early part of the twentieth century largely fell into the "independence" model. As such, it revealed a Kantian strategy of compartmentalizing the spheres of science and faith.[20] Jeffrey Stout argues that at this point theology fell into two responses, both of which have failed.[21] One was the Barthian route of retreat into fideistic revelation, a realm of *Heilsgeschichte* (salvation history) inaccessible to historiography. The other was to evacuate the meaning of faith so much that it could hardly be distinguished from nonbelief, an accusation he brings against Paul Tillich.

Yet a third approach has more clearly emerged that Stout did not identify, an approach significant for our purposes. This is the foundationalist appeal to a universal religious experience. In some ways, it is like the Barthian appeal to revelation, but it actually represents the view of Barth's nemesis, Friedrich Schleiermacher, and as such is at the core of the nineteenth-century liberalism that Barth passionately rejected. George Lindbeck has described this strategy most eloquently in *The Nature of Doctrine* as the "experiential-expressive" approach.[22] Schleiermacher grounded religion in the feeling of absolute dependence, which he thought was

18. Thomas Hobbes, *Leviathan,* ed. Michael Oakeshott, 2d ed. (New York: Macmillan Co., 1947), pt. 1, chap. 4.

19. Ludwig Wittgenstein, *Tractatus Logico-Philosophicus,* trans. D. F. Pears and B. F. McGuinness (London: Routledge & Kegan Paul, 1961), 4.116 (refers to the numbering of the paragraphs of the text, not the page numbers).

20. Ian G. Barbour, *Religion and Science: Historical and Contemporary Issues,* rev. ed. (San Francisco: HarperSanFrancisco, 1997), 45–47, 68–70, 84–89. He places conservatives (whom he terms "biblical literalists") in the conflict model—along with scientific materialists. He rightly sees the way in which the univocal hermeneutic of the nineteenth-century conservatives and their modern creation-science descendants led to conflict with modern science. He does not, however, treat the fideistic strand of conservative theology that fits also into his independence model.

21. Jeffrey Stout, *Ethics after Babel: The Languages of Morals and Their Discontents* (Boston: Beacon Press, 1988), chap. 7.

22. George Lindbeck, *The Nature of Doctrine: Religion and Theology in a Postliberal Age* (Philadelphia: Westminster Press, 1984).

common to all religions but was expressed most clearly in the Christian faith.[23] This provides the unity of all religion in a common experience that is simply described in different ways.

Both Gadamer and Ricoeur pay a great deal of attention to Schleiermacher also as the chief representative of Romantic hermeneutics, as we briefly noted in chapter 1. Schleiermacher increasingly moved toward the goal of interpretation as divining the intentions of the author. Even more, the idea was to re-create the creative experience of the author's genius. Wilhelm Dilthey, as Schleiermacher's successor, called explicitly for re-experiencing the author's creative act. To be sure, both saw that one reaches the author's experience through exegesis of the text, but the focus is on the empathetic understanding of the author.

The critique of authorial intent by Gadamer and Ricoeur represents the formidable obstacles that this approach to hermeneutics has encountered in the twentieth century, which we take up further later in this chapter. For the moment, it suffices to note with Murphy that the common liberal appeal to the experience of the author or to fundamental religious experience in general is a foundationalist move on the liberal side in order to make the religious claim impregnable.[24] It is an "inside-out" Cartesian appeal to indubitable experiences in the religious sphere. Lindbeck and Murphy trace such an appeal to fundamental experiences in contemporary theologians such as David Tracy and Gordon Kauffman. While their interpretation of Tracy has been sharply contested, due to his hermeneutical turn, they undoubtedly identify a persistent tendency in modern theology.[25] Dependence on an experience that is expressed in a variety of ways is also exceedingly difficult to criticize and is protected from attack by scientific and historical investigation. Lindbeck's criticism is that words are not so malleable that the same word can depict such varied experiences.[26] In the end, the experiential-expressive view can make the text mean almost anything, thus losing hermeneutical constraints.

On the liberal side of modern theology, the challenge is thus to find a non-foundationalist hermeneutic that accepts pluralism and biblical criticism

23. Friedrich Schleiermacher, *The Christian Faith,* ed. H. R. Mackintosh and J. S. Stewart (Philadelphia: Fortress Press, 1928), esp. par. 32.

24. Murphy, *Beyond Liberalism and Fundamentalism,* 19–28.

25. See especially Tracy's own rejection of this characterization of himself in David Tracy, "Lindbeck's New Program for Theology: A Reflection," *The Thomist* 49 (1985): 460–72. The criticism is probably more pertinent to the Tracy of his earlier work—David Tracy, *Blessed Rage for Order: The New Pluralism in Theology,* The Seabury Library of Contemporary Theology (New York: Seabury Press, 1979)—than to his later—David Tracy, *Plurality and Ambiguity: Hermeneutics, Religion, Hope* (San Francisco: Harper & Row, 1987).

26. Lindbeck, *Nature of Doctrine,* 39–41.

while taking the text seriously and not lapsing into vacuousness and fideism. Conservatives have overemphasized the hermeneutical constraints of the text; liberals have underemphasized it. In response, Lindbeck has called for a "postliberal" theology; some evangelicals have now called for a "postconservative" theology.[27] This work is an effort to show how Ricoeur's hermeneutical philosophy can contribute to both of these much-needed endeavors.

Ricoeur and the Surplus of Meaning

The contribution of Ricoeur to the problems raised by modern biblical hermeneutics is manifold. One addressing of these problems is his development of a discourse theory that affirms the surplus of meaning of texts, which will engage us for the rest of this chapter. Another part of the response is his creative approach to metaphor and narrative, which the next chapter will treat. Yet a third important component is chapter 5's account of the problem of the conflict of interpretations.

Gadamer and Belongingness to the Text

As we have seen in the context of Ricoeur's development of his hermeneutical arc, Ricoeur repeatedly takes his cue from Gadamer but then moves in a more critical direction. This is what he does in the course of developing his notion of a text and its surplus of meaning.

In *Truth and Method,* Gadamer severely criticizes the Romantic hermeneutics of Schleiermacher and Dilthey. Moving away from their author-centered hermeneutics, he turns to a focus on the text. It is the text itself that has a subject matter *(die Sache)* that must be interpreted. The fusion of horizons is not between the author and the reader, it is between *die Sache* and the reader.

Ricoeur similarly argues that Schleiermacher and Dilthey never reconciled their focus on divining the experience of the author and the desire to make hermeneutics objective and respectable. Indeed, they could not. The text, however, provides a focus and substance that are not so elusive as the internal thoughts and experiences of an author. Gadamer's and Ricoeur's view agrees with much twentieth-century literary criticism, which has charged Romantic hermeneutics with the intentional fallacy, that is, with

27. Roger E. Olsen, "Postconservative Evangelicals Greet the Postmodern Age," *Christian Century* (May 1995): 480–83.

identifying the meaning of the text with what the author experienced in writing.[28]

Gadamer furthermore recognizes that even the text itself cannot simply be repeated but must be interpreted. The fusion of horizons guarantees that discerning the meaning of a text is always at some level a creative act—not repetition but interpretation. He emphasizes that, because of the commonality of human experience and tradition, if we can read a text at all, we have some common ground. In other words, there is a "belongingness" to human tradition that makes it possible for our horizons to connect at some level.

Gadamer's point has been echoed by others who reject the idea that our cognitive frameworks separate us into incommensurable camps, living in the aftermath of the mythical tower of Babel. Perhaps Donald Davidson has made this point the most strongly in arguing for the impossibility of such isolated conceptual schemes,[29] followed by the neopragmatists Jeffrey Stout and Richard Rorty.[30]

At the same time, Gadamer perhaps does not do justice to the possibility of misunderstanding. Most dramatically, the French poststructuralist Jacques Derrida, in a notorious encounter with Gadamer, illustrated the possibility of "nonencounter."[31] They both agreed to a celebrated meeting and never seemed to understand each other. Derrida especially seemed intent upon showing that dialogue and agreement do not proceed as amicably as Gadamer suggests.

As we shall see in chapter 5, Ricoeur also believes that Gadamer does not allow adequately for a hermeneutic of suspicion. While agreeing with a dimension of belongingness, he also thinks Gadamer does not allow enough for distanciation and alienation, which Ricoeur thinks especially arise in the distinction between direct speech and texts.

28. For example, see Leland Ryken, "Formalist and Archetypal Criticism," in *Contemporary Literary Theory: A Christian Appraisal,* ed. Clarence Walhout and Leland Ryken (Grand Rapids: Wm. B. Eerdmans Publishing Co., 1991), 6.

29. Donald Davidson, "On the Very Idea of a Conceptual Scheme," in *Inquiries into Truth and Interpretation* (Oxford: Clarendon Press, 1984), 183–98.

30. Stout, *Ethics after Babel,* chap. 1; Richard Rorty, *Consequences of Pragmatism: Essays, 1972–1980* (Minneapolis: University of Minnesota Press, 1982), 3–18.

31. Diane P. Michelfelder and Richard E. Palmer, eds., *Dialogue and Deconstruction: The Gadamer-Derrida Encounter* (Albany: State University of New York Press, 1989).

Distanciation of a Text

In an important essay in 1973, "The Hermeneutical Function of Distanciation," Ricoeur elaborated what he called a "productive notion of distanciation."[32] He was reacting to what he considered to be Gadamer's unproductive opposition between alienation and belonging. As Ricoeur put it, "My own reflection stems from a rejection of this alternative and an attempt to overcome it."[33] He began by laying out five criteria of textuality that mark the move from direct speech to writing.[34]

1. One criterion relates the dialectic of event and meaning. Drawing on the French linguist Emile Benveniste, Ricoeur emphasizes equally the importance of the event of language and the system of language.[35] He is here addressing structuralism, perhaps the major French philosophical movement of the time, which puts all emphasis on the *system* of language.[36] In Ricoeur's theory of discourse, both dimensions are irreplaceable.

A word is concretized in the event, the now, of language. In fact, a word may never have been coined before, as in the case of a new metaphor. The system of words, however, of which a dictionary consists, is drawn from such usage and in turn shapes such usage. The relations of words that we see in a dictionary and the often polysemic variety of definitions of words condition use but represent only latent potentiality apart from use. For example, the shades of meaning in the word *love* cannot be determined apart from use in a particular context, whether it be romantic love or Christian agape love. Ricoeur summarizes, "To say that discourse is an event is to say, first, that discourse is realised temporally and in the present, whereas the system of language is virtual and outside of time."[37] As he

32. Paul Ricoeur, "The Hermeneutical Function of Distanciation," in *Hermeneutics and the Human Sciences: Essays on Language, Action, and Interpretation,* ed. John B. Thompson (Cambridge: Cambridge University Press, 1981), 131–44.

33. Ibid., 131.

34. I am adding the qualifier *direct* because Ricoeur does not allow for the way in which speech, as in a recording or a broadcast, functions in his terms very much like a text. Speech is not always direct, in other words. Nicholas Wolterstorff, in fact, sharply remarks, "Ricoeur conducts his discussion as if we were living in a pre-Edisonian age!" See Nicholas Wolterstorff, *Divine Discourse: Philosophical Reflections on the Claim That God Speaks* (Cambridge: Cambridge University Press, 1995), 143.

35. Emile Benveniste, *Problems in General Linguistics,* trans. Mary Elizabeth Meek (Miami: University of Miami Press, 1971).

36. See Dan R. Stiver, *The Philosophy of Religious Language: Sign, Symbol, and Story* (Cambridge: Blackwell, 1996), chap. 8, for an account of structuralism and its sequel, poststructuralism. Structuralists make the distinction, following Ferdinand de Saussure, between *langue,* referring to the system of words, and *parole,* the event of speech.

37. Ricoeur, "Hermeneutical Function of Distanciation," 133.

suggests, the event of discourse, while concretizing words, fades away, leaving behind the word as meaning, which can be used again and again. If stabilized, it becomes an item in the dictionary. Again, both dimensions of the dialectic are important. "Just as language, by being actualised in discourse, surpasses itself as system and realises itself as event, so too discourse, by entering the process of understanding, surpasses itself as event and becomes meaning."[38]

Beyond the role of the meaning of words as implied by events of discourse, words appear only in sentences. Their meaning is structured and concretized not only by their codified meanings but by the rules of grammar. Grammatical rules, too, represent the dialectic of usage. Usage conveys grammatical practices that in turn shape further usage. In terms of grammar, too, "[t]he very first distanciation is thus the distanciation of the saying in the said."[39]

In this sense, the author is indispensable. "The objectification of discourse," Ricoeur says, "in a structured work does not abolish the first and fundamental feature of discourse, namely that it is constituted by a series of sentences whereby someone says something to someone about something."[40] While we have yet to specify the role of the author, it is important to note, in light of criticisms of Ricoeur, that Ricoeur does not imagine speech or writing as authorless. Rather, he carefully locates the role of the author. The system of language makes no reference to an author. Only in the event of discourse, where language is actualized, does an author play a role. What that role is, we shall see.

2. The second criterion is the realization of discourse as a structured work. At this point, a work goes beyond the analysis of a sentence to the identification of genres and styles. It complexifies the dialectic of event and meaning, which Ricoeur expresses deftly:

> By introducing the categories of production and labour into the dimension of discourse, the notion of work appears as a practical mediation between the irrationality of the event and the rationality of meaning. The event is stylisation itself, but this stylisation is in dialectical relation with a complex, concrete situation presenting conflictual tendencies. Stylisation occurs at the heart of an experience which is already structured but which is nevertheless characterised by openings, possibilities, indeterminacies. To grasp a work as an event is to grasp the relation between the situation and the project in the process of restructuration.[41]

38. Ibid., 134.
39. Ibid.
40. Ibid., 138.
41. Ibid., 137.

One can see here the basis of what Ricoeur later, in *Time and Narrative,* refers to as the act of configuration.

3. The first criterion dealt primarily with speaking, the second with writing. How do they relate? Ricoeur's main point is that in the fixation of discourse in writing, the subjective experience and intentions of the author are left behind. The work is distanciated from the author. As Ricoeur observes, whether we like it or not, "henceforth, textual meaning and psychological meaning have different destinies."[42] This does not, however, imply an incoherent notion of an authorless text. As Ricoeur says, "Not that we can conceive of a text without an author; the tie between the speaker and the discourse is not abolished, but distended and complicated."[43]

We can add several examples of this distension and complication in terms of scripture. In many cases we do not know the author, as in the case of Hebrews. Moreover, the time frame is often inexact, as in the case of Malachi or the book of Job. Job raises the issue of composite works, where someone has drawn on earlier material to compose a new work. This "redaction" may go beyond what we think of as simple editing to the creative proposal of distinctive theologies, as in the common understanding of Matthew and Luke drawing on Mark. Both Matthew and Luke utilize Mark in the service of their own distinctive theological emphases. Another instance is the final redactor of the Pentateuch, who apparently combined a JE document, which had already been creatively refigured, with a P and D document.[44] And what do we do with "books" that contain single oracles that have been combined in seemingly haphazard form, as in much of the Prophets, and which also apparently include the work of different authors at different times, as in Zechariah and Isaiah? This is not to mention larger problems of authorial intent that go beyond the Bible itself, for instance, determining the intentions behind a document propounded by a group, such as the Nicene Creed or the Constitution of the United States. Whose intentions are determinative? What if we have little idea of the specific people who authorized a document and of their intentions, as is the case for many of the creeds of the churches? How do we determine the meaning of a document such as the Bill of Rights that is constantly being reinterpreted in case law? Whose intentions count? Problems like these have led many to follow Gadamer and Ricoeur in turning to the

42. Ibid., 139

43. Paul Ricoeur, "The Model of the Text: Meaningful Action Considered as a Text," in *Hermeneutics and the Human Sciences,* ed. Thompson, 201.

44. A prominent hypothesis for this person is Ezra, which is also based in ancient tradition. See Richard Eilliot Friedman, *Who Wrote the Bible?* 2d ed. (San Francisco: HarperSanFrancisco, 1997).

text. As Ricoeur notes, "The'world' of the *text* may explode the world of the *author*."[45]

The significance of Ricoeur's point is that this distanciation of the text from the writer is not necessarily negative but is constitutive of writing. It is what enables the text to be available to others, often centuries later in quite different contexts, in a way that direct speech is not. Against Gadamer, who puts much more weight on speech and on "belongingness" than on distance, Ricoeur argues that this autonomy of the text is not just "the product of methodology and hence something superfluous and parasitical. . . . It is the condition of interpretation."[46]

4. The distanciation of the work from the intentions of the author makes it possible for the text itself to be seen as projecting a world, which may or may not coincide with the actual, conscious intentions of the author. This fourth criterion of Ricoeur's puts the emphasis not on the world behind the text but on the world in front of the text. "To interpret," Ricoeur says in this connection, "is to explicate the type of being-in-the-world unfolded *in front of* the text."[47]

Ricoeur's thesis cuts across several boundaries. On the one hand, it clashes with the tendency of modern theology, in both its conservative and liberal forms, to focus on the world behind the text. The consequent eclipse of biblical narrative has occurred across the board. The narrative shape was neglected by historical-critical scholars, who simply used the configured text to reconstruct the historical world behind it. Conservatives also conflated the meaning of the text with modern historiography by defending the text's historical assertions, thus neglecting its narrative shape.

Ricoeur also rejects structuralism's evasion of any world at all in its search for the deep structures of a text. He explicitly says that he is attempting to transcend not only the way in which Romantic hermeneutics sought to grasp the experience of genius behind the text but also structuralism's comfort in dealing only with internal analysis of basic structures. Ricoeur asks, after noting the problems of Romantic hermeneutics, "But is this to say that, renouncing any attempt to grasp the soul of an author, we shall restrict ourselves to reconstructing the structure of a work?"[48] He replies, "The principal task of hermeneutics eludes the alternative of genius or structure."[49]

45. Ricoeur, "Hermeneutical Function of Distanciation," 139.
46. Ibid., 139f.
47. Ibid., 141.
48. Ibid., 140.
49. Ibid.

Ricoeur emphasizes that texts refer to reality and not only to their internal structure. His thought here also runs against the grain of New Criticism in literature, which restricts interpretation to the internal world of the text. In contrast, Ricoeur asserts a dimension of appropriation, as we saw in terms of his hermeneutical arc. Not only does Ricoeur want to transcend the desert of criticism whereby readers lose themselves in a whirlwind of dissected texts, but he wants to recognize the power of texts to project a world that can possibly reconfigure the world of the reader. As he puts it, "For what must be interpreted in a text is a proposed world which I could inhabit and wherein I could project one of my ownmost possibilities."[50]

The hermeneutical arc reveals, however, that Ricoeur does not understand appropriation in any simple way. With respect to fiction in particular, the route we must travel is one that traverses the paths of criticism, including structuralism. As Ricoeur recognizes, much modern literature distances itself from the everyday world precisely in order to convey another world. In fact, he observes that "the role of most of our literature is, it seems, to destroy the world."[51] Nevertheless, this suspension of a direct connection with reality opens up an indirect—what he will call "metaphorical"—connection with reality. He states:

> My thesis here is that the abolition of a first order reference, an abolition effected by fiction and poetry, is the condition of possibility for the freeing of a second order reference, which reaches the world not only at the level of manipulable objects, but at the level that Husserl designated by the expression *Lebenswelt* [life-world] and Heidegger by the expression "being-in-the-world."[52]

5. Ricoeur concludes by noting how such self-understanding occurs only as mediated through distanciation. Appropriation occurs only through the distanciation of the writing from the writer. Unlike the situation of conversation, "appropriation is quite the contrary of contemporaneousness and congeniality: it is understanding at and through distance."[53] It is mediated by the structures of the work. He notes the broader philosophical significance: "In contrast to the tradition of the *cogito* and to the pretension of the subject to know itself by immediate intuition, it must be said that we understand ourselves only by the long detour

50. Ibid., 142.
51. Ibid., 141.
52. Ibid.
53. Ibid., 143.

of the signs of humanity deposited in cultural works."[54] We have immediacy neither with the writer nor with ourselves. The focus lies first of all not with what the writer might have wanted to express but with what was expressed.

Additionally, the distanciation of the work makes possible the self-criticism of the reader. The work enables readers to be distanced also from themselves, in order that they may attain an "enlarged self."[55] This allows for a genuine reading of the text as well as a genuine confrontation with the text that is not simply a repetition of the prejudices of the reader. "As reader, I find myself only by losing myself."[56]

Ricoeur's insight into the productivity of distanciation thus moves him beyond the liberal emphasis on an experience or intention behind the text and toward the conservative emphasis on the text. At the same time, it moves him away from a simple univocal reading of the text to a conception of a text rich in depth of meaning, with a larger role for the reader.

The Surplus of Meaning

With Ricoeur's notion of the distanciation of texts in hand, we can turn specifically to his idea of a surplus of meaning. Rather than trying to delimit the text to a specific conscious intention of the author or to a univocal meaning, Ricoeur sees that texts are fertile. Especially with religious texts that involve a great deal of figurative language, it is difficult to confine their meaning within one reader's interpretation. In fact, a familiar experience with scripture is the same reader coming back again and again to find more meaning. In early Separatist and Baptist history, this idea was celebrated by the alleged saying of the Separatist John Robinson that "the Lord had more Light and Truth yet to break forth out of His Holy Word."[57]

Ricoeur thus looks at texts in terms of a "principle of plenitude," which he defines oracularly: "A text means all that it can mean."[58] He therefore attempts to stake out a middle ground between the extremes of tyranny and anarchy. The history of interpretation of significant texts shows that meaning is irreducible to simple, perspicuous meanings, as in the conser-

54. Ibid.
55. Ibid.
56. Ibid., 144.
57. J. H. Shakespeare, *Baptist Congregational Pioneers* (London: Kingsgate Press, 1906), 165.
58. Paul Ricoeur, "Metaphor and the Central Problem of Hermeneutics," in *Hermeneutics and the Human Sciences,* ed. Thompson, 176.

vative hermeneutics of the nineteenth century. Beyond a strictly historical reading of a biblical text on its terms, theologians call for canonical and theological readings that place a particular work in the larger context of the canon and the reflection of the church.[59] Charles Scalise, for example, sees Ricoeur's hermeneutical arc as pointing to levels of meaning that represent a contemporary understanding of canonical hermeneutics and of appropriating the levels of meaning of medieval exegesis.[60]

Do these various readings leave us in the end with relativism? Some readings of French poststructuralism imply that any reading goes. Whether that is the case or not, Ricoeur certainly resists such a position. Consistent with his general postmodern approach, he tries to avoid the modern dilemma between objectivism and relativism.

His hermeneutical arc reveals the way in which he strives to avoid the dilemma. The first moment of understanding and a second moment of explanation correspond to an initial guess at meaning and then an attempt at validation. He argues that the latter, while not as precise as empirical verification in the sciences, is a logic of probability that could still be termed science. As we mentioned in chapter 2, Ricoeur at this point does not reflect the best understandings of contemporary philosophy of science, but if anything, current conceptions of science help his cause. Evaluation of scientific research programs involves critical comparisons that yield one conclusion more probable than another, making science itself hermeneutical. Ricoeur says similarly of texts, "The role of falsification is played here by the conflict between competing interpretations. An interpretation must not only be probable, but more probable than another. There are criteria of relative superiority which may easily be derived from the logic of subjective probability."[61] The criteria that he here invokes are especially native to the interpretation of texts, such as evaluating a text in terms of its language, its genre, its context, its time and place, and its relation to human self-understanding.

Ricoeur says more specifically, like Gadamer, that "validation is an argumentative discipline comparable to the juridical procedures of legal interpretation."[62] We will see how he develops this much further in the

59. See Stephen E. Fowl, *Engaging Scripture: A Model for Theological Interpretation,* Challenges in Contemporary Theology, ed. Gareth Jones and Lewis Ayres (Malden, Mass.: Blackwell, 1998); Kevin Vanhoozer, *Is There a Meaning in This Text? The Bible, the Reader, and the Morality of Literary Knowledge* (Grand Rapids: Zondervan Publishing House, 1998).

60. Charles J. Scalise, *Hermeneutics as Theological Prolegomena: A Canonical Approach,* Studies in American Biblical Hermeneutics 8 (Macon, Ga.: Mercer University Press, 1994).

61. Ricoeur, "Model of the Text," 213.

62. Ricoeur, "Metaphor," 175.

direction of a full-blown epistemology in chapter 7, but at this point, he explains the dynamic in terms of texts:

> In conclusion, if it is true that there is always more than one way of construing a text, it is not true that all interpretations are equal and may be assimilated to so-called "rules of thumb." The text is a limited field of possible constructions. The logic of validation allows us to move between the two limits of dogmatism and scepticism. It is always possible to argue for or against an interpretation, to confront interpretations, to arbitrate between them, and to seek for an agreement, even if this agreement remains beyond our reach.[63]

This lengthy analysis illuminates several important dimensions of the surplus of meaning. Meanings are not so exhaustible that "new light springing forth" is impossible. Neither are we left with incommensurate interpretations in "cold war" camps. Continuation of the dialogue is almost always possible. This is a salutary observation that the neopragmatists Stout and Rorty make, contending that the specter of relativism is an Enlightenment chimera in practical cases. In theory, disputes are difficult to settle in any kind of binding, universal way, even in the hard sciences. Nevertheless, at the practical level, discussion can continue. New evidence turns up. A new look at old data is possible. A fresh twist arises. In practice, changing people's minds is an individual thing. One person will be persuaded while another will not, and it is not predictable in advance what will trigger the change. The advantage of this view is that it does justice to the actuality of many differing interpretations, while not succumbing to relativism.

Ricoeur suggests that the text means all that it can mean, but it is nevertheless limited; it cannot mean anything one wants. One might imagine here a vector sweeping out from a central point; it extends even to infinity, but this is a "bounded" infinity. Ricoeur implies something like this in intimating that a text's potential interpretation is almost unlimited—but it does not include everything. For example, one cannot turn "God is love" into "God is hate." While people have appealed to the Bible as a source for white supremacy, most would say it is impossible legitimately to do so. What one has, then, is some hermeneutical control that avoids univocal limitation. As Ricoeur says, one is not condemned "to oscillation between dogmatism and scepticism."[64]

63. Ibid.
64. Ibid.

We explore in the next chapter how the surplus of meaning is further deepened by contemporary understanding of metaphor and of narrative. Before turning in that direction, however, we need to examine another, related issue: Can Ricoeur's notion of a text be expanded to nontexts?

Texts and Nontexts

One of the most important moves of Ricoeur in the 1970s was the application of his hermeneutical model to human action in "The Model of the Text: Meaningful Action Considered as a Text."[65] This extension of his hermeneutic has resulted in seminal application of both his and Gadamer's work in the area of sociology.

In this article he argues that actions are enough like texts that they involve similar hermeneutical dynamics. First, he contends that actions involve a certain distanciation from their agents parallel to the way in which writing is distanced from oral discourse. As he says, "In the same way that interlocution is overcome in writing, interaction is overcome in numerous situations in which we treat action as a fixed text."[66] Second, the meaning of an action, like writing, becomes detached from the author and takes on new significance, which Ricoeur terms "the *social* dimension of action."[67] Actions leave traces in history, which then become "read." "Thanks to this sedimentation in social time, human deeds become 'institutions,' in the sense that their meaning no longer coincides with the logical intentions of the actors."[68] We could add here Gadamer's notion of a game as involving players but being more than the players.

Third, the meaning of actions constitutes or projects a "world" that can be appropriated by others besides the original actors. For example, the French Revolution and the American Revolution have been appropriated again and again by later generations. Actions thus become "quasi texts." Ricoeur adds, fourth, that contemporaries at the time are not inherently privileged in their interpretation.

Ricoeur then shows that his hermeneutical arc can be applied to human actions. Actions are interpreted, and the interpretation involves an initial guess in a first understanding. The need for critical explanation follows, but it must, in turn, lead to a postcritical understanding that involves appropriation of the referential meaning. Ricoeur summarizes:

65. Ricoeur, "Model of the Text."
66. Ibid., 203.
67. Ibid., 206.
68. Ibid.

> In the same way as language-games are forms of life, according to the famous aphorism of Wittgenstein, social structures are also attempts to cope with existential perplexities, human predicaments, and deep-rooted conflicts. In this sense, these structures, too, have a referential dimension. They point toward the *aporias* of social existence, the same aporias around which mythical thought gravitates. And this analogical function of reference develops traits very similar to what we called the non-ostensive reference of a text, i.e., the display of a *Welt* which is no longer an *Umwelt,* the projection of a world which is more than a situation. May we not say that in social science, too, we proceed from naïve interpretations to critical interpretations, from surface interpretations to depth interpretations *through* structural analysis?[69]

The implication of a surplus of meaning would hence also apply. An action may engender multiple interpretations that themselves allow for further development and ramifications. The crucifixion of Jesus is an example of how an action is itself an object of interpretation. Centuries of reflection have led to different interpretations and at times to a narrowing of possible interpretations. Nevertheless, ever-new responses continue. One might also think in this connection of the exodus, of Jesus' healings, of Pentecost, and so on.

What we have in these events is a rich interplay between actions and texts that interpret the events. Actions already involve meaning. In terms of the first stage of Ricoeur's narrative arc, prefiguration, he draws on Clifford Geertz to say, "If, in fact, human action can be narrated, it is because it is always already articulated by signs, rules, and norms. It is always already symbolically mediated."[70] The interpretation of an action is, as such, a text that calls for its own history of interpretation. For instance, a surplus of meaning lies in the event of Jesus' crucifixion as reflected in the various Gospel accounts, but a surplus of meaning also applies to each Gospel taken by itself. In turn, the appropriation of significant texts plays back into the network of symbols upon which agents of action draw. One may try to act in accordance with the serene faith of Psalm 23 or respond to suffering with the pathos of Job. Seeing events as at least quasi texts undergirds the close relation between the two.[71]

While treating events or actions as texts seems obviously fruitful, some cautions are in order. Events are not as clearly communication as discourse. We are thinking of events involving human actions, which include intentionality and purpose, but not all events are as open to hermeneutics.

69. Ibid., 220.

70. Paul Ricoeur, *Time and Narrative,* vol. 1, trans. Kathleen McLaughlin and David Pellauer (Chicago: University of Chicago Press, 1984), 57.

71. Ibid., 58.

How does one factor in the natural events that accompany human actions, such as courageous survival from a shipwreck in a storm? The human actions may be intentional reactions to nature but certainly do not control all the circumstances. At the same time, characters and plot in stories usually also deal with such events beyond human control, even in fiction but certainly in historical narratives, so the distinction is relative and not absolute.

Further, some have wondered whether the paradigm should run in the opposite direction; that is, should we not consider discourse from the perspective of action rather than the other way around?[72] The one, however, does not disallow the other. Especially if one does not emphasize Ricoeur's third stage of application, one can miss the concrete dimension of praxis in hermeneutics. Hermeneutics thus cannot be understood apart from action. Likewise, hermeneutics enriches the understanding of action.

The value of this move by Ricoeur is that his hermeneutical model is considerably broadened. It opens up the door for treatment not only of religious texts but of religious experiences and actions. Theology can be considered as an aspect of the critical moment in the interpretation of texts but also in the interpretation of religious action. In contemporary life, the latter is as important as the former. Theology's critical role in the discernment of actions is as crucial as its role in the critical appropriation of texts.

With the idea of Ricoeur's paradigm of the text well in front of us, with its manifold dynamics, we can turn more specifically to Ricoeur's groundbreaking work on the nature of figurative language, which is extremely significant in interpretation of the primary discourse of scripture. This will allow us to return to the nature of scripture and the complex relationship of scripture to its authors.

72. See Roger Lundin, Clarence Walhout, and Anthony C. Thiselton, *The Promise of Hermeneutics* (Grand Rapids: Paternoster Press, 1999); Joseph Rouse, *Knowledge and Power: Toward a Political Philosophy of Science* (Ithaca, N.Y.: Cornell University Press, 1987), 22, 134.

CHAPTER FOUR

Forms of Discourse

Ricoeur's pilgrimage led him to stretch the boundaries of phenomenology into the realm of the involuntary and the unconscious. From there he burst its boundaries altogether as he moved beyond the realm of literal and essential phenomenological description into the realm of the figurative: the symbol, metaphor, and narrative. He found that essential and prosaic phenomenological description was inadequate to express all the dimensions of human life.

As he turned to closer examination of the different forms of figurative language such as metaphor and narrative, he participated in groundbreaking developments that indicated their fundamental epistemological significance. This new interest sharply contrasted with the traditional suspicion and sometimes outright dismissal of figurative language as of no epistemological value at all. The linguistic turn, therefore, in the twentieth century was not only a new recognition of the significance of language for thought; it also began to see figurative language, which heretofore had often been seen as largely ornamental, as perhaps of even greater significance than nonfigurative language for understanding, especially in religion. The significance for theology is evident, in that theology reflects on the more figurative language of scripture and usually has attempted to express its conclusions in nonfigurative language. Accordingly, theologians have sometimes seen their theologies not as second-order language but as a better and preferable expression. The revolutionary challenge to these assumptions that occurred in the twentieth century has had enormous impact on theology, the results of which are ongoing. The nature of this change can be traced in an impressively full way in Ricoeur's work. We therefore, in this chapter, trace Ricoeur's path from symbolism through metaphor and narrative. From there we turn to the significance of these shifts for scriptural interpretation. We explore the kind of significance that

Ricoeur places on the forms of discourse in scripture, the ways in which Ricoeur's thought enables us to bring together historiography and fiction in the Gospels, and how Ricoeur's approach relates to a contemporary hermeneutic of divine discourse in scripture advanced by Nicholas Wolterstorff. The last direction is significant because in developing his own hermeneutic, Wolterstorff extensively criticizes Ricoeur. Responding to Wolterstorff will reveal some common misconceptions of Ricoeur but will also show how Wolterstorff and Ricoeur can mutually complement one another, rather than their hermeneutics necessarily being in opposition.

Symbolism

In *Freedom and Nature* in 1950, Ricoeur attempted to provide a phenomenological description of the will.[1] Already he was extending phenomenology to include what he called a "diagnostic" relation to embodiment. That is, our embodiment includes much that is not conscious and not intentional, but which our conscious intentions appropriate. Ten years later he published a two-part second volume of his projected three-part philosophy of the will.[2] The first part of the second volume, *Fallible Man,* moves as close as phenomenology can to an account of the freedom involved in willing good and evil.[3] He concluded, like theologians such as Reinhold Niebuhr and Paul Tillich, that human beings are in a tension between finite and infinite dimensions. We walk on a fault line that renders us fallible. To deal with our actual "fault," however, Ricour felt that he had to leave behind phenomenology and deal with symbolic language in *The Symbolism of Evil.*[4] This led to a preoccupation with figurative language and narrative that would last three decades and represents some of the most significant and innovative philosophical work in the twentieth century.

The guiding thread in *The Symbolism of Evil* is Ricoeur's conviction that the instrumentality of prosaic essential description cannot capture the

1. Paul Ricoeur, *Freedom and Nature: The Voluntary and the Involuntary,* trans. Erazim Kohák, Northwestern University Studies in Phenomenology & Existential Philosophy (Evanston, Ill.: Northwestern University Press, 1966).

2. As indicated in the introduction, the third volume, which was to be a poetics of the will, was never completed, although his later work in metaphor, narrative, and anthropology may be a transposed fulfillment.

3. Paul Ricoeur, *Fallible Man,* trans. Charles Kelbley, rev. ed. (New York: Fordham University Press, 1986).

4. Paul Ricoeur, *The Symbolism of Evil,* trans. Emerson Buchanan, Religious Perspectives 17 (New York: Harper & Row, 1967).

free but irrational phenomenon of evil. Only symbolic language, with its richer texture, can hope to frame such an enigma. He first looks at how more physical symbols in the Hebrew Bible, such as "stain" and "defilement," gave way to the less physical and more ethical symbols of "sin" and "guilt."[5] In this process, he also sees that the earlier symbols continue in the later. The full panoply of symbols are necessary to complement and deepen one another.

These symbols, he thinks, were then taken up in myths, which require a narrative context, involving the gods. In particular Ricoeur examines the traditional Babylonian myth of chaos and creation, the Greek myth of tragedy, the Orphic myth of the exiled soul in the body so influential on Plato's philosophy, and the biblical myth of the Fall.[6] In the end, he suggests that the biblical myth contains in a fuller way the themes of the others but leaves a creative tension.[7] On the one hand, evil seems already present before the act, symbolized by the serpent in the Garden of Eden. This idea is also represented in the Orphic myth of the fall into the body, which is the cause of evil. On the other hand, evil is not something that happens to us but something we choose and do. Sin *befalls* us, and we *fall into* it. The tense fallibility that he chronicles in *Fallible Man* becomes actual fault in this twofold drama. As Ricoeur spells out his reasoning:

> The concept toward which the whole series of the primary symbols of evil tends may be called the *servile will.* But that concept is not directly accessible; if one tries to give it an object, the object destroys itself, for it short-circuits the idea of will, which can only signify free choice, and so free will, always intact and young, always available—and the idea of servitude, that is to say, the unavailability of freedom to itself. *The concept of the servile will, then, cannot be represented as the concept of fallibility.* . . . That is why the concept of the servile will must remain an indirect concept, which gets all its meaning from the symbolism that we have run through which tries to raise that symbolism to the level of *speculation.*[8]

The conclusions that Ricoeur draws from this study are significant for his later work on metaphor and narrative. First, he realizes that the primary language of faith and of life is marked by symbolic language. Long before we possess the speculative theory of original sin in theology, we

5. Ibid., part 1.
6. See, for example, ibid., 171–74.
7. Ibid., 309. Ricoeur adds, "The pre-eminence of the Adamic myth does not imply that the other myths are purely and simply abolished; rather, life, or new life, is given to them by the privileged myth" (309).
8. Ibid., 151.

have the stain and defilement of sin that is also connected to a narrative drama of fallenness. This undergirds his sense that theology is second-order, reflective language.

Second, he realizes that one cannot exhaust the symbol. The symbol not only says in a compact way what would take prose much longer to say, but it says what prose could not fully say. Rich symbols are not completely reducible to literal language, and their meaning is inexhaustible. This undergirds in yet another way the surplus of meaning of rich texts. Ricoeur expresses this idea in his final reflective chapter by taking up a suggestion by Immanuel Kant that "the symbol gives rise to thought."[9] "Thought" is second-order reflection on the constant fruitfulness of symbols. Theology and philosophy, then, rather than being foundational disciplines, live from the primary symbols that arise in the experience of life and of faith. As Hegel said of philosophy, "The owl of Minerva spreads its wings only with the falling of the dusk."[10] Reflection comes too late to start itself in the way that Descartes and the modern project dreamed.

Third, such reflection must return again and again to be tested and funded by these basic symbols. Already Ricoeur was pointing to the dynamic of his later hermeneutical arc. It is in the concluding chapter of *The Symbolism of Evil* that he suggests the provocative idea of a "second naïveté," which marks an understanding that appreciates the symbolic mode of thought, yet with the help of critical reflection. He especially explicates the significance for hermeneutics in this passage:

> But if we can no longer live the great symbolisms of the sacred in accordance with the original belief in them, we can, we modern men, aim at a second naivete in and through criticism. In short, it is by *interpreting* that we can *hear* again. Thus it is in hermeneutics that the symbol's gift of meaning and the endeavor to understand by deciphering are knotted together.[11]

What Ricoeur had not yet done was to develop his full-blown hermeneutical arc. Neither had he distinguished symbols, which he later saw as more experiential and nonverbal, from the literary nature of metaphors. Nor had he seen how symbols and metaphors are caught up in broader narratives. He tended to see the symbols as standing alone and

9. Ibid., 347–57.

10. Georg Wilhelm Friedrich Hegel, *Hegel,* ed. Robert Maynard Hutchins, vol. 9: *The Philosophy of Right,* trans. T. M. Knox, Great Books of the Western World (Chicago: Encyclopaedia Britannica, 1952), 7.

11. Ricoeur, *Symbolism of Evil,* 351.

narratives as secondary. He later saw that this was a mistake; the reverse is more likely true, that is, that symbols arise in the context of larger narratives.

In his later *Interpretation Theory* (1976), Ricoeur distinguished symbol from metaphor in seeing metaphor as a more linguistic, literary phenomenon. A symbol possesses a greater nonlinguistic dimension, as in a mountain, a cross, or a flag. Ricoeur observes, "Metaphor occurs in the already purified universe of the logos, while the symbol hesistates [*sic*] on the dividing line between *bios* and *logos.* It testifies to the primordial rootedness of Discourse in Life. It is born where force and form coincide."[12] Although symbols share the same dynamic of irreducibility as metaphors and thus are closely related, he feels that a distinction can be made in the way that symbols are more "bound to the cosmos."[13] In dreams, in sacred spaces and objects, symbols give rise to their own kind of prelinguistic semantic shift.

For a French philosopher in the early 1960s, the logical direction in which to turn in order to continue exploration into symbols was to Sigmund Freud. Ricoeur originally projected a short excursus but ended up with another landmark book. Titled *Freud and Philosophy,* it concerned Freud as a hermeneutical thinker.[14] One of the striking themes of the book is what has come to be known as a "hermeneutic of suspicion."[15] The Freudian probing of manifest meaning for latent, unconscious, infantile illusions points to a general dimension of critique that is as important applied to symbols as to any kind of work. We especially treat the issue of critique in the next chapter. At this point, the related aspect of Freud that interested Ricoeur was the idea of double meaning, which he saw at play in symbols and in metaphors. *Freud and Philosophy* consequently led Ricoeur to more and more rethinking of the nature of metaphor, which he saw as the key to understanding figurative language.

12. Paul Ricoeur, *Interpretation Theory: Discourse and the Surplus of Meaning* (Fort Worth: Texas Christian University Press, 1976), 59.

13. Ibid., 61.

14. Paul Ricoeur, *Freud and Philosophy: An Essay on Interpretation,* trans. Denis Savage, Terry Lectures (New Haven, Conn.: Yale University Press, 1970). Recall that Jacques Lacan was offering in the 1960s a prominent structuralist interpretation of Freud, which sparked a painful interchange between him and Ricoeur concerning influence. See Charles E. Reagan, *Paul Ricoeur: His Life and His Work* (Chicago: University of Chicago Press, 1996), 25–31. Recall that Jürgen Habermas also in the 1960s appropriated Freud in support of his critical theory.

15. Ricoeur, *Freud and Philosophy,* 32–36.

Metaphor

In 1972, Ricoeur published an essay titled in English "Metaphor and the Central Problem of Hermeneutics."[16] In doing so, he was participating in a virtual revolution in how both metaphor and hermeneutics were being understood. What he discerned was that metaphor is the hermeneutical key, so to speak, to hermeneutics.

In his work on metaphor, *The Rule of Metaphor* (published in French in 1975 as *La Métaphore vive),* Ricoeur begins with Aristotle.[17] Although at many points critical of Aristotle, and especially of the way in which Aristotle has been traditionally appropriated, Ricoeur quotes approvingly Aristotle's observation in the *Poetics* that "the greatest thing by far is to be a master of metaphor."[18] This capacity for imaginative judgment is at the heart of Ricoeur's approach. Aristotle's influence, however, led to quite a different understanding of metaphor in the tradition. Aristotle also saw metaphors as substitutions for literal terms. Thus he approached metaphor in terms of individual words and in terms of a reduction to literal language. In the background to Aristotle was Plato's criticism of the poets and of their use of inflammatory figurative language that does not literally depict the gods. Despite the ironic fact that Plato was a master of metaphor in Aristotle's terms, Plato's and Aristotle's influence led to a denigration of metaphor in favor of prose for the sake of expressing truth.[19] In the modern period, with its quest for clarity and exactness, metaphor particularly has been relegated to the ornamental and incidental. Sometimes it has been seen, as in Plato, as positively dangerous. John Locke, for example, expresses this antagonism very lucidly:

> Since wit and fancy find easier entertainment in the world than dry truth and real knowledge, figurative speeches and allusion in language will hardly be admitted as an imperfection or abuse of it. . . . But yet if we would

16. Paul Ricoeur, "Metaphor and the Central Problem of Hermeneutics," in *Hermeneutics and the Human Sciences: Essays on Language, Action, and Interpretation,* ed. John B. Thompson (Cambridge: Cambridge University Press, 1981), 165–81. Originally published in French as "La Métaphore et la problème central de l'herméneutique," *Revue philosophique de Louvain* 70 (1972): 93–112.

17. Paul Ricoeur, *The Rule of Metaphor: Multi-Disciplinary Studies for the Creation of Meaning in Language,* trans. Robert Czerny, Kathleen McLaughlin, and John Costello (Toronto: University of Toronto Press, 1977).

18. Aristotle, *On Poetics,* trans. Ingram Bywater, in *The Works of Aristotle,* ed. Robert Maynard Hutchins, Great Books of the Western World 9 (Chicago: Encyclopaedia Britannica, 1952), sec. 22.

19. Mark Johnson, "Introduction: Metaphor in the Philosophical Tradition," in *Philosophical Perspectives on Metaphor,* ed. Mark Johnson (Minneapolis: University of Minnesota Press, 1981).

> speak of things as they are, we allow that all the art of rhetoric, besides order and clearness; all the artificial and figurative application of words eloquence hath invented, are for nothing else but to insinuate wrong ideas, move the passions, and thereby mislead the judgment; and so indeed are perfect cheats.[20]

Even in preaching, metaphor was seen sometimes as a necessary evil, requisite in a sense only to keep people alert and to aid their memory. Figurative language was ornamental in relation to the more desirable straightforward, prosaic exposition.[21]

Mark Johnson, writing in 1981, lucidly captures the dramatic shift that occurred in the latter half of the twentieth century with respect to the philosophical significance of metaphor:

> In the last decade or so the study of metaphor has become, for an ever-increasing number of philosophers, a way of approaching some of the most fundamental traditional concerns of philosophy. Metaphor is no longer confined to the realm of aesthetics narrowly conceived; it is now coming to be recognized as central to any adequate account of language and has been seen by some to play a central role in epistemology and even metaphysics. This burgeoning of interest is a curious phenomenon. Why is it that as recently as twenty years ago (and for centuries before that) it was imprudent to say nice things about metaphor in respectable philosophical circles? And why is it now an embarrassment to be caught without an account of the nature, function, and proper role of metaphor?[22]

As a major shaper of this new approach, Ricoeur and others developed a *tension* or *interaction* theory of metaphor over against the traditional *substitution* theory.[23] Ricoeur emphasizes that metaphors involve at least the sentence, if not an entire work, and cannot be understood in terms of the substitution of individual terms. Rather, out of the interaction between the clash of literal meanings, a "semantic impertinence" ensues that gives rise to new meaning.[24] Ricoeur calls this dynamic a "split reference" in which the literal meaning is denied in order to construct an imaginative

20. John Locke, "An Essay concerning Human Understanding," in *Locke, Berkeley, Hume,* ed. Robert Maynard Hutchins, Great Books of the Western World 35 (Chicago: Encyclopaedia Britannica, 1952), 3.10.34.

21. A good example is Merrill R. Abbey, *Communication in Pulpit and Parish* (Philadelphia: Westminster Press, 1973), 181, where the "illustration" is "support material" that comes only after having the idea and design. The title of the chapter indicates that the illustration helps communicate the substance, which is separate.

22. Johnson, "Introduction," 3.

23. Ricoeur, *Interpretation Theory,* 52.

24. Paul Ricoeur, "Biblical Hermeneutics," *Semeia* 4 (1975): 78, 27–138.

new meaning.[25] This "semantic innovation" is often irreducible to literal paraphrase—at least in terms of significant metaphors, which Ricoeur refers to as "living metaphors."[26] The result is a dynamic and elusive "is/is not."[27] Metaphor must be both affirmed and denied, which contributes to its exasperating capacity to elude cognitive nets that call for precision and determinacy. The capacity to erect, from the clash of "the systems of associated commonplaces" associated with disparate words, a distinct new meaning is a mysterious, creative event not fully explicable, a reason for Aristotle's encomium that being a master of metaphor is the greatest thing by far.[28]

The new interactionist approach thus allows for metaphorical meaning to be created and grasped without being wholly explained in terms of univocal language or method. Ricoeur says, "To say that a metaphor is not drawn from anywhere is to recognise it for what it is: namely, a momentary creation of language, a semantic innovation which does not have a status in the language as something already established, whether as a designation or as a connotation."[29] In fact, the best explication of a metaphor may be another metaphor. Meaning is let loose, therefore, and escapes the corral of careful hermeneutical control. The power of metaphor, as Janet Soskice suggests, perhaps lies in its very vagueness and fluidity.[30] Because it cannot be pinned down, it cannot be exhausted and thus die the death of much less than a thousand qualifications.[31] Living metaphors have a way of provoking new meanings and insights. Instead of metaphors being secondary ornaments to univocal language, it may be that language arises

25. Ricoeur, *Rule of Metaphor,* 224. Janet Martin Soskice criticizes this phraseology because she says that a reference is not ever actually constructed at the literal level. Rather, people notice the problem of reference at the literal level and thus move on to metaphorical reference. She is technically correct on this point, but Ricoeur's phraseology, if not pressed too literally, is suggestive and quite useful when he applies it to narrative. See Janet Martin Soskice, *Metaphor and Religious Language* (Oxford: Clarendon Press, 1985), 84–90.

26. Ricoeur, "Biblical Hermeneutics," 78–79. The French title of *The Rule of Metaphor, La Métaphore vive,* meant "the living metaphor."

27. Ibid., 88.

28. Aristotle, *On Poetics,* sec. 22; Ricoeur, "Metaphor," 172. The reference to a "system of associated commonplaces" is to Max Black, "Metaphor," in *Philosophical Perspectives on Metaphor,* ed. Johnson, 74.

29. Ricoeur, "Metaphor," 174.

30. She is thinking especially here of its role in science. Soskice, *Metaphor and Religious Language,* 133.

31. The reference is to Antony Flew's charge, in his famous criticism of God-language in his parable of the invisible gardener, that believers make so many allowances for their beliefs that they "die the death of a thousand qualifications." See Antony Flew, "The University Discussion," in *New Essays in Philosophical Theology,* ed. Antony Flew and Alasdair C. MacIntyre (London: SCM Press, 1964), 96–99.

originally from metaphorical language. Univocal language is thus easily seen as largely composed of "dead" metaphors. The metaphorical and, more generally, poetic function of language allows us to say and imagine something new. It may be, moreover, that we cannot reach the new apart from the semantic innovation of metaphorical language. The "ontological vehemence" of metaphor is its capacity to project new worlds, tying in with Ricoeur's general hermeneutical theory in which one looks for the world projected by a work.[32]

Ricoeur speaks of "root" metaphors that organize a whole network of metaphors. Examples in scripture are the "kingdom of God" and God as "Father." Ricoeur says, "Root metaphors assemble and scatter. They assemble subordinate images together, and they scatter concepts at a higher level."[33] Metaphor's potency thus also lies in the focused way in which it can frame an entire discourse. It is in this sense that it is now more commonly recognized that neither science nor philosophy nor theology, with all their univocal discourse, can do without metaphor. One can thus say of a metaphor what Ricoeur says of a text: It "means all that it can mean."[34]

Furthermore, given the philosophical tradition's suspicion toward the emotions as a rival to cognition, an important postmodern dimension of Ricoeur's work on metaphor is how he understands the emotions and imagination as essential to cognition. He therefore suggests that part of metaphor's vigor is its capacity to frame and focus, in a holistic way, the cognition and the emotions together.[35] All of these characteristics challenge the primacy of univocal and highly rational language in the philosophical tradition.[36] As a centerpiece of epistemology, the interaction approach to metaphors clearly points to a postmodern epistemology and away from the demand for Cartesian clarity and certainty.

The worrisome problem, however, concerning this interaction approach to metaphors is the question of hermeneutical control. Is there any limit to the interpretation of a metaphor? Is such interpretation rule-

32. Ricoeur, *Rule of Metaphor*, 299.

33. Ricoeur, *Interpretation Theory*, 64.

34. Ricoeur, "Metaphor," 176.

35. See especially Paul Ricoeur, "The Metaphorical Process as Cognition, Imagination, and Feeling," in *Philosophical Perspectives on Metaphor*, ed. Johnson, 228–47. For another important book on the subject, see Mark Johnson, *The Body in the Mind: The Bodily Basis of Meaning, Imagination, and Reason* (Chicago: University of Chicago Press, 1987).

36. See Dan R. Stiver, *The Philosophy of Religious Language: Sign, Symbol, and Story* (Cambridge: Blackwell, 1996), chaps. 1–2, for a historical account of the centrality of univocal language, especially in philosophy. In other words, it is not just Christian fundamentalists and conservatives like Carl F. H. Henry who have insisted on literal language; it is a facet of the entire philosophical tradition of the West.

governed at all? If not, how is it that people can use metaphors meaningfully? In *The Rule of Metaphor,* Ricoeur documents a progressive taming of the wild power of metaphor. Remembering that Aristotle places metaphor within rhetoric, Ricoeur says:

> Thus, before taxonomy of figures of speech, there was Aristotle's far more embracing rhetoric; but even before the latter, there was undisciplined common speech . . . and the wish to harness its dangerous power by means of a special technique. Aristotle's rhetoric is already a domesticated discipline, solidly bound to philosophy by the theory of argumentation, from which rhetoric, in its decline, severed itself.[37]

Despite the way in which he bound metaphor, Aristotle went on to say, "It is the one thing that cannot be learnt from others; and it is also a sign of genius, since a good metaphor implies an intuitive perception of the similarity in dissimilars."[38] What Aristotle apparently means by the unteachability of metaphor is something like what modern metaphorists mean by saying metaphors are irreducible. He apparently assumes that teachability depends on a repeatable, explicit operation, what Gadamer would term "method."[39]

In his article on metaphor and hermeneutics, Ricoeur suggests that the nature of explanation in metaphor should be a guide to explanation in hermeneutics in general. As we saw in chapter 1 concerning the hermeneutical arc, now undergirded by his understanding of metaphor, the "explanation" of which Ricoeur speaks is not the stereotype of positivist scientific explanation; it is less verification than validation. As we noted, the logic of this kind of method is one of probability, of better or worse, rather than of empirical verification. Even then, it is "a logic of uncertain and qualitative probability" rather than quantitative probability.[40] Like juridical interpretation, one can follow the clues of a text, but in the final analysis, personal hermeneutical judgment that cannot be conclusively demonstrated will determine the interpretation. As Eva Feder Kittay claims, "To say a thing is not subject to a given set of rules is not to say that it is subject to no rules."[41] Metaphors obviously do not have the precision of univocal language, but neither are they anarchic. They

37. Ricoeur, *Rule of Metaphor,* 10.

38. Aristotle, *On Poetics,* sec. 22. Aristotle also says in the *Rhetoric* that metaphor is of "great value" and "is not a thing whose use can be taught by one man to another." See Aristotle, *Rhetoric,* trans. W. Rhys Roberts, in *The Works of Aristotle,* ed. Hutchins, 3.2.

39. See chapter 1, above.

40. Ricoeur, "Metaphor," 175.

41. Eva Feder Kittay, *Metaphor: Its Cognitive Force and Linguistic Structure* (Oxford: Clarendon Press, 1987), 68.

imply the validity of judgment irreducible to strict method. The interpretation of metaphor thus fits in with Ricoeur's general hermeneutical arc and, in fact, is a key to the particular way in which he develops it.

One possible misunderstanding of both Aristotle and Ricoeur is that metaphors are so creative and vague that they can hardly be used. In other words, perhaps it takes a genius not only to create but also to understand them. To make a Wittgensteinian point, however, our *use* of metaphor belies this concern. Judging from the way in which our common language is laced with metaphor, it actually suggests that it takes a genius neither to create a metaphor nor to understand one. Otherwise, the enterprise of poetics and persuasion would never get off the ground. Some hearers are better than others, to be sure, but Aristotle seems to assume that the common populace of his day are able to grasp and judge the fittingness of metaphor. The point is that, despite Aristotle's implication that metaphorical ability is rare and unusual, the capacity to use and understand metaphor is commonplace. It is something that virtually all people do and, for the most part, do rather well. Perhaps the ability to make metaphors cannot be taught, but the capacity to understand metaphors is surely learned by virtually everyone, just as they learn language in general.

What Aristotle is lacking in this context is the concept of something that can be taught without being totally explicit. In a Christian context we might speak of discipleship or spiritual formation, which is more tacit than explicit. Ironically, Aristotle had something like this idea in his ethics, since he saw character as something that must be educated without it being a demonstrable activity; not enough rules can be created to determine the judgments of a wise person.[42] Ethics, however, is far from being anarchic. Likewise, the meaning of metaphor is perhaps not as mysterious and remote as Aristotle's words about genius suggest. We see here another similarity between Aristotle's notion of practical wisdom for ethics and hermeneutical judgment.

For both Aristotle and Ricoeur, therefore, metaphors cannot be exhaustively explained, but they can be understood. In other words, people use metaphors quite well without having a thorough explanation, method, or decision procedure to determine their meanings. Metaphors are thus not common in the sense of being literal, but they are in terms of use. The lack of any explicit hermeneutical control does not limit hermeneutical reliability at all. Metaphors are used to telling effect without being reducible to univocal language. For example, it was accurate to say of Michael

42. Aristotle, *Nichomachean Ethics,* trans. W. D. Ross, in *The Works of Aristotle,* ed. Hutchins, 2.3.

Jordan that he "soared" through the air, but not of Magic Johnson. It was accurate to speak of Ronald Reagan as the "Teflon" president, but not of Jimmy Carter. Our discourse is shot through with metaphors, and people use them, understand them, and appraise them with surprising ease and without a lot of fanfare. The reliability of metaphors seems to emerge from their being part of common linguistic practices in which people develop competency as a part of linguistic fluency. Again, most people develop expertise without necessarily being geniuses in Aristotle's sense. The lack of an algorithmic method does not undermine reliable usage.

Further support for the role of metaphor in ordinary language comes from George Lakoff and Mark Johnson in *Metaphors We Live By.*[43] They argue that everyday language is interlaced with metaphors and that we commonly think in terms of metaphors. Even more than Ricoeur, they maintain that metaphor is something we use often and well, yet without being rule-governed. Ricoeur notes that much discussion about metaphor uses familiar metaphors, which he pejoratively calls "trivial metaphors."[44] For the most part, he is interested in more powerful, "living" metaphors and tends to see a sharp distinction between these powerful metaphors and trivial or dead metaphors. Lakoff and Johnson, by contrast, add a category of common or conventional metaphors that frame much of our speech, realizing that these may be background assumptions rather than foreground assertions. For example, they analyze an "argument is war" metaphor and point out that, apart from some such a basic operative framework, we cannot see the relationship of otherwise unrelated propositions. To give their examples:

> ARGUMENT IS WAR
>
> Your claims are *indefensible.*
> He *attacked every weak point* in my argument.
> His criticisms were *right on target.*
> I *demolished* his argument.
> I've never *won* an argument with him.
> You disagree? Okay, *shoot!*
> If you use that *strategy,* he'll *wipe you out.*
> He *shot down* all of my arguments.[45]

43. George Lakoff and Mark Johnson, *Metaphors We Live By* (Chicago: University of Chicago Press, 1980). Mark Johnson, interestingly, was a student of Ricoeur's. I owe some of the insights that follow to a former student, Greg Johnson, who explored the difference between Ricoeur's approach and that of Lakoff and Johnson in a paper delivered at the 1993 meeting of the Baptist Association of Philosophy Teachers, Las Vegas, Nevada.

44. Ricoeur, "Metaphor," 172.

45. Lakoff and Johnson, *Metaphors We Live By,* 4.

This approach furthermore helps us understand the creation of new inferences. For example, if argument is war, the spin-offs are almost endless: One can add newer permutations such as "I nuked my opponent" or "They need a Star Wars defense." They also point out that it is not just that we talk about war, but this metaphor structures our actions and practices as well. "We see the person we are arguing with as an opponent. We attack his positions and we defend our own. We gain and lose ground."[46] This metaphor can be contrasted with another metaphorical frame, such as "argument is dance," where we might say, "You move, then I'll move," or "We're out of sequence or rhythm." They explore numerous such metaphorical frames to show how our everyday speech trades on our ability to maneuver around metaphors. They therefore emphasize the dense metaphorical background even to our use of literal language. Rather than being an optional item in our linguistic arsenal, useful in poetics and rhetoric but not in description or science, metaphors pervade all our language. Even if Lakoff and Johnson's claims are exaggerated, they convincingly show how metaphors are more prevalent in our language than we might think. Others have similarly pointed out how significant metaphors are in science, questioning the traditional picture of science as using solely highly univocal and precise language.[47] Scientific language is actually full of metaphors, especially metaphorical models that guide thought and research. The implication for religious and theological language is that the metaphors are not dispensable but essential for understanding. In preaching, for example, the so-called illustration may be the point rather than the ornament. Theology especially can be seen as orienting itself around key metaphors, for instance, relating to the atonement in ransom imagery, in terms of a legal case, or as personal sacrifice. Rather than trying to eliminate these metaphorical dimensions in an attempt to attain univocal precision, it may be more fruitful to explore concepts such as grace and sin in terms of their metaphorical significance and network than to examine them in a prosaic, conceptual way.

Sallie McFague, who is heavily influenced by Ricoeur, has in fact made metaphor the model for theology itself, seeing it as an effort, at best, to portray the indescribable God in human language. Theology, too, has an "is/is not" structure. She then sees theology's role as exploring the metaphors of the tradition and also as creating new metaphorical models.

46. Ibid.

47. For example, see Ian G. Barbour, *Religion and Science: Historical and Contemporary Issues,* rev. ed. (San Francisco: HarperSanFrancisco, 1997); Mary Hesse, *Revolutions and Reconstructions in the Philosophy of Science* (Bloomington: Indiana University Press, 1980).

One of her major efforts has been to develop the metaphors of God as Mother, Lover, and Friend, which she sees as explicating and extending the tradition by means of metaphor more than by univocal discourse.[48]

Ricoeur was already in the 1970s relating metaphor to the longer work of narrative. His reflections at this point, in his article on metaphor and hermeneutics in 1972 and in his book on metaphor in 1975, formed the bridge to his full-scale treatment of narrative in the early 1980s. It was at this point that he broadened his understanding of hermeneutics from the treatment of double-meaning expressions, symbol, and metaphor to the wider arena of interpretation in general.[49] Specifically, in light of the hermeneutical arc that he was constructing in the 1970s, he pictured the intricate relationships between it, metaphor, and narrative in the following way:

> From one point of view, the understanding of metaphor can serve as a guide to the understanding of longer texts, such as a literary work. This point of view is that of explanation; it concerns only that aspect of meaning which we have called the "sense," that is, the immanent pattern of discourse. From another point of view, the understanding of a work taken as a whole gives the key to metaphor. This other point of view is that of interpretation proper; it develops the aspect of meaning which we have called "reference," that is, the intentional orientation towards a world and the reflexive orientation towards a self. So if we apply explanation to "sense," as the immanent pattern of the work, then we can reserve interpretation for the sort of inquiry concerned with the *power of a work* to project a world of its own and to set in motion the hermeneutical circle, which encompasses in its spiral both the apprehension of projected worlds and the advance of self-understanding in the presence of these new worlds. Our working hypothesis thus invites us to proceed from metaphor to text at the level of "sense" and the explanation of "sense," then from text to metaphor at the level of the reference of a work to a world and to a self, that is, at the level of interpretation proper.[50]

This statement reveals especially well the state of his thinking at the time and how he was already pushing beyond metaphor to narrative, without leaving behind their reciprocal relationships. Some things he would modify, but the basic pattern he has retained.

48. Sallie McFague, *Metaphorical Theology: Models of God in Religious Language* (Philadelphia: Fortress Press, 1982); Sallie McFague, *Models of God: Theology for an Ecological, Nuclear Age* (Philadelphia: Fortress Press, 1987); Sallie McFague, *The Body of God: An Ecological Theology* (Minneapolis: Fortress Press, 1993).

49. Paul Ricoeur, "On Interpretation," trans. Kathleen Blamey and John B. Thompson, in *From Text to Action: Essays in Hermeneutics,* vol. 2, Northwestern University Studies in Phenomenology & Existential Philosophy (Evanston, Ill.: Northwestern University Press, 1991), 17.

50. Ricoeur, "Metaphor," 171.

Narrative

Ricoeur's massive *Time and Narrative,* published in French between 1983 and 1985, is a highly acclaimed, magisterial work on narrative.[51] Given that it is a three-volume work, however, it is rather narrowly focused on issues relating to fiction, historiography, and temporality. Its significance is carried further, in a more succinct way, in *Oneself as Another.*[52] We therefore will not summarize all of Ricoeur's work on narrative but draw from it select themes.

Ricoeur sees in the longer works of narrative some of the same dynamics of metaphor that represent such a challenge to the philosophical and theological traditions. Narratives are not reducible to prosaic paraphrase; they say things that cannot be said in any other way; they are creative acts of the productive imagination; they convey meaning about reality but cannot be explicated or evaluated in the terms of positivistic science; and their interpretation follows the contours of the hermeneutical arc.

What he adds, as we saw in chapter 2, is a narrative arc. Without recapitulating the previous discussion *in toto,* Ricoeur thinks in terms of a threefold mimesis that involves the preunderstanding, or prefiguration, that we bring to a text ($mimesis_1$); the configuration of a text, involving characterization and plot ($mimesis_2$); and the refiguration of a world in front of the text, which involves a fusion of horizons ($mimesis_3$). Recall that I synthesized in chapter 2 his two arcs, retaining the fundamental dynamic in the earlier arc of a movement from a precritical naïveté, through criticism, to a postcritical appropriation. I added some nuances to Ricoeur's discussion by seeing that the configured world of the text must be more carefully distinguished from the refigured world in front of the text.

Ricoeur focuses in *Time and Narrative* on the significance of narrative for relating human existence to the aporias of temporality. He sees this exemplified particularly by Augustine in the last chapters of his *Confessions,* where he said, "What then is time? If no one asks me, I know; if

51. Paul Ricoeur, *Time and Narrative,* vol. 1, trans. Kathleen McLaughlin and David Pellauer (Chicago: University of Chicago Press, 1984); Paul Ricoeur, *Time and Narrative,* vol. 2, trans. Kathleen McLaughlin and David Pellauer (Chicago: University of Chicago Press, 1985); Paul Ricoeur, *Time and Narrative,* vol. 3, trans. Kathleen Blamey and David Pellauer (Chicago: University of Chicago Press, 1988).

52. Paul Ricoeur, *Oneself as Another,* trans. Kathleen Blamey (Chicago: University of Chicago Press, 1992).

I wish to explain it to one that asketh, I know not."[53] With the aid of reflection on Aristotle's *Poetics,* Ricoeur sees a tension between discordance in Augustine and concordance in Aristotle. He extends this tension to the interplay between chronological time and human time, suggesting finally that "speculation on time is an inconclusive rumination to which narrative activity alone can respond."[54] He thus concludes that human beings are inherently narratively shaped, or story-shaped, with narrative offering a way of configuring a discordant concordance of time.[55] As with metaphor, rather than seeing narrative as ornamental and dispensable in serious philosophical discourse, Ricoeur sees that narrative is necessary. Human identity and existence cannot be understood apart from the way in which we "story" our lives.

In this he joins many others, particularly theologians. In my *Philosophy of Religious Language,* I described three types of narrative theologies.[56] Ricoeur is like all three in emphasizing that theology is second-order reflection on first-order narratives and cannot ever leave them behind, Like them, he also rejects the previous generation's existentialist theologies, which were "indifferent to the historical dimension, which would be exclusively attentive to the irruption of the word in the instant of the decision of faith."[57]

Each type, however, has its distinctive emphasis. Perhaps the most well known is the Yale school of narrative theology. They focus on "The Story," that is, the biblical story, which, as we noted in chapter 1, they see as the world that should absorb our world, rather than the reverse. The "California school," inspired by James McClendon, focuses on "Your Story and My Story," that is, on biographies and autobiographies. McClendon argues that the meaning of theological concepts cannot be understood apart from their narrative shape in people's lives, particularly that of contemporaries. Ricoeur is a central figure in what is often called the Chicago school of narrative theology, which is seen as connecting theology not so much to The Story or My Story but "Our Story," that is, the broader cultural narrative in which our identities are formed.

In actuality, however, Ricoeur's work relates to all three. He focuses at times on the narratives in scripture but is careful to note that they are not

53. Augustine, *The Confessions,* trans. Edward Bouverie Pusey, in *Augustine,* ed. Robert Maynard Hutchins, Great Books of the Western World 18 (Chicago: Encyclopaedia Britannica, 1952), 11.14.17.

54. Ricoeur, *Time and Narrative,* vol. 1, 6.

55. Ibid., 72.

56. Stiver, *Philosophy of Religious Language,* chap. 7.

57. Paul Ricoeur, "Toward a Narrative Theology: Its Necessity, Its Resources, Its Difficulties," trans. David Pellauer, in *Figuring the Sacred: Religion, Narrative, and Imagination,* ed. Mark I. Wallace (Minneapolis: Fortress Press, 1995), 236.

the only genre in scripture. He certainly recognizes, like the Yale school, that scripture projects a world that we must appropriate—or be appropriated by. The import of his work is that our identity is formed by texts, including those other than scripture. That is, like the California school, each of us has a story that is shaped by the stories of others. This includes all the particularity that comes from our individual plots. Ricoeur says, "If theological discourse does not consist in extracting anemic generalities from the narratives recorded in the Scripture, it has to disentangle the intelligibility immanent in the recounted stories from our own individual and communal histories and stories."[58] Ricoeur himself can hardly be understood apart from the particularities of his French background in the twentieth century, losing a father to World War I, becoming a prisoner of war in World War II, suffering student revolts in the 1960s, and turning to North America in the 1970s and 1980s.

What he does is set narrative concerns in a wider philosophical framework. We explore in a later chapter the significance of narrative for identity; but in this context he notes how narratives hold together the tension that he saw in his work on the symbolism of evil, where a symbol could express acts of freedom that are conditioned but not determined. Narratives, he indicates, function to hold together the tension between concordance, for which we strive, and discordance, which we continuously experience. The interplay between chance and necessity, as a chaos theorist might put it, is a feature of our lives taken up narratively in our continuing story.[59]

Ricoeur sees as a further feature of the discordant concordance of narrative the interweaving between fiction and historiography. Rather than typically seeing these as strictly opposed, he knits them closely together. Both involve a configurative or mimetic element, both are works of the productive imagination, and both involve reference to history. The fact that they do so in different ways does not remove them from the basic dynamic of interpretation. As we saw in chapter 2, historiography involves what Ricoeur calls a "debt to the past" that must be paid even as any historical account involves a creative, even "fictive," rendering that, in its own way, includes plot and characterization. Fiction does not directly attempt to pay this debt, but its power also stems from its redescription of the world in a more subtle way. Ricoeur points back to Aristotle, who saw

58. Ibid.

59. See, for example, the work by Nobel Prize–winning scientist Jacques Monod, *Chance and Necessity: An Essay on the Natural Philosophy of Modern Biology,* trans. Austryn Wainhouse (New York: Vintage Books, 1972). For a more positive view of the implications of chaos theory, see Barbour, *Religion and Science,* 312–13; John Polkinghorne, *Science and Providence: God's Interaction with the World,* New Science Library (Boston: Shambhala, 1989), 38–41.

fiction as more "philosophical" than historiography because historiography deals with particulars whereas fiction represents the general or universal.[60] Fiction also represents what *could be* the case and is not tied to what *was* the case. In its own way, however, as we have seen, fiction projects a world in which we might live. It involves a complex split reference, as in metaphor, where, in an act of fusion of horizons, we move from the fictional world to relate it to our world. Ricoeur thus identifies "an interpenetration of history and fiction, stemming from the criss-crossing processes of a fictionalization of history and historization of fiction."[61] This complex interplay is what makes it possible, he thinks, to integrate the otherwise discrepant dimensions of time—lived time, chronological time, and broader historical time—into a narrative identity.[62]

Ricoeur draws on reader-response theory to focus on how a text does not exist apart from the reader. The merit of reader-response theory is to show how a text does not say everything. If a text did, it would be too long and boring. An artful text says enough to help the reader be an accomplice in the production of its meaning. In this way, the reader's imagination is unavoidably engaged. Each reader thus renders his or her own distinctive fusion of horizons that shares much in common with others but in other ways is distinctively unique. The scripture's narratives, for example, are notable in their reticence and in what they leave up to the reader. The accounts of Peter and of Judas in the Gospels are filled in by readers in ways both common and individual. This dynamic indicates how the idea of simply being absorbed by the biblical world apart from the contemporary world, as the Yale school suggests, is an impossible notion. The fusion of horizons must occur for there to be a text. At the same time, the text guides the configuring and refiguring work of the reader.

Ricoeur's own scholarly itinerary has thus led him to deal with first symbol, then metaphor, and then narrative. As such, he is one of the first philosophers to place such figurative language at the center of his philosophy. This philosophical reflection on figurative language is, in turn, one of the most obvious resources for theologians.

Scripture

The reconfiguration of metaphor and narrative that one finds in Ricoeur is of immense significance for the interpretation of scripture. I explore

60. Aristotle, *On Poetics,* 3.9.
61. Ricoeur, *Time and Narrative,* vol. 3, 246.
62. Ibid.

here two applications that stem from Ricoeur, as well as another that Ricoeur strangely did not explore but that is enriched by his work.

The Parables as Extended Metaphors

One of the most important applications of Ricoeur's work on metaphor in particular was its extension to the parables of Jesus. Ricoeur engaged the parables in a seminal monograph in 1975 titled "Biblical Hermeneutics."[63] His work paralleled similar groundbreaking work by other New Testament scholars such as John Dominic Crossan, Robert Funk, Dan Via Jr., and Norman Perrin. Collaborating on a new understanding of the parables in the mid-1970s, their work focused on the parable of the Good Samaritan.[64] Essentially, they took the new understanding of metaphor that was found in Ricoeur and others and applied it to the parables. The parables had long been understood as allegories, but in the nineteenth and twentieth centuries, this view was discarded. Particularly in the work of Adolf Jülicher, C. H. Dodd, and Joachim Jeremias, the parables were seen as having one basic point rather than many allegorical and often fanciful points.[65]

In the 1970s, this view was questioned. The parables convey a message, but like the significance that Ricoeur saw in other biblical genres, the medium is also the message. As "extended" metaphors, parables likewise began to be seen as not fully translatable into literal language, into theological "points"; as containing a surplus of meaning; and as catalysts of new meaning rather than as ornamental figures of meaning best expressed in prosaic language. In addition, in the hands of Jesus, they possessed further qualities that took advantage of the metaphorical dynamic. In Crossan's terms, the parables "subvert world," as opposed to myths that "establish world" or other stories that simply "investigate world."[66] Parable is "the dark night of story."[67] In the case of the parable of the Good Samaritan, this approach opened up the way to see it not as was customary, as a simple example story, but as a clash of worlds. An example story

63. Ricoeur, "Biblical Hermeneutics."

64. This story is well told in Norman Perrin, *Jesus and the Language of the Kingdom: Symbol and Metaphor in New Testament Interpretation* (Philadelphia: Fortress Press, 1976), 132–81.

65. Ibid., 91–107.

66. See especially John Dominic Crossan, *The Dark Interval: Towards a Theology of Story* (Allen, Tex: Argus Communications, 1975), chap. 2. For his further, much more elaborate treatment of parables, see John Dominic Crossan, *In Parables: The Challenge of the Historical Jesus* (New York: Harper & Row, 1973).

67. Crossan, *Dark Interval,* 60.

would have had a common Jew as the helper. The story ends up, however, with the common Jew as the one needing help but desperately not wanting to be helped by a hated, unclean Samaritan. The question is left: Would a good Jew accept help from a most unlikely and unwanted source?[68] The larger messianic context portrays the question thus: Could the people welcome help from a most unlikely messianic candidate, namely, Jesus of Nazareth? This kind of approach dramatically reshapes parable interpretation.

Ricoeur additionally emphasizes that an unnoticed aspect of the parables is their extravagant nature.[69] They speak of small seeds growing unusually large, of workers being paid far beyond what they have earned, of a prodigal son being welcomed home virtually without repentance, and so on. These represent an "intensification" of the metaphorical nature of the parables and result in a "transgression," in which "these forms of discourse point beyond their immediate signification toward the Wholly Other."[70] Crossan sees this movement primarily in terms of "shattering world."[71] Ricoeur agrees but also sees a "re-orientation by disorientation."[72] Theologically, he identifies this reorientation with the eschatological scandal that responds to evil with a "no longer" and a hope of "how much more" we may anticipate from God, in faith but not by sight—or knowledge, as in a Hegelian philosophy of history or a Christian theology of glory.[73]

More recently, Ricoeur has connected the extravagance in the parables with a logic or economy of superabundance that is also a logic of the "gift," opposed to an economy of equivalence, thus joining a lively current philosophical discussion.[74] As such, this analysis is a way in which, despite his protestations, he integrates his Christian reflection with his philosophical reflection. It also reveals his point, however, that religious

68. Perrin, *Jesus,* 168–81.
69. Ricoeur, "Biblical Hermeneutics," 99.
70. Ibid., 108.
71. Crossan, *In Parables,* 76.
72. Ricoeur, "Biblical Hermeneutics," 114.
73. Ibid., 121.
74. Paul Ricoeur, "Love and Justice," trans. David Pellauer, in *Figuring the Sacred,* ed. Wallace, 326. He makes a profound connection here between the logic of the parables and what he calls the prose of justice and the poetics of love. For introduction to the philosophical discussion, see Stephen H. Webb, *The Gifting God: A Trinitarian Ethics of Excess* (New York: Oxford University Press, 1996); Jacques Derrida, *Given Time: I. Counterfeit Money,* trans. Peggy Kamuf (Chicago: University of Chicago Press, 1992); Jacques Derrida, *The Gift of Death,* trans. David Wills, Religion and Postmodernism (Chicago: University of Chicago Press, 1995). Ricoeur was already speaking of a logic of superabundance and excess in 1968, without using the language of "gift." See Paul Ricoeur, "Freedom in the Light of Hope," trans. Robert Sweeney, in *Essays on Biblical Interpretation,* ed. Lewis S. Mudge (Philadelphia: Fortress Press, 1980), 164.

hermeneutics, such as parable interpretation, is not reducible to hermeneutics in general. It is not a simple subcategory of hermeneutics, but while sharing many characteristics, it also stretches hermeneutics to the breaking point as it attempts to interpret discourse about God.

The Forms of Discourse in Scripture

One of the advantages of Ricoeur's approach to narrative is that he has a balanced approach that values it more highly than is traditional. As a result, he contributes to reconfiguration of the theological task by narrative theologians. His sensitivity to literary genre, however, prevents him from collapsing everything into narrative or a one-dimensional conception of narrative. He affirms what he calls the "magisterial work"[75] of Hans Frei in *The Eclipse of Biblical Narrative,*[76] but he does so in the sense of rejecting with Frei a monovalent theology of history, *Heilsgeschichte,* in which a Hegelian pattern is imposed on scripture and theology. He explains:

> In fact, *the* biblical narrative has reached the shores of our culture as a grandiose but frozen one-dimensional narrative in which all the varieties of discourse are leveled off. The creation story, the fall story, and the patriarch stories are held as equally authentic accounts as say, the story of the succession to David's throne or the story of the dramatic encounter between Jesus and his opponents. The biblical narrative that collapsed is, in fact, this flat linear account that amounts to a world-history and that competed with newly conceived world-histories from the renaissance time down to Hegel.[77]

Instead, Ricoeur calls for attention to the variety of forms of discourse in scripture in a way that goes beyond Frei and Lindbeck, who tend to speak in terms of one biblical world. Ricoeur, like Frei, is concerned with the recovery of biblical narrative, but he sets the specific biblical narratives in the context of several other forms of discourse.

He first examines *prophetic* discourse, where there is an explicit sense in which the prophet speaks for God, and we thus have a "double author."[78] Both God and the prophet are the speakers. This type of biblical discourse raises for some the notion of dictation. As Ricoeur says, however, "Any

75. Ricoeur, *Figuring the Sacred,* 237.

76. Hans W. Frei, *The Eclipse of Biblical Narrative: A Study in Eighteenth and Nineteenth Century Hermeneutics* (New Haven, Conn.: Yale University Press, 1974).

77. Ricoeur, *Figuring the Sacred,* 237.

78. Paul Ricoeur, "Toward a Hermeneutic of the Idea of Revelation," trans. David Pellauer, in *Essays on Biblical Interpretation,* ed. Mudge, 75.

access to a less subjective manner of understanding revelation is prematurely cut off."[79] This move is actually forestalled by the other forms of biblical discourse.

Ricoeur notes that in biblical *narrative* discourse "the author often disappears and it is as though the events recounted themselves."[80] The focus is now not on God as the speaker but on God as the actor, a "double actant," if you will, that balances the double author of prophecy.[81] This is where the neo-orthodox emphasis on scripture as the record of God's acts in history fits best.[82] A further balance, or sometimes tension, between these two discourses lies in the challenge that prophecy often brings to history. "The same history which narration founds as certain is suddenly undercut by the menace announced in the prophecy."[83] Ricoeur argues that no system can assuage this dialectic; only hope can.[84] Beyond this, Ricoeur reminds us that "the polysemy and polyphony of revelation are not yet exhausted by this coupling of narration and prophecy."[85]

A third genre is *prescriptive* discourse, legal discourse. Ricoeur is especially concerned to overcome the way in which the Law has been increasingly understood in terms of Kantian heteronomy, a set of Pharisaic, arbitrary, external demands.[86] He reminds us that the Law is set within the narrative of the exodus. It is also set within the broader framework of a relational covenant that goes beyond simple command and obedience. In addition, there is a dialectic in the Law that moves from increasing detail to summary in terms of loving God. Ricoeur point out, "The Sermon on the Mount proclaims the same intention of perfection and holiness that runs through the ancient Law."[87]

According to Ricoeur, this deepening of the Law is extended and almost shattered by *wisdom* discourse. Wisdom aims at every human being and thus "overflows the framework of the Covenant."[88] Like the other discourses, wisdom further joins "ethos and cosmos, the sphere of human action and the sphere of the world."[89] But it joins them in suffering and

79. Ibid., 76.
80. Ibid., 77.
81. Ibid., 78.
82. See, for a classic explanation of this approach, John Baillie, *The Idea of Revelation in Recent Thought* (New York: Columbia University Press, 1956).
83. Ricoeur, "Toward a Hermeneutic of the Idea of Revelation," 80.
84. Ibid., 81. We examine the role of hope in Ricoeur's thought in chapter 7, dealing with epistemology.
85. Ibid.
86. Ibid., 82–84.
87. Ibid., 84.
88. Ibid., 85.
89. Ibid., 86.

hope. The tragedy of the unexplained suffering of Job, who wishes that he had never been born, and the futility of the Preacher of Ecclesiastes, who saw no point in being born, mark the obscure shadow and the evil in life that has preoccupied Ricoeur from the beginning. Despite the different kinds of despair in Job and in the Preacher, their canonical context nevertheless opens up a fragile hope. As Ricoeur says:

> We should begin to see at what point the notion of God's design—as may be suggested in different ways in each instance, it is true, by narrative, prophetic, and prescriptive discourse—is removed from any transcription in terms of a plan or program; in short, of finality and teleology. What is revealed is the possibility of hope in spite of. . . . This possibility may still be expressed in the terms of a design, but of an unassignable design, a design which is God's secret.[90]

The sage moreover does not profess to speak for God but is nevertheless regarded as inspired by God.[91]

The final genre at which Ricoeur looks is *hymnic* discourse, which he sees as not simply added to narration; rather, its "celebration elevates the story and turns it into an invocation."[92] Ricoeur notes that the I-Thou relation of Martin Buber may have been exaggerated, but it finds its home in this discourse.[93]

Attention to these forms of discourse is extremely significant. The "medium is the message" in large part and shows in yet another way how theology cannot "take these forms of discourse as simple literary genres which ought to be neutralized so that we can extract their theological content."[94] Ricoeur's analysis cautions against overextending any particular genre and certainly against taking one model of authorship, such as the prophetic, and applying it woodenly across the board.

Having passed through these literary fires, Ricoeur comes back to assert that there is a larger sense in which all of the canon is set within a narrative framework, remembering that this is an unfinished history that is discordant as well as concordant. He emphasizes, "The story of the partnership between God and Israel is, as such, not only open and ongoing but unfathomable and unspeakable."[95] This biblical story parallels the

90. Ibid., 87.
91. Ricoeur suggests that in this characteristic, prophecy and wisdom join in the apocalyptic literature. Ibid., 88.
92. Ibid., 88f.
93. Ibid., 89.
94. Ibid., 90–91.
95. Ricoeur, "Toward a Narrative Theology," 242f.

way in which our human stories and identities are finally story-formed while they are yet unfinished and full of discordance—and hope.

History and Fiction in Scripture

Another delicate issue of balance with respect to genre concerns the relationship of fiction and historiography in scripture. A tendency of the literary approach to the scriptures is to see them as fictive and to prescind altogether their historical reference.[96] Ricoeur's way of drawing both fiction and historiography together, in seeing them both as mimetic and historical, provides a way beyond the impasse of a heavily historical concern found in traditional historical-critical approaches versus a nonhistorical literary approach. In *Time and Narrative,* Ricoeur focuses on modern fiction and modern historiography and does not deal with the Gospels, which have been variously interpreted as more akin to fiction or more akin to historiography. While it is understandable that he did not deal with biblical literature in *Time and Narrative,* it is surprising that he has not elsewhere applied his hermeneutic to the vexed nature of the Gospels. Several have seen, however, that Ricoeur's work on history and fiction opens up a fresh way of relating the literary and historical dimensions of the Gospels.[97] Tim Maddox has creatively applied Ricoeur's work in *Time and Narrative* to the Gospel of Luke with the idea that the Gospel genre is a unique interweaving itself of fiction and historiography.[98] The Gospels can be seen thus as inherently configured, in other words, as interpretations, but sharing important characteristics of both fiction and historiography. The Gospels bear a debt to the past. They are both about events in the past and interpretations of what happened. John Van den Hengel points out that Ricoeur's own inclinations are, like Hans Frei's, to see the Gospels as history-like and not to delineate how they are historical. But Van den Hengel also argues that Ricoeur's framework provides a fruitful way to

96. For a discussion of this problem and a balanced response, see R. Alan Culpepper, *Anatomy of the Fourth Gospel: A Study in Literary Design,* ed. Robert Funk, Foundations and Facets: New Testament (Philadelphia: Fortress Press, 1983).

97. Timothy Donald Fletcher Maddox, "Paul Ricoeur's *Time and Narrative* as a Model for Historical Reference in Biblical Narrative" (Th.M. thesis, Southern Baptist Theological Seminary, 1992); John Van den Hengel, "Jesus between History and Fiction," in *Meanings in Texts and Actions: Questioning Paul Ricoeur,* ed. David E. Klemm and William Schweiker, Studies in Religion and Culture (Charlottesville: University Press of Virginia, 1993), 133-53; Francis Watson, *Text and Truth: Redefining Biblical Theology* (Grand Rapids: Wm. B. Eerdmans Publishing Co., 1997), 54–63.

98. Maddox, "Paul's Ricoeur's *Time and Narrative.*"

understand the historicity of the Gospels.[99] Ricoeur himself at one point indicates that the question about the reference of the resurrection cannot be avoided.[100]

It is evident, however, that in the Gospels, the primary focus is not on the debt to the past but on the configuration of a world in which we might live. As John most clearly puts it, "But these are written so that you may come to believe that Jesus is the Messiah, the Son of God, and that through believing you may have life in his name" (John 20:31). The Gospels reveal that many details are capable of being moved around, reshaped, and elaborated in order to convey the reality of what Jesus Christ brought to the world. But, there is no *carte blanche.* A historical dimension is present throughout. Moreover, the specific rootage in history is, *in the Gospel accounts themselves,* crucial. One can say that the details of the crucifixion vary, but the testimony to its happening does not. Details of Jesus' life vary, but the testimony to his sign working and parabling does not. Certain events such as death on the cross and the resurrection are implied by the text as non-negotiable referents in a way that others are not. As such, these historical markers are not contrary to the world of the text but required by it. The debt to the past, as it were, must be "paid off," but the larger debt is to the configuration of a redemptive world in which we are called to live. The vexing polarity between the Gospels as history or as fiction can be relaxed through Ricoeur's matrix of the inherent interweaving of history and fiction. The Gospel genre can thus be fruitfully understood as a complex and particular interweaving of the two.

99. Van den Hengel, "Jesus between History and Fiction." Francis Watson also says, "Ricoeur enables us to conceive of a historiography enriched by fiction and not subverted by it." See Watson, *Text and Truth,* 57. I am using the term *historicity* guardedly, aware that a creative, even "fictive," rendering of an event can be truer to the historical meaning than a flat chronicle. I am using the term in the modern sense of recounting what happened, not so much the meaning of what happened. I am assuming at the same time Ricoeur's criticism of positivist historiography, which sees such an account as supremely objective and factual, realizing that historiography itself is at the very least highly configurative, imaginative, and theory-laden, just as scientific "facts" are. Nevertheless, the value of Ricoeur's middle way is to see this mimetic dimension of historiography while still allowing for a difference between the genres of modern fiction and modern historiography. Of course, these issues similarly arise for the history of the Hebrew Bible. See Karl Möller, "Renewing Historical Criticism," in *Renewing Biblical Interpretation,* ed. Craig Bartholomew, Colin Greene, and Karl Möller, vol. 1, Scripture and Hermeneutics Series (Grand Rapids: Zondervan Publishing House, 2000), 145–71; Iain W. Provan, "Ideologies, Literary and Critical: Reflections on Recent Writing on the History of Israel," *Journal of Biblical Literature* 114, 4 (1995): 585–606.

100. Ricoeur, *Essays on Biblical Interpretation,* 44. I deal with criticisms of Ricoeur's position on history and biblical hermeneutics in chapter 7 and argue that his position is much less subjective and much more historical than some believe. I emphasize, however, that my focus is on his philosophical, not his theological, position. His philosophical framework allows for diverse theological appropriations.

Divine Discourse

In his Gifford Lectures, Nicholas Wolterstorff proposes a creative way in which to appropriate scripture as "divine discourse," the title of the book in which he published the lectures in 1995.[101] He drew on speech-act theory, suggesting that it provides "finally, after all these centuries," for a way to understand God's authorship adequately.[102] In the process, he uses Ricoeur as a foil for his views. While Wolterstorff's idea is very creative and worth developing, he misconstrues Ricoeur's work at several points, which is ironic since Ricoeur is compatible with his proposal in many ways. Analysis of Wolterstorff's work reveals some common misconceptions of Ricoeur on the contemporary scene, while also showing how Ricoeur's work is actually more adaptable than is often thought.

Speech-act theory derives from the British philosopher John Austin, who understood speech as actions, that is, things we do with words.[103] One of Austin's primary criticisms is what he called the "descriptive fallacy," where we traditionally look at speaking as primarily describing.[104] In actuality, we do many things with words, probably most things, that are not simple descriptions. Austin further recognized that even descriptions are actions that involve the backing of the speaker, who is making a kind of commitment. He analyzed all speech acts as involving "locutionary" elements of grammar and syntax; "illocutionary" elements that involve conventions to indicate the speech act is one of promising, affirming, questioning, requesting, and so on; and "perlocutionary" elements that involve how the speech act is received, that is, the effect intended by the speech act. Austin's work has been further appropriated as grounds for understanding narrative theology and as a promising postmodern philosophy in general.[105] Austin's thought was influenced by the work of the later Wittgenstein, who emphasized that meaning is a function of public

101. Nicholas Wolterstorff, *Divine Discourse: Philosophical Reflections on the Claim That God Speaks* (Cambridge: Cambridge University Press, 1995).

102. Nicholas Wolterstorff, "The Importance of Hermeneutics for a Christian Worldview," in *Disciplining Hermeneutics: Interpretation in Christian Perspective,* ed. Roger Lundin (Grand Rapids: Wm. B. Eerdmans Publishing, Co., 1997), 30.

103. John L. Austin, *How to Do Things with Words,* ed. J. O. Urmson and Marina Sbisà, 2d ed. (Cambridge, Mass.: Harvard University Press, 1975). This work is based on the William James Lectures delivered at Harvard University in 1955.

104. Ibid., 1.

105. See Michael Goldberg, *Theology and Narrative: A Critical Introduction* (Nashville: Abingdon Press, 1982); and Nancey C. Murphy, *Anglo-American Postmodernity: Philosophical Perspectives on Science, Religion, and Ethics* (Boulder, Colo.: Westview Press, 1997).

use. This common background implies connections with the Yale school of narrative theology, which also draws heavily on Wittgenstein.[106] Ricoeur himself draws on speech-act theory at certain points.[107]

Wolterstorff argues that theology has focused too much on the category of scripture as revelation, which is to misunderstand the nature of divine discourse. Wolterstorff's prime insight is that speaking is more complex than is often recognized, which gives us room to understand scripture as divine discourse without recourse to a divine dictation theory of revelation. He points out that Jews, Christians, and Muslims understand God in their scriptures to be making such things as commands, promises, and assurances. Wolterstorff maintains:

> The theory of interpreting for divine discourse which I will articulate and defend . . . implies that, unless there is good reason to act otherwise, the writers of scripture should be interpreted as speaking literally on this matter; and implies that, unless there is good reason to do otherwise, God should be interpreted as saying what the writers said.[108]

How is this possible?

Wolterstorff offers a novel approach. In human conventions, he reminds us, people can "deputize" others to speak for them.[109] For example, a president can authorize or deputize an ambassador to represent him or her to a foreign dignitary. The speech is literally that of the ambassador, but it functions as the words of the president. This categorization could apply to some biblical discourse, such as prophetic oracles, in a way similar to Ricoeur's analysis of them as involving a "double author," where the prophet speaks God's word; but it would not help with most of the biblical literature.[110] So a second kind of speech act is noted. Here someone "appropriates" another's work or words as his or her own.[111] An example would be a speech written for the president. Or it could be a work written independently on a subject, which the president later designates as representing his or her position. In both cases, the words are regarded as

106. See, for Wittgenstein, Stiver, *Philosophy of Religious Language,* chap. 4; and for Wittgenstein and speech-act theory, ibid., chap. 7.

107. For example, Paul Ricoeur, "The Hermeneutical Function of Distanciation," in *Hermeneutics and the Human Sciences,* ed. Thompson, 134–35. Ricoeur believes that the three locutionary acts can be inscribed and marked to some degree in writing as well as in oral speech. He says, "Thus the propositional act, the illocutionary force and the perlocutionary action are susceptible, in decreasing degrees, to the intentional exteriorisation which renders inscription by writing possible" (135).

108. Wolterstorff, *Divine Discourse,* 101.

109. Ibid., 42–51.

110. Ricoeur, "Toward a Hermeneutic of the Idea of Revelation," 75.

111. Wolterstorff, *Divine Discourse,* 51–54.

the president's in this conventional sense. Wolterstorff wonders why we could not see the Bible as a whole as works that God has similarly appropriated. This allows for the individuality of the writers and for it to be divine discourse. With this ingenious insight, Wolterstorff has done no more than draw on recognized human conventions to make a radical point, namely, that scripture is God's word in a literal sense that is nevertheless far from a dictation or inerrantist theory of inspiration.

Divine Discourse and Revelation

Drawing on this idea, Wolterstorff critiques Ricoeur at two major points, one having to do with the nature of revelation and the other with the role of the author. In the first case, he charges Ricoeur, and many others, with confusing the act of "revealing" with "speaking." Over and over he maintains that "speaking is not revealing."[112] He is correct, of course, in the particular sense that a certain kind of speech act of revealing is not the same as speaking. He raises the example of a patriarch of the family revealing a secret about his will. One can do this with words or without words, which he calls, respectively, nonmanifestational (propositional) and manifestational revelation. In a certain sense, some of the Bible can be regarded as this kind of making known of something that has been hidden—but not all of it. The act of commanding or promising is not one of revealing. One could say that in commanding, God is revealing a divine command, but the illocutionary act itself is "commanding," not "revealing."[113] Wolterstorff especially criticizes Karl Barth and other neo-orthodox theologians for using *revelation* to refer to God's action primarily in Jesus Christ and only secondarily as the expression of that action in words.[114] In so doing, they miss out on nonmanifestational revelation and totally omit divine discourse.

While Wolterstorff is technically correct, it seems that he misses the point of most talk of revelation. More seriously, in his own terms, he has misconstrued theologians' speech acts in which they talk of revelation. Theologians use *revelation* more broadly, as the way in which scripture conveys truth about God. In traditional terminology, *special revelation* refers to the way in which we have knowledge of God through the special history of God's dealing with Israel, culminating in Jesus Christ. As such,

112. This is the title of chapter 2 in Wolterstorff's *Divine Discourse.*
113. See ibid., 20–21. The perlocutionary effect, however, may be one of revealing.
114. See especially ibid., chap. 4.

special revelation easily can be seen as including God's speech acts toward humans. Even if one emphasizes the Barthian idea that God's Word is primarily Jesus Christ, the scripture is still regarded as the Word of God in a derivative sense. *Revelation* is simply the label or category for dealing with the way in which we understand scripture, or more broadly, the way God is known in and speaks through scripture. This broad notion of revelation is akin to the doctrine of creation including a variety of understandings of creating, perhaps even a process view that denies *creatio ex nihilo.* Revelation's function as one of the major divisions of systematic theology gives it a use different from the technical speech act of a dying person revealing a secret, to which Wolterstorff refers. It is the label for the section of systematic theology that deals with God's speaking and revealing in various ways, not so much a descriptive characterization of a particular kind of speech act.

Even with this broader conception of revelation in mind, we can still see that Wolterstorff has offered an ingenious new way to think of scripture as God's Word that does justice both to its human and divine elements. He still does not, however, address the issues with which Ricoeur deals. Even if one accepts scripture as a whole as God's authorized speech, one still has to interpret it. One still has to deal with its meaning, which involves understanding its genre, its figures of speech, its context, and all the other standard issues of interpretation. Wolterstorff acknowledges this when he speaks of a first and second hermeneutic.[115] The first involves understanding what the human authors were saying and doing. The second concerns what God is doing in appropriating their work. Especially in the first case, but also in the second, one has to understand the meaning by interpreting the text.

In fact, as we have seen, Ricoeur makes major contributions to these hermeneutical issues in understanding the Bible as involving many different genres that cannot simply be collapsed into one another. Wolterstorff's theory does not particularly deal with these dimensions of hermeneutics. He provides a certain framework for looking at scripture, but this is only the beginning of the work of understanding. One may understand scripture as God's speech, but what God is saying must still be interpreted, and it must be interpreted, as both agree, as a human work quite apart from divine dictation. One may pass through Wolterstorff, but that does not mean that one need not pass through Ricoeur.

115. Ibid., chaps. 11–12; Wolterstorff, "Importance of Hermeneutics," 44.

Wolterstorff's proposals should be understood as a distinctive approach to the traditional notion of the theory of inspiration, and Ricoeur's as an aspect of the traditional notion of the interpretation or hermeneutic of scripture.[116] Both are included within the doctrine of revelation.

It is true that Ricoeur does not particularly offer a view of inspiration; he focuses on interpreting the meaning of the scriptural texts. In this sense, Wolterstorff points out a lacuna in Ricoeur's thought. At the same time, if one is disposed to accept Wolterstorff's account of inspiration, Ricoeur fills a lacuna in Wolterstorff's approach.

After criticizing Ricoeur for dealing with revelation and not divine discourse, Wolterstorff criticizes Ricoeur's understanding of revelation itself as a manifestational and "projective" approach to revelation. The first problem with this criticism is that Wolterstorff draws on an equivocal use of manifestation, just as he did with revelation. He takes manifestation to be showing or revealing something by some natural sign.[117] It is akin to revealing one's nervousness by one's hurried speech or gestures. As such, this is what Wolterstorff terms "manifestational," as opposed to "nonmanifestational" or propositional, revelation. It is correct that many in the biblical theology movement and neo-orthodox movement saw revelation in this way. God reveals God's self by God's mighty acts, which are to be distinguished from the reports or records of them. This is not Ricoeur, however. Ricoeur takes very seriously the message communicated by the text as a structured work, representing syntax, genre, and so on. He uses "manifestation" in this context in a Heideggerian sense that has to do with truth being disclosed through language in a way not reducible to simple correspondence.[118] The issue is disclosure through a

116. This may seem odd, since Wolterstorff maintains, characteristically, that to inspire is a different speech act than to reveal; see Wolterstorff, "Importance of Hermeneutics," 37. The doctrine of inspiration, however, is a broader category that includes the various theories about how the Bible comes to be God's Word. In this sense, Wolterstorff's idea is such a theory. This is true despite the fact that, in contrast to traditional theories of inspiration, as I. Howard Marshall points out, Wolterstorff does not deal at all with the divine activity at the time of writing or production of the biblical writings. See I. Howard Marshall, "'To Find Out What God Is Saying': Reflections on the Authorizing of Scripture," in *Disciplining Hermeneutics,* ed. Lundin, 51.

117. Wolterstorff, *Divine Discourse,* 28.

118. Paul Ricoeur, "Naming God," trans. David Pellauer, in *Figuring the Sacred,* ed. Wallace, 223. An element of confusion may arise from another discussion by Ricoeur, where he deals in the phenomenology of religion with religions of "proclamation," such as Christianity and Islam, and religions of "manifestation," such as tribal religions of the sacred. See Paul Ricoeur, "Manifestation and Proclamation," trans. David Pellauer, in *Figuring the Sacred,* ed. Wallace 48–67. In the latter article, he opposes a symbolism of the sacred to revelation through the prophetic word and written texts. Perhaps Ricoeur's usage of "manifestation" in this article is close to Wolterstorff's usage; the problem is that Wolterstorff references Ricoeur's other usage, rather than this one.

work.[119] (This can include acts, which, as we have seen, also have to be interpreted.) In effect, Ricoeur's manifestion is not at all manifestation in Wolterstorff's sense, that is, indirectly by some natural sign. It is directly, so to speak, in words.

Moreover, the idea of a manifested truth in a world projected by the text allows for revelation that is asserted in Wolterstoff's terms but also for divine discourse in the sense of God's speaking. It is telling that Wolterstorff omits, in his usually careful discussion of Ricoeur, the fact that Ricoeur continues to assume both the role of a human author and divine authorship of scripture, which as a whole names God in manifold ways as well as reveals God's promises, assurances, and other speech acts.[120] It reveals truth about God as well as conveying what God says—at least, it can be so regarded. A liberal might resist the idea of God speaking through scripture and see it simply as fallible human efforts to represent God. Ricoeur's hermeneutic is open to both this view and a higher view of scripture, although Ricoeur himself points beyond the liberal view to a more traditional view of scripture as God's revealed Word. What Ricoeur resists is a divine dictation view or any similar view that avoids regarding these as incarnate, human works, embedded in their situation, that call for interpretation. Wolterstorff actually suggests at one point that one could think of a projected world in which God speaks—precisely the implication of Ricoeur's work.[121] This shows that the manifestation or projective model does not inherently preclude the divine speech model.

This can be seen in several ways. First, Ricoeur sees that scripture can be seen as a whole as referring to God. He says, "God is in some manner implied by the 'issue' of these texts, by the world—the biblical world—that these texts unfold."[122] Second, Ricoeur indicates that insofar as the texts are regarded as inspired by God, an analogy to the idea of prophetic discourse, where God speaks through the prophet, holds throughout all the various biblical genres.[123] He predictably qualifies this by saying that the prophetic model is complemented by other models, but in general this view allows for divine speech in such a projected world. For example, in

119. Ricoeur, "Toward a Hermeneutic of the Idea of Revelation," 99–100. For extensive discussion of a disclosure theory of truth in Heidegger, Gadamer, and Ricoeur, in contrast to traditional correspondence and coherence theories of truth, see James DiCenso, *Hermeneutics and the Disclosure of Truth: A Study in the Work of Heidegger, Gadamer, and Ricoeur* (Charlottesville: University Press of Virginia, 1990).

120. See Ricoeur, "Toward a Hermeneutic of the Idea of Revelation," 92–93, 103–4.

121. Wolterstorff, *Divine Discourse,* 62. He says, "To use Ricoeur's conceptuality: an aspect of the world projected by all these texts is that of God speaking."

122. Ricoeur, "Naming God," 221.

123. Ricoeur, "Toward a Hermeneutic of the Idea of Revelation," 103.

Ricoeur's several reflections on the meaning of the First Commandment, to love God, he assumes the legitimacy of the command even as he emphasizes the relational and divine dimensions of the command—as he puts it, "You—love me."[124] Third, he reminds us, in a way that Wolterstorff does not, that a biblical hermeneutic involving this reference to God is a unique hermeneutic, not reducible without strain to any particular hermeneutic, including speech-act theory. This comes actually from the sense in which God is the author and referent of the biblical canon.

When one realizes that Ricoeur thinks of the text as projecting a world in which God promises, comforts, and does many other speech acts, then the difference between him and Wolterstorff collapses. There is nothing in Ricoeur's approach that prohibits understanding the text as one in which God speaks. In fact, it is clearer to see in Ricoeur's approach how one would interpret a text as doing such a thing. Conversely, it is difficult to imagine how Wolterstorff can move through the interpretation of the text to a conclusion about what the text is doing and avoid a complex hermeneutical analysis such as Ricoeur's. One way Wolterstorff attempts to soften the problem of interpretation is to call upon the author, which brings us to the second major criticism that he makes of Ricoeur.

Divine Discourse and Textual-Sense Interpretation

Wolterstorff's second major objection concerns Ricoeur's rejection of authorial intent in favor of the distanciation of the text from the author. Wolterstorff favors what he considers a traditional "authorial discourse interpretation" over against Ricoeur's "textual-sense interpretation."[125] Wolterstorff objects to the latter because, he speculates, the text might be seen as a deliberate attempt at deception.[126] The words might be seen as obscure codes for something entirely different. He argues, then, that we assume the authors of the biblical texts have no such intentions, and we could not make that assumption without regard for the author. *Ipso facto,* Ricoeur's and others' rejection of the author is misguided. Wolterstorff also considers it important that the author is making a commitment in communicating, especially, as one might expect, when promises or covenants are being made. The author is thus important as the one making the commitment.[127]

124. André Lacocque and Paul Ricoeur, *Thinking Biblically: Exegetical and Hermeneutical Studies,* trans. David Pellauer (Chicago: University of Chicago Press, 1998), 67, 121.

125. Wolterstorff, "Importance of Hermeneutics," 38–42.

126. Ibid., 42–43.

127. Wolterstorff, *Divine Discourse.*

Again, Wolterstorff misconstrues Ricoeur. Although he might be more on target concerning the French poststructuralists whom he also criticizes, his reprobation of Ricoeur is wide of the mark.[128] What is ironic is that Wolterstorff rejects Romantic hermeneutics for the same reasons as do Ricoeur and Gadamer.[129] Wolterstorff argues that we cannot get into someone else's mind and thus must turn to the text, which has a public meaning of its own. To communicate, writers must use public words and conventions in accord with speech-act theory. We know that Ricoeur agrees with Wolterstorff in rejecting Romantic hermeneutics. What Wolterstorff neglects is that we do not know the authors of most of the biblical books, and that many of the books have a history of construction that involves multiple authors or editors, such as the Pentateuch, which generally is regarded as composed of at least four different works. The Synoptic Gospels are generally regarded as Matthew and Luke drawing on Mark and another document, Q. The actual author of any of those documents is not known. What we have are texts that have been taken up by the church as accounts of the meaning of Jesus Christ (in the case of the Gospels) and of the way of God with a special people (in the case of the Pentateuch). Despite Wolterstorff's requirements of knowing the author's intended speech acts, we simply do not always know. We can only appeal to the text and the way it has been received as a sincere construal of God's revelation. Ricoeur addresses this issue in a way that allows us to go on with the texts without worry, while Wolterstorff, one might say, leaves us with deep anxiety about whether the scripture is trustworthy, since in so many cases we know nothing of the authors' identities, much less their intentions.

Wolterstorff seems to escape the dilemma that he unwittingly raises by seeing scripture as authorized divine discourse mediated by the early church's acceptance of it as canon.[130] Ironically, this is very similar to Ricoeur's own reasoning. All of scripture, Ricoeur argues, refers back to

128. His criticism may also miss on Jacques Derrida. As Merold Westphal notes in a review of *Divine Discourse,* "I think his interpretations of these two thinkers (and traditions) would be more compelling if they were more charitable." Merold Westphal, "Review Essay: Theology as Talking about a God Who Talks," *Modern Theology* 13, 4 (1997): 532.

129. See, for example, Wolterstorff, *Divine Discourse,* 76; "But I also dissent from the expressionist (Romanticist) view of speaking as consisting in the intentional expression of inner states by way of uttering or inscribing some bit of language"; and "But even more important for our subsequent purposes is the fact that to speak is not, as such, to express one's inner self but to take up a normative stance in the public domain. The myth dies hard that to read a text for authorial discourse is to enter the dark world of the author's psyche" (93).

130. Ibid., 288–96. Note how Wolterstorff's language in this section shifts subtly from focus on the author to the evaluation of the church.

God as the one who speaks in it, which is argued on the basis of the text and the reader's evaluation, and not on the basis of knowing the authors' intentions. The problem that makes this option a blind alley for Wolterstorff is that he calls for a "double discourse" and a "first" and "second hermeneutic," where we need first to interpret the human author's meaning and then the divine.[131] On this reasoning, we could not interpret most of the Bible. We have no idea who the authors were and whether they might have tried to deceive us or not; thus we cannot get the first hemeneutic off the ground, much less the second.

When Wolterstorff turns to the second hermeneutic, with God as the appropriator, he implies that the particular writings are distanciated from their human authors and fill a role authorized by God, mediated, of course, through the church's adoption of these writings as canonical and by their place in the canon. For example, the Song of Solomon has a role in the canon, however problematic, larger than its particular meaning in its historical context. This is true in the Christian canon of the entire Hebrew Bible as related to the New Testament. It is true of James as related to Romans, and the list goes on and on. In these ways, the text takes on a life of its own beyond the human author, in a way not dissimilar to Ricoeur.

Wolterstorff unnecessarily distances himself from Ricoeur by seeing Ricoeur as implying a kind of incoherent notion of an "authorless text." As we have seen, this is too extreme. In fact, Ricoeur's discourse theory is predicated on the basic paradigm of "someone saying something about something to someone." Wolterstorff confuses the distanciation of texts from their authors with denial of authors altogether. In general, Ricoeur is such an "incarnational" philosopher, in the sense of emphasizing how all our knowledge and language is rooted in embodied and worldly beings (related to Martin Heidegger's understanding of *Dasein* as a being-in-the-world), that he can hardly suppose a disembodied and transhuman, Platonic view of texts.[132] Ricoeur makes it clear that texts are human works produced by humans and must be interpreted as such. Despite the complicated and what he calls "playful" relationship of the author to the work, this "does not imply the elimination of the author."[133] In fact, Ricoeur can speak of fulfilling the intent of Friedrich Schleiermacher's

131. Wolterstorff, "Importance of Hermeneutics," 44; Wolterstorff, *Divine Discourse,* chaps. 11–12.

132. See especially Ricoeur, *Freedom and Nature.*

133. Paul Ricoeur, "Appropriation," in *Hermeneutics and the Human Sciences,* ed. Thompson, 188.

desire to understand authors better than they understood themselves.[134] His practice of interpretation reveals that when we know the author and an author's corpus, we can draw on that knowledge in interpretation, as in the case of the apostle Paul or Plato or Hegel.[135] Nevertheless, the focus is on the public meaning of the text in the public way in which it is configured, which is a very Wittgensteinian kind of point. Texts and their modes of configuration, as we have seen in the case of metaphor and narrative, are conveyed in public ways. Their public nature does not preclude their creativity but indeed makes it possible. In terms of scripture, this frees us to interpret scripture as texts with integrity, and without worry that we do not know their author or authors. We could interpret, moreover, a creed that was adopted by a group without worry about the individual intentions of people whom we can never know. The public language and context of the time, along with the affirmation of the text as having integrity, gives us enough. What Ricoeur allows us to see is that such texts then are interpreted again and again in other contexts, without necessarily doing violence to the texts. Their public meaning opens them up to fusion with other horizons, in Gadamer's terminology. Rather than decrying this dynamic, hermeneutical philosophy sees it as a part of the nature of a text from the beginning. This is the way in which texts can take on classic status as texts that speak to every horizon, rather than being limited and confined within their original horizons.

Wolterstorff adds yet another, related concern. He objects to the analogy that Ricoeur and Gadamer use of a text having multiple interpretations akin to the way in which a musical piece can be variously interpreted, which Wolterstorff calls "performance" interpretation rather than authorial discourse interpretation.[136] This, however, is to take the analogy literally rather than figuratively. The concern of both Ricoeur and Gadamer in most circumstances is for what they call the "issue" of the text. This can be understood in many ways as it fuses with many different horizons, but the point is to understand the meaning of the text and *not* to see how many different creative variations are possible.[137] The surplus

134. Ibid., 189. To repeat a quotation cited in chapter 3, above, "Not that we can conceive of a text without an author; the tie between the speaker and the discourse is not abolished, but distended and complicated." See Paul Ricoeur, "The Model of the Text: Meaningful Action Considered as a Text," in *Hermeneutics and the Human Sciences,* ed. Thompson, 201.

135. See, for example, on Freud, Ricoeur, *Freud and Philosophy;* and on Marx, Paul Ricoeur, *Lectures on Ideology and Utopia,* ed. George H. Taylor (New York: Columbia University Press, 1986).

136. Wolterstorff, *Divine Discourse,* chap. 10.

137. Westphal also agrees that Wolterstorff misconstrues Ricoeur and Gadamer on this point but is more eager to defend performance interpretation as altogether consistent with Wolterstorff's authorial discourse interpretation. Westphal, "Review Essay," 534–35.

of meaning does not necessarily point in the direction of creative artistry; rather, it points to the unavoidable fecundity of meaning of a rich text. The comparison to a musical score is a comparison to illuminate a particular point, but it is clear from the context that they are not collapsing the two together. In other words, Gadamer and Ricoeur are making a metaphorical point while Wolterstorff is making a univocal one.

Wolterstorff even argues that because of the complexity and richness of the texts, our interpretations are forever incomplete, which he refers to, without reference to Ricoeur, as a "surplus of significance."[138] He means that we can use the text in many ways in many contexts, but he also means what Ricoeur means, that is, that texts have a richness of meaning that is virtually inexhaustible. It is striking in the end how close he comes to Ricoeur, given the role of Ricoeur as a foil to his views.

Wolterstorff desires that we see the texts as appropriated discourse in which God sometimes speaks to us, and that in interpretation we attempt to understand what God is saying, promising, assuring, and so on. I suggest that this approach differs little from that of Ricoeur and other theologians as they attempt to understand the meaning of the texts in their role in the canon as divine revelation, that is, as revelation of God. This revelation is sometimes about God and sometimes understood as revealing what God is saying, promising, assuring, and so on. Theologians may be remiss in lumping everything they do under the rubric of revelation and in not doing justice to the particularities of the way in which God speaks through scripture, but this is often more a labeling problem than a substantive one. It is true that Wolterstorff's approach clarifies greatly, and he should be commended for it. It is also true that he exaggerates the extent to which his approach differs from the practice of contemporary theologians.

The difficulty with Wolterstorff's view is that he seems to suggest we need a proper theory of inspiration and also need to know the authors before we can safely regard scripture as trustworthy. I think Wolterstorff would be shocked at these implications, but they follow from his reflections. At this point, his own high view of scriptural integrity and authority would be buttressed by adopting an approach to the text like Ricoeur's.

In the end, the irony is that Wolterstorff's understanding of scripture as divine discourse quite apart from knowing the biblical authors or their intentions, and as related to the canonization process of the early church, undergirds Ricoeur's basic theory more than it does Wolterstorff's appeal

138. Wolterstorff, *Divine Discourse,* 185.

to authorial interpretation. Wolterstorff's novel approach, in the final analysis, is complementary to Ricoeur's, and perhaps needs Ricoeur's, rather than being opposed to it—despite Wolterstorff's authorial intentions. I also argue, however, that Ricoeur's views are clarified and augmented in dialogue with Wolterstorff's.

In this chapter, we have seen how Ricoeur's phenomenological efforts led him to turn to figurative language. As a result, he has made major contributions to contemporary understanding of symbol, metaphor, and narrative. His attention to the significance of these and other forms of discourse opens up numerous fresh approaches to scripture. With this much more ample grasp of Ricoeur's positive appreciation of the variety in discourse, as well as his high estimation of scripture, we are in better position to turn to one of his most distinctive contributions that may seem to fly in another direction, namely, his emphasis on criticism and suspicion.

CHAPTER FIVE

The Hermeneutic of Suspicion

Ricoeur has accepted the modern mantle of criticism, to take nothing for granted and to test everything. So far, he is with Descartes. With other postmodernists, however, he has turned his critical eye upon modernity itself, questioning the human capacity to arrive at the Cartesian idea of a single, clear and distinct, God's-eye point of view. The converse of the surplus of meaning, which in many ways can be regarded as positive and not so threatening, is "the conflict of interpretations," which is more threatening. His move away from the emphasis on the essential and certain in phenomenology was already dissatisfaction with the modern project, of which Husserl's phenomenology represented something of a last effort. And while Ricoeur has continued to make philosophical and religious affirmations of meaning and of hope, he has passed through the refining fires of atheism and nihilism. Thus, Ricoeur's hermeneutic of suspicion is a major dimension of his philosophical project, one whose extent sets him apart from more conservative postmodern projects and yet one whose critical reluctance to eliminate meaning altogether sets him apart from the more radical postmoderns.

To understand this important aspect of Ricoeur's thought, we trace the development of his seminal notion of a hermeneutic of suspicion by first setting it in the context of his hermeneutical arc. We return then to its inception in his concern with human evil and its clear arrival in his treatment of Freud. We see how he further develops it in positioning himself both with regard to the Continental debate between Gadamer and Habermas and with regard to ideology and utopia. The latter offers his perspective on Karl Marx and on critical theory, of which Habermas is a central figure. Finally, we connect Ricoeur's hermeneutic of suspicion with the theological categories of prophetic critique and hope, which point ahead to chapter 7 on epistemology.

The Moment of Criticism

In the hermeneutical arc, there is a threefold movement from a first understanding, through a critical middle moment, to a postcritical understanding that involves appropriation. Even in my revised version of his arc, incorporating Ricoeur's later work on narrative, I retain this threefold dynamic.

To recall, Ricoeur elaborated the hermeneutical arc in light of two issues. One was the Continental tension between the *Geisteswissenschaften* and *Naturwissenschaften,* the humanities and the natural sciences, which involved two different epistemologies: "understanding," related to the *Geisteswissenschaften,* and "explanation," related to the *Naturwissenschaften.* As we saw, Ricoeur brought them together in a dialectic where the more intuitive and holistic understanding is necessary at both ends of the arc, but he felt that the more analytical explanation has its own place in conjunction and not in disjunction with understanding.

Ricoeur saw the problem of what he called the "desert of criticism." Criticism arises everywhere in modernity, with the result that, increasingly, at the end of modernity, affirmation has been difficult to find. In biblical studies, a common concern is that historical-critical studies, which dominated the academy over the past two centuries, have in their erudition lost sight of what brought them into being in the first place, namely, a worthwhile subject matter. Increasingly, criticism has become valuable for its own sake. One can be a lifelong biblical scholar whose passion is not in the subject matter but in the analysis of it. Certainly, there is nothing wrong per se with this possibility. But sometimes this critical preoccupation has seemed the only alternative for the academy, and often outside the academy; in the pulpit, for example, this has also been the case, as theological students have tried to move from the minutiae of critical knowledge to some kind of affirmation of the gospel. Karl Barth began a theological revolution in the early twentieth century with his own similar experience of trying to move from his theological studies to proclamation of the gospel, but it only slowed down the tide. What is still needed is further integration of "affirmation and critique," to use the title of one of Ricoeur's recent books. This dialectic has engaged Ricoeur virtually for his entire career. His hermeneutical arc was an attempt to show how the two can be brought together. Many have found his approach, culminating in a postcritical naïveté, a promising way out of the desert of criticism.

Focus on the third stage of the arc should not, however, cause us to lose sight of the fact that Ricoeur saw no way of avoiding the stage of criticism. He is quite opposed to a complacent or reactionary return to a precritical stance. Such a possibility is an existential reality for theological students caught in the previously described situation of attempting to relate their critical studies to unreceptive congregations. In their frustration, students sometimes repress their theological education and revert to their earlier, precritical mode in order to engage the congregation. Ricoeur is as adamant that we cannot avoid the critical stage as he is about passing beyond it to a postcritical stage. The possibility, however, of moving to a postcritical stage can help free a person to engage more fully the critical stage. If the other side is already in view, however dimly, one may venture more willingly into the desert.

Ricoeur's conviction is that the middle moment of explanation, as objective, external, and analytical as it may be, represents gain in the end, not loss. He was especially concerned with structuralism in the construction of his hermeneutical arc. Rather than joining or dismissing structuralism, he appropriated it. He argued that structuralism is an instrument or tool to deal with the analysis of the structure of the text. It moreover is textual in nature and thus brings a native and not a foreign tool to deal with texts. For example, in the study of the parables in the 1970s, structuralism was heavily applied. Debate arose about how fruitful it was in the study of the parables,[1] but it undoubtedly brought some insight into what the structuralists called the deep structures that tied various parables together and, in turn, contrasted them with other genres such as myth.[2]

As I mentioned in chapter 2, Ricoeur's focus on structuralism's emphasis on codes and deep structures caused him to leave very vague the status of the "surface structure" or individual story of a text. That is, Ricoeur tended to equate the identification of semiotic codes with the narrative world of the text. From a current perspective, it is more obvious that structuralism is yet another possible tool in religious studies, helpful in some ways and limited in others. In this sense, structuralism complements but does not at all replace more straightforward literary analysis of a text. In terms of Ricoeur's arc, therefore, structuralism need not be the universal method that he suggested in the 1970s. Rather, it can take its place along

1. Norman Perrin, *Jesus and the Language of the Kingdom: Symbol and Metaphor in New Testament Interpretation* (Philadelphia: Fortress Press, 1976), 169–81.

2. John Dominic Crossan, *The Dark Interval: Towards a Theology of Story* (Allen, Tex.: Argus Communications, 1975).

with source criticism, form criticism, redaction criticism, sociological criticism, and so on.

All of these critical tools in the field of biblical studies, as an example, can be extremely helpful, but they can also become ends in themselves. The major observation of canonical criticism, which is akin to Ricoeur's, is that there was so much attention to the world behind the text that the canonical text was left in tatters.[3]

Ricoeur wants to affirm critical approaches, but he also desires to point beyond them to a rereading of a text in the third moment, now holistically, with all the criticism in the background. The focus on the rereading is on the holistic meaning, not what may have contributed to it behind the text. Perhaps a good analogy is the relation of a film criticism to a film. A critique can bring to light things we may not have seen, but even if a critical piece is especially insightful, few would want to replace the film with the criticism. In terms of Ricoeur's hermeneutic, the idea is that we are first grasped by the film, in a sense being judged by it. Then we judge it through criticism. Finally, we return to it, hopefully to grasp and be grasped by it in a deeper way. Of course, we may judge something we first thought of as highly significant to be of little significance after the critical moment. The claim of classical literature or of scripture, however, is that it will stand up to the test. The role of criticism is still somewhat vague, but it can be fleshed out to some extent by looking at other contexts where Ricoeur dealt with critique.

Evil

Related to the move from pure phenomenology to a more existential and practical phenomenology, Ricoeur raised suspicion of any clear-cut, rational grasp of human evil. In the previous chapter, we saw how this precipitated his turn to the figurative language of symbol, metaphor, and narrative. The horrors of the twentieth century launched a massive assault on Enlightenment optimism in the power of rationality, in the end providing one of the major battering rams that brought down the modern and Enlightenment project.[4] The two issues of evil and knowledge intertwine

3. See especially Brevard Childs, "The Canonical Shape of the Prophetic Literature," *Interpretation* 32 (1978): 46–55.

4. See Paul Ricoeur, *The Just* (Chicago: University of Chicago Press, 2000), for Ricoeur's reflective view concerning how the evils of the twentieth century have preoccupied us. He confesses that he has similarly been preoccupied, but in this book he wants to recover something that has been lost in that focus, namely, the "just" or "juridical."

in Ricoeur's thought, just as they have been intertwined in his life and in the events of the twentieth century.[5]

Ricoeur considers the outbreak of evil to be an irrational act, incapable of essential analysis. While his treatment of the various myths of the Fall show that evil is "always already there," before the act, the most powerful account in his opinion, the biblical Eden story, shows the combination of that sense of fatedness with human choice and responsibility. The result is a "servile will." Focus on human responsibility itself reveals the radicality of the sinful act, as in Kant.[6] Even this focus, however, cannot do justice to the tragic and fated dimension of evil that is larger than the particular human. Philosophically speaking, Ricoeur says, "[a]t its base the symbolism of evil is never purely and simply the symbolism of subjectivity, of the separated human subject, of interiorized self-awareness, of man severed from being, but symbol of the union of man with being."[7] There is a mystery here, even if it is a mystery of iniquity.[8] Beyond that, there is a divine mystery that can hardly be plumbed. Ricoeur confesses, "Against the juridicalism of accusation and justification, the God of Job speaks 'out of the whirlwind.'"[9] The irrationality of the evil act, along with the mystery of divine response, reveals the incapacity of the Enlightenment theodicy project to "make sense" of evil.[10]

In terms of general philosophy, Ricoeur points out that evil undermines any "philosophy of totality," which is the thrust of the modern project. As he explains:

> [I]t must be admitted that no great philosophy of the totality is capable of giving an account of this inclusion of the contingency of evil in a meaningful schema. For either the thought of necessity leaves contingency aside, or it so includes it that it entirely eliminates the "leap" of evil which posits itself and the "tragic" of evil which always precedes itself.[11]

5. Remember the loss of his father as MIA in World War I and Ricoeur's captivity in World War II, noted in the introduction.

6. Paul Ricoeur, "The Hermeneutics of Symbols and Philosophical Reflection: I," trans. Denis Savage, in *The Conflict of Interpretations,* ed. Don Ihde, Northwestern University Studies in Phenomenology & Existential Philosophy (Evanston, Ill.: Northwestern University Press, 1974), 303–4.

7. Ibid., 309.

8. Ibid.

9. Ibid.

10. For a devastating critique of the Enlightenment theodicy project, see Terrence W. Tilley, *The Evils of Theodicy* (Washington, D.C.: Georgetown University Press, 1991). For a defense of a more nuanced and modest theodicy, see Dan R. Stiver, "The Problem of Theodicy," *Review and Expositor* 93, 4 (Fall 1996): 507–17.

11. Ricoeur, "Hermeneutics of Symbols I," 311.

We take up these wider philosophical ramifications further in the next section on Freud.

So Ricoeur's phenomenological project of a philosophy of the will, which normally entailed an essential description of the will, foundered at several points. First, he could not purely describe the will without including the role of the body, which provided context and motives for action, much of which is not accessible to consciousness. This resulted at the outset, in *Freedom and Nature,* in an impure "diagnostic" methodology, combining essential phenomenological description with attention to the more indirect and external understanding of the body, much of which comes from scientific investigation. In other terminology, he had to combine at the beginning understanding and explanation.

In order then to treat the servile will, he had to turn away from prosaic description altogether to figurative treatment in terms of symbol and myth. These figurative accounts, he concluded, could not be fully translatable into philosophical prose, even though, as Ricoeur put it, they "give rise to thought." In the end, this spelled doom to any theodicy project. He says, "The failure of all theodicies, of all systems that attempt to deal with the problem of evil, is testimony to the failure of absolute knowledge in the Hegelian sense."[12] Suspicion thus was raised at every moment in our typical attempt to comprehend and explain. This suspicion was heightened as Ricoeur began to consider the modern project in the context of Freud's assault on consciousness.

Freud and Philosophy

A consciousness fully conscious of itself, transparent to itself, was a part of the Cartesian and modern dream. It was essential to Husserl's phenomenological project. This dream fittingly died one of its many deaths at the hands of Ricoeur, one of Husserl's major expositors, in Ricoeur's exploration of Freud in the 1960s.

As Ricoeur sees it, the modern project combined the idea of a transparent consciousness with the capacity to fully grasp the object of consciousness. These were the twin goals at the heart of Husserl's phenomenology, which focused on essential description of the *noesis* (the act of consciousness) and the *noema* (the object of conscious intentional-

12. Paul Ricoeur, "The Hermeneutics of Symbols and Philosophical Reflection: II," trans. Charles Freilich, in *Conflict of Interpretations,* ed. Ihde, 332.

ity). In fact, phenomenological psychology—for example, in Jean-Paul Sartre—was sharply opposed to Freud, and to depth psychology in general, because of Freud's questioning of the transparency of consciousness.

In Ricoeur's work on Freud, he engaged Freud's critique in ways that transcended typical Freudian understanding. In other words, he made Freud into a philosopher and a hermeneutician,[13] often in the face of great opposition by the French Freudians of the 1960s.[14] Ricoeur refers to Freud's own estimation that the latter's insights provided a kind of third strike against human pride and consciousness in the modern era, along with the Copernican and Darwinian revolutions.[15] As Ricoeur says, "What emerges from this reflection is a wounded *cogito,* which posits but does not possess itself, which understands its originary truth only in and by the confession of the inadequation, the illusion, and the lie of existing consciousness."[16] As such, Freud represents the demise of a philosophy of consciousness or immediacy, as opposed to what Ricoeur calls a "philosophy of reflection."[17] A contemporary philosophy of reflection therefore must pass through the night of suspicion, of illusion, and of guile if it is to be possible at all.

Ricoeur positions Freud with respect to the criticism of philosophy and of consciousness in several ways that strikingly portray the tenor of Ricoeur's thought. First, Ricoeur points out that Freud is significant on the contemporary scene because *language* is the meeting place of all philosophies.[18] Whether it be phenomenology, existentialism, structuralism, logical positivism, or even, as Ricoeur mentions, religious studies, all have turned to language. Second, it is not just language that is significant, but figurative or symbolic language has risen to prominence, as we saw in the case of metaphor and narrative.[19] This already points to the significance of hermeneutics; philosophy has become hermeneutical in order to deal with language.

Third, however, figurative language is not straightforward and is capable of distortion, illusion, and deception. Ricoeur says, "Language itself is

13. See especially, for a concise account, Paul Ricoeur, "A Philosophical Interpretation of Freud," trans. Willis Domingo, in *Conflict of Interpretations,* ed. Ihde, 160–76.

14. This story is told in Charles E. Reagan, *Paul Ricoeur: His Life and His Work* (Chicago: University of Chicago Press, 1996), 25–31.

15. Ricoeur, "Philosophical Interpretation of Freud," 172.

16. Ibid., 173.

17. Paul Ricoeur, *Freud and Philosophy: An Essay on Interpretation,* trans. Denis Savage, Terry Lectures (New Haven, Conn.: Yale University Press, 1970), 43–44.

18. Ibid., 3.

19. Ibid., 8.

from the outset and for the most part distorted: it means something other than what it says, it has a double meaning, it is equivocal."[20] Ricoeur thus sounds like he harbors the suspicion that philosophers have held against figurative language from the beginning. Moreover, Ricoeur agrees that what Freud has done is to raise this suspicion against all language. After Freud, the modern philosopher cannot appeal to a universal rationality, to what is clear and distinct, or to a foolproof methodology. Language is everywhere, and thus, so are suspicion and guile. As Ricoeur points out, even when outright deception is not involved, interpretation cannot be avoided, and so the problem of the conflict of interpretations is raised. Without direct access to transparent consciousness of truth, there is no escape from hermeneutics. This, in a nutshell, is the essence of the postmodern paradigm change.

The haunting question that is thus raised by this hermeneutic of suspicion is whether anything is left of notions of truth or knowledge. Ricoeur's version of postmodernism affirms a positive answer to this question, but only in and through the crucible of criticism. He mentions three masters of suspicion: Freud, Nietzsche, and Marx.[21] Ricoeur reminds us that each takes up Cartesian doubt, but in a higher key. Then Ricoeur asserts, "After Marx, Nietzsche, and Freud, this too [Descartes's affirmation of consciousness] has become doubtful. After the doubt about things, we have started to doubt consciousness."[22] Nietzsche particularly raises the specter of relativism and nihilism. Ricoeur contends, however, that each of these men posited something beyond suspicion. They were three great destroyers, but Ricoeur sees them as finding meaning beyond their doubt. Significantly, though, this was achieved only through interpretation, an "exegesis of meaning." Ricoeur says, "Beginning with them, understanding is hermeneutics."[23] At this point, hermeneutics in Ricoeur's hands becomes what Josef Bleicher terms "critical hermeneutics."[24] Ricoeur does not believe, however, that this spells the end of meaning. Hermeneutics cannot avoid the guile of false consciousness, but "guile will be met by double guile."[25]

20. Ibid., 7.
21. Ibid., 32.
22. Ibid., 33.
23. Ibid.
24. Josef Bleicher, ed., *Contemporary Hermeneutics: Hermeneutics as Method, Philosophy, and Critique* (London: Routledge & Kegan Paul, 1980), part 3. Note, however, that Bleicher tends to identify critical hermeneutics with the critical theory approach of Habermas, though he seems to suggest, very cautiously, that it transcends the distinction between Gadamer and critical theory (233–35).
25. Ricoeur, *Freud and Philosophy*, 34.

Ricoeur sets this discussion in the context of the tension between phenomenology of religion and psychoanalysis. The former is a recollection of meaning and calls to a participation in meaning. Ricoeur acknowledges that he breaks with the alleged neutrality of the phenomenological method at this point: "The similitude in which the force of symbols resides and from which they draw their revealing power is not an objective likeness, which I may look upon like a relation laid out before me; it is an existential assimilation."[26] It involves a recharging of language in the modern critical landscape, a possibility of being addressed anew by the sacred. Ricoeur revealingly confesses:

> Is not the expectation of being spoken to what motivates the concern for the object? Implied in this expectation is a confidence in language: the belief that language, which bears symbols, is not so much by men as spoken to men, that men are born into language, into the light of the logos "who enlightens every man who comes into the world." It is this expectation, this confidence, this belief, that confers on the study of symbols its particular seriousness. To be truthful, I must say it is what animates all my research.[27]

Against this hope, Ricoeur sets the formidable array of the great masters of suspicion. Far from this hope being a naive assumption in the spirit of Enlightenment optimism, Ricoeur sees that we are not only in but must pass through the desert of criticism. He finds in Freud at this point a telling example. He maintains that Freud is primarily a hermeneutician, in part because he must have recourse to a diagnostic or mixed discourse, as did Ricoeur in *Freedom and Nature.* Freud relates the double meaning of dreams and of slips of the tongue to an "energetics" of forces.[28] He offers a quasi-physical explanation that involves pent-up energy that must be released through language. However simplistic it may seem, this positivist explanation accompanies the attempt to deal with double meaning of words. Such a reductionist "archaeology of meaning" Ricoeur takes very seriously as a threat and challenge to any transparent meaning.

Fourth, at the same time, Ricoeur concludes that such archaeology is not sufficient. Freud himself could not do without the discourse of meaning to go along with his discourse of energy.[29] As Ricoeur says, "Psychoanalysis never confronts one with bare forces, but always with forces in

26. Ibid., 31.
27. Ibid., 28–29.
28. Ibid., 62.
29. Ibid., 117.

search of meaning."[30] Freud also does not fail to transcend his own withering criticism of the pretensions of consciousness, pointing to a mature consciousness that has been "educated into reality." He looks to a consciousness won on the far side of unconsciousness. The difference is that, unlike Enlightenment rationalists, he never leaves the unconsciousness behind. Ricoeur also believes that such a reductionism cannot do justice to the possibility of meaning in the symbols. Much like Carl Jung, Freud's erstwhile protégé, Ricoeur wants to be open to more meaning in the symbols. Ricoeur at this point turns to Hegel, arguing that an *archaeology* must be balanced by a *teleology,* or as Ricoeur sometimes expresses it, an *eschatology.*[31] As Werner Jeanrond puts it, Ricoeur's hermeneutic is one of both *suspicion* and *retrieval.*[32] The archaeology nevertheless forbids the teleology from being absolute knowledge and leaves valid knowledge as a wager and a hope.

Fifth, the result of the Freudian suspicion of symbols in contrast to the Cartesian dream of clarity is that consciousness is more a task than it is a given. Ricoeur aligns himself to some extent with modern philosophy in seeing that it begins with the positing of the self.[33] He parts company from Descartes, however, and takes sides with Kant in seeing that the apprehension of the self is not by a direct and clear intuition but only by mediated reflection.[34] The original positing is more a vague feeling, he says, than a possession.[35] Freud adds that our awareness of ourselves may be not only vague but deceitful. Thus, "a reflective philosophy is the contrary of a philosophy of the immediate."[36] Ricoeur opposes in this sense what we may call a philosophy of reflection to a modern philosophy of consciousness.[37]

Despite his appreciation of Kant, Ricoeur sees Kant as too rationalistic and focused on epistemology. So Ricoeur turns to Johann Gottlieb Fichte and Jean Nabert, who see that reflection has to do not only with justification of knowledge, of science, and of practical reason but with our holistic desire to exist. We begin not by self-possession but by dispossession. Desire does not imply attainment. Reflection follows awareness of what we do not have. Ricoeur is comfortable in this philosophical context of

30. Ibid., 151.
31. Ricoeur, "Hermeneutics of Symbols II," 333.
32. Werner Jeanrond, *Theological Hermeneutics: Development and Significance* (New York: Crossroad, 1991), 70ff.
33. Ricoeur, *Freud and Philosophy,* 43.
34. Ibid., 44.
35. Ibid.
36. Ibid., 43.
37. Ibid.

using the language of being lost. For him, "the ego must lose and find itself."[38] Here again, "the positing of self is not given, it is a task, it is not *gegeben,* but *aufgegeben.*"[39] Ricoeur sums up his approach in this way: "Reflection is the appropriation of our effort to exist and of our desire to be, through the works which bear witness to that effort and desire."[40] This means, again, that reflection must become interpretation and hermeneutics, "because I cannot grasp the act of existing except in signs scattered in the world."[41]

Sixth, while the need for interpretation means that all the critical tools are necessary, it does not result in absolute knowledge. The suspicion of false or infantile consciousness is a barrier on the one hand; on the other is the barrier of the mystery of hope and eschatology.[42] Both leave us with hope, not sight; a wager, not proof.

So Ricoeur concludes, "After Freud's work it is no longer possible to speak of consciousness in the same way that we did before. . . . Consciousness is not the first reality which we can know but the last."[43] The knowledge we attain is itself permanently under the sign of suspicion.

Gadamer and Habermas

In the 1960s, Gadamer and Habermas engaged in a critical interchange between the two traditions of hermeneutical philosophy and neo-Marxist critical theory. Habermas in fact appropriated Gadamer's approach as the way to fulfill our "interest" in public dialogue but finally thought Gadamer's approach as a whole was too uncritical to fulfill our "emancipatory" interest.[44] Gadamer assumed meaning and was not critical enough of the deep distortions of knowledge that a Freud or a Marx could see. What happens when one is subject unconsciously to a pernicious ideology? What happens when communication is systematically distorted such that the interloctors are unaware of it? These were Habermas's questions, and he resorted to a "quasi-transcendental" norm of an ideal speech

38. Ibid.
39. Ibid., 45.
40. Ibid., 46.
41. Ibid.
42. Ricoeur, "Hermeneutics of Symbols II," 333.
43. Ibid., 323.
44. Jürgen Habermas, "The Hermeneutic Claim to Universality," in *Contemporary Hermeneutics,* ed. Bleicher, 181–211. For Habermas's appropriation of Gadamer, see Jürgen Habermas, *Knowledge and Human Interests* (London: William Heinemann, 1968). See, for a fuller account of the debate, David Couzens Hoy, *The Critical Circle: Literature, History, and Philosophical Hermeneutics* (Berkeley: University of California Press, 1978), 117–30.

situation to answer them. Interestingly, he also appealed earlier to Freud, in the sense that a therapist must have an overarching explanatory method in order to detect what is deception and what is truth.

Gadamer responded to Habermas by saying that hermeneutics allows for critique in terms of the encounter of different perspectives.[45] In any case, Gadamer charged, no method such as Habermas desired could guarantee knowledge or enable one to escape from interpretation. Outside the therapeutic situation, for example, there is no agreed-upon framework for adjudicating what is true or what is not. Gadamer saw Habermas's offering as yet another appeal to a method to extricate us from the inextricable, that is, our human, hermeneutical situation. Outside the counseling session, in other words, agreement does not exist concerning who is the therapist and who is the patient. Freudian theory itself is sharply contested, from within and from without. Because of his appeal to an objective standpoint, however carefully qualified, Habermas is frequently classified as a modernist rather than a postmodernist. While Habermas's view is certainly sophisticated, it shares in this sense what Richard Bernstein calls Enlightenment nostalgia for the Enlightenment dream of certain knowledge.

Ricoeur responds to this interchange with sympathy on both sides. He first agrees with Habermas that Gadamer was too one-sided. As we have seen, he sees Gadamer as emphasizing belonging and participation to such an extent that Gadamer did not do justice to distanciation and alienation. Ricoeur did not at the time have the chance to take into full account Gadamer's reply to Habermas, which ameliorated this charge to some extent. Nevertheless, Bernstein, who was sympathetic to Gadamer, still concluded in 1985, "Gadamer's philosophical hermeneutics is virtually silent on the complex issues concerning domination and power."[46] Ricoeur took pains in various ways to redress this lack. Besides his deeper treatment of fault and evil, Ricoeur was quite concerned in his hermeneutical arc to allow for critical methodologies in a way that Gadamer did not. Gadamer said that his own thought preceded method and was consistent with using critical methodologies; he just did not give much direction in using them.

Ricoeur explicitly, however, wanted to make room for criticism, including the deep Freudian level of unconscious distortion and false conscious-

45. Hans-Georg Gadamer, "On the Scope and Function of Hermeneutical Reflection (1967)," in *Philosophical Hermeneutics,* ed. David E. Linge (Berkeley: University of California Press, 1976), 18–43.

46. Richard J. Bernstein, *Beyond Objectivism and Relativism: Science, Hermeneutics, and Praxis* (Philadelphia: University of Pennsylvania Press, 1985), 156.

ness. In the next section, we see that he is sympathetic to Marx's critique of ideology that also occurs behind the back, so to speak. Ricoeur's concern for taking account of deep dissimulation ties in with his religious sense of the pervasiveness and extent of evil and is part of the reason that he does not see an easy rational "answer" to the problem of evil.

In the end, however, Ricoeur comes down on the side of Gadamer in Gadamer's insistence on the universality of hermeneutics. Ricoeur points out that even Habermas's neo-Marxist, and increasingly neoliberal, ideology critique is rooted in a tradition, cannot free itself from interpretation, and cannot find an objectivist foundation. He concludes, "The task of the hermeneutics of tradition is to remind the critique of ideology that man can project his emancipation and anticipate an unlimited and unconstrained communication only on the basis of the creative reinterpretation of cultural heritage."[47] More specifically, he points out with respect to Habermas, "This tradition is not perhaps the same as Gadamer's; it is perhaps that of the Aufklärung, whereas Gadamer's would be Romanticism. But it is a tradition nonetheless, the tradition of emancipation rather than that of recollection. Critique is also a tradition."[48] Thus, critique cannot escape the fundamental dynamics of hermeneutics. Rather than hermeneutics representing one of three kinds of interest, as in Habermas, hermeneutics represents the basic kind of knowing on which all the others rest, as in Gadamer. Ricoeur thus resists the opposition between hermeneutics and critique, explaining:

> First, I cannot conceive of a hermeneutics without a critical stage itself. . . . Second, the critical sciences are themselves hermeneutical, in the sense that besides tending to enlarge communication they presuppose that the distortions of which they speak are not natural events but processes of desymbolization. The distortions belong to the sphere of communicative action.[49]

Nevertheless, it is important to be suspicious of ideology and to utilize critical methodologies, but as an aid and not a foundation. Ricoeur concludes, "Hermeneutics without a project of liberation is blind, but a project of emancipation without historical experience is empty."[50] Ricoeur

47. Paul Ricoeur, "Hermeneutics and the Critique of Ideology," in *Hermeneutics and the Human Sciences: Essays on Language, Action, and Interpretation,* ed. John B. Thompson (Cambridge: Cambridge University Press, 1981), 97.

48. Ibid., 99.

49. Paul Ricoeur, *Lectures on Ideology and Utopia,* ed. George H. Taylor (New York: Columbia University Press, 1986), 236.

50. Ibid., 237.

deepened his "critical hermeneutics" by further extensive dialogue with the issue of ideology critique in the Marxist and Frankfurt school tradition, in lectures in the mid-1970s that became a book, *Lectures on Ideology and Utopia.*[51]

Ideology and Utopia

In this work, Ricoeur desired particularly to engage the master of suspicion Karl Marx but also wanted to pursue the issue of ideology further in its relation to utopia, looking not only to Habermas but especially to Karl Mannheim. The problem that Marx's thought raises, as does Freud's and also the thought of contemporary counterparts such as Michel Foucault and Jacques Derrida, is how to get out of the circle of suspicion. In Marx's case, if beliefs tend to be ideological because of the underlying play of vested interests and large, impersonal forces, how does even the Marxist critique avoid being tarred with the same brush? This is the problem that Mannheim especially raised, one that Habermas countered by his appeal to an objective ideal speech situation.

Ricoeur's response is complex and impressive. He begins by conceding the significance of Marx's characterization of ideology as a pernicious and widespread distortion of beliefs. As a Frenchman who experienced the devastation of two world wars, followed by the cold war, Ricoeur does not doubt the destructive power of ideology; hence his own emphasis on a hermeneutic of suspicion. What he does doubt, however, is the orthodox Marxist solution as it developed into a position of "scientific" Marxism against everyone else's ideology.[52] Ricoeur sees in this "scientistic" position, however far removed it is from science per se, a variant on the modernist desire for objectivism, ironically, a God's-eye point of view, which cannot be had. It runs against Ricoeur's entire hermeneutical stance that we cannot extricate ourselves from the responsibility and the risk of interpretation by recourse to an external and independent epistemological platform.

Ricoeur further questions the way in which Marxism developed away from a certain interest in the self and in praxis toward impersonal structures, as exemplified by Louis Althusser. Ricoeur finds in his reading of Marx adequate grounds for locating the fundamental dynamic between the life of praxis and theoretical reflection, as opposed to the dynamic of

51. Ricoeur, *Lectures on Ideology and Utopia.*
52. Ibid., 76.

"science" against ideology.[53] One can easily see how this pattern fits Ricoeur's hermeneutical arc, where we begin by drawing on first-order expressions that are close to praxis and can never get beyond them. In this case, the arc reveals the way in which Ricoeur sees even first-order expressions as grounded in the practical activity of life, in "labor" taken in a broad sense, in a way that cannot be surpassed.[54] By thus reducing the clash between his approach and that of a praxis-centered approach, Ricoeur fits very well what Joseph Rouse terms a "practical hermeneutics" as opposed to a "theoretical hermeneutics," bringing the hermeneutical tradition close to the praxis tradition rather than seeing the two as antithetical.[55] This is an important emphasis that perhaps marks a shift in Ricoeur's thought. In the preface to a collection of his works in 1991, appropriately titled *From Text to Action,* Ricoeur provocatively says, "Little by little, a dominant theme asserts itself in this enterprise of militant hermeneutics, namely, the gradual reinscription of the theory of texts within the theory of action."[56]

In this practical emphasis, Ricoeur agrees with Habermas's interpretation of Marx as pointing to the basic reality of praxis—praxis, however, not understood as dealing only with instrumental action. In Kantian terms, Habermas believes that Marx's great insight was that it is really labor, or "the productivity of a working subject," instead of the schematism of the imagination that fundamentally establishes the Kantian synthesis of an object.[57] Habermas then argues that Marx mistakenly collapsed all action into technical production rather than including the full range of hermeneutical and emancipatory action.[58] Ricoeur significantly agrees with this criticism of Marx but, as noted above, sees all action as hermeneutically or symbolically mediated in a more extensive way than does Habermas. Apart from this emphasis on the person in praxis, Ricoeur believes that one cannot do justice to the idea of alienation, since alienation consists in workers having a distorted relation to the works of their hands. Such an emphasis shows the Marxist basis for an approach that does not eliminate the subject, as do Althusser and contemporary

53. Ibid., 77.

54. See ibid.

55. Joseph Rouse, *Knowledge and Power: Toward a Political Philosophy of Science* (Ithaca: Cornell University Press, 1987), ch. 3.

56. Paul Ricoeur, *From Text to Action: Essays in Hermeneutics, II,* trans. Kathleen Blamey and John B. Thompson, Northwestern University Studies in Phenomenology & Existential Philosophy (Evanston, Ill.: Northwestern University Press, 1991), xiv.

57. Ricoeur, *Lectures on Ideology and Utopia,* 217.

58. Ibid., 218–21.

poststructuralists like Foucault. Rather, it allows for what Ricoeur considers his reflective philosophical approach that affirms but also criticizes the subject.[59]

In the process, one sees an excellent example of Ricoeur's interpretative practice at work. Far from disregarding the author altogether when appropriate and known in a corpus of works, he is concerned to interpret Marx, but he focuses on his works, not on Marx's unknown inner intentions. He considers the chronological development of Marx's thought in his works through five chapters of his own, concluding with a well-argued reading of Marx. Ricoeur acknowledges that the other, more objectivist reading is possible, but he thinks it not as well grounded as his own. He is careful to distinguish not only different readings of Marx but also the development of Marx's thought into orthodox Marxism.[60]

At this point, Marx has a basis for criticism of theory, or the superstructure, that is tenuously lodged on the basis of practice and its symbolic expression, much in the way that criticism in Ricoeur's hermeneutical arc is continually tested itself by returning to its adequacy in relation to first-order language. Ricoeur goes further, however, and much more radically. Ricoeur questions the monovalent understanding of ideology as inherently negative. He purposely begins with its hardly challengeable status as distortion, for example, in fascism, but he then moves, with the help of Max Weber, to show how it could play a necessary, legitimizing role in society. Finally, with the help of Clifford Geertz, Ricoeur shows how ideology can play a necessary, constitutive role in society.[61] If there is to be a society, there must be establishment and preservation of legitimate authority. Since Ricoeur follows Geertz in emphasizing that even the fundamental level of practice is ineluctably symbolic, then human life together is inevitably symbolically shaped.[62] It is praxis all the way down, but it is also hermeneutical all the way down. Given the hermeneutic of suspicion, this means that not only meaning but also conflict and distortion are inherent in human life.

Moreover, any society relies on founding stories, narratives, that shape its identity, just as narratives shape individual identities.[63] For example, George Washington's crossing of the Delaware River in the Revolutionary

59. See ibid., 131, where Ricoeur sees the Althusserian type of Marxism as making common cause with contemporary structuralists and poststructuralists like Foucault.

60. For example, ibid., 183.

61. For a succinct summary, see ibid., 181–82.

62. Ibid., 256.

63. Ibid., 261.

War is a story told from the American perspective that has left a permanent imprint on the American self-understanding of a beleaguered, underdog nation striving to overcome great odds with "Yankee ingenuity." Every nation has its own stories, most of which go much farther into the past than that. Ricoeur questions whether this activity is dispensable or somehow wrong. Rather, it seems to be a necessary condition for human society, and society seems to be a necessary condition for being human, as we explore in chapter 6.

So far from "ideology" always being "ideological," therefore, it can also be constructive and constitutive. Similar to the way in which Ricoeur understands human beings to be fallible and prone to misuse of their freedom, he sees the necessary constitutive role of ideology to be fallible and constantly threatening to fall into the negative sense of ideology. Why is this so? Ricoeur sees the reason in the "surplus of meaning" inherent in ideology, which in this Marxist context he terms its "surplus-value."[64] It always calls for more than it can deliver. The ideology is always idealistic enough that it outstrips the reality, as witnessed by the American pledge to a country "with liberty and justice for all." In this sense, the Marxist recognition that there is always distortion in ideology is correct. It is unavoidable, but it has a positive dimension that Marxism does not recognize. As in the Cain and Abel story in Genesis, however, where God reminds Cain that "sin is lurking at the door" (4:7), ideology is always prone to destructive distortion. This "overvalue" of meaning is necessary to motivate the support of the citizenry, but it makes ideology vulnerable to the concealment of vested interests and the legitimization of illegitimate power.[65]

This is why Ricoeur goes to some lengths to challenge the major Marxist notion that action is due to mechanistic causation, again by impersonal forces, rather than the motivation of agent causation. As he says, "The function of ideology at this stage is to fill the credibility gap in all systems of authority. This argument is coherent, though, only in a motivational and not in a mechanistic model."[66] Ricoeur is concerned to protect the integrity of the individual human's freedom and responsibility, while always acknowledging our fallibility and servility. Ricoeur's emphasis on motivation rather than mechanism is crucial to his understanding of

64. Ibid., 183. He points out that the idea of legitimation is in Weber, but not the idea of surplus-value.

65. Paul Ricoeur, "Ideology and Utopia," trans. Kathleen Blamey and John B. Thompson, in *From Text to Action,* 315.

66. Ricoeur, *Lectures on Ideology and Utopia,* 183.

ideology as a possible good that is nevertheless prone to great evil. Although he is able to ground his views in Marx's writings, it fits the basic biblical pattern that Ricoeur saw in the Adamic story, where a basic good is deeply distorted and deranged but also capable of restoration.

What restoration is possible for an ideology that has fallen into distortion? At this point, Ricoeur turns to utopia as a balance. Mannheim saw the paradox of Marxism, namely, that it could not stand above the fray and avoid itself being ideological. Ricoeur in fact observed in 1974, "The sclerosis of Marxism provides the most striking example of ideology in modern times."[67] Marxism's claim to be objective and neutral science is patently self-serving, but it raises the deeper and troubling question of whether any way to elude ideology is possible. The radicality of Ricoeur's response is now further manifested in that, with Mannheim, he takes the problem of criticism to another level by criticizing critique.

He looks to Mannheim first. Mannheim attempted an uneasy escape that ultimately failed, in Ricoeur's view, but it was an instructive failure. In fact, Ricoeur concedes, "I consider Mannheim's attempt to overcome this paradox one of the most honest and perhaps the most honest failure in theory."[68] Mannheim's solution verged on the position of hermeneutical philosophy. He thought that if an intellectual could see things from enough perspectives, this would guard against the domination of ideology. In a sense, this is Gadamer's idea that dialogue, especially with the Other, widens our horizon enough to provide substantive critique. Ricoeur's problem with Mannheim's solution in the end is that Mannheim thought this awareness of different positions in a sociology of knowledge yielded an objective position, outside the fray, so to speak, as an intellectual looking down from above.[69] Neither Gadamer nor Ricoeur believes that such disengagement and objectivity are possible. Such a position is yet another manifestation of the Enlightenment dream of a universal standpoint unaffected by passionate human involvement. Habermas attempted to evade this problem by a sophisticated appeal to the norms of an ideal speech situation. As we saw, this, too, is not possible as a neutral standpoint.

And this is the problem: It is not possible to avoid tradition. Utopia, though, is complementary to tradition. It does not avoid it but lives off of it. Literally, it is "no-place," one might say, "no-tradition." More exactly,

67. Paul Ricoeur, "Science and Ideology," trans. John B. Thompson in *Hermeneutics and the Human Sciences,* 236.

68. Ricoeur, *Lectures on Ideology and Utopia,* 166.

69. Ibid., 312.

it is a revision of tradition or a reclaiming of an old tradition in order to counter current ideology. Ideology establishes and preserves a tradition; utopia challenges it. One may see here a connection with Ricoeur's work on metaphor at this time. In Crossan's terms, myth establishes world, whereas parable (as extended metaphor) subverts world. Utopia also undoes world by telling a new story whose purpose is to call the old into question. In this sense, it serves a "parabolic" function. Ricoeur sees that the overreaching of ideology inevitably leads to the challenge of utopia: "It is always from the point of view of a nascent utopia that we may speak of a dying ideology."[70] Ricoeur suggests that Habermas's ideal speech situation actually functions as a utopia.[71] Moreover, religion may play an ideological role, as Marxists are wont to see, but in an age when "this function has been superseded by the ideological role of the market and technology," then "perhaps a utopian use of religion may be a part of the critique of ideology."[72] This is what liberation theologians have seen so well. Their vision of the kingdom of God calls into question the complacency of the kingdoms of this world.

Both ideology and utopia are works of the productive imagination and are symbolic representations of life. Utopia is more obviously creative, but ideology is also a configured narrative that is "fictive." Witness the "history" taught to generations of U.S. students about Columbus's "discovery" of America. This story is told quite differently by native Americans and, now, by revisionist historians.

The symbolic function of ideology and utopia represents both promise and peril. The distortions of ideology are self-evident, so much so that Ricoeur has to labor to find a constructive notion of ideology. Utopia, however, is also subject to the ambiguity afflicting any human production. Sometimes before stories are ideologies, they are utopias. Utopias, like metaphors that have died, can fall into ideology. The messianic dreams of the Hebrew Bible were appropriated as the basis for the Christian church, sometimes to good effect and sometimes to ill, as the church often attempted to bring about the kingdom of God by force. Acts famously pictures a "communistic" fulfillment of messianic-age prophecies, where all shared according to their means, a vision not lost on the much later Karl Marx. Ever since that day, such Christian communes have been prone to abuse by leaders who use the utopia as a pretext to be dictators. The

70. Ibid., 180.
71. Ibid., 252–53.
72. Ibid., 231.

Puritan dream of a "city set on a hill" is commonly (mis)appropriated in American elections. Ricoeur points out that the concept of freedom in the modern period was "alternatively utopian, conservative, and utopian once more."[73] These examples reveal how utopia alternately inspires revolutions and is abused by revolutions. What are the most infamous cults but utopias turned ideologies and then gone awry?

In this dialectic, ideology can guard against the neurotic wish-fulfilling hopes of utopia, to use Freudian language, and utopia can guard against repressive ideological regimes. When one looks for more, as in Althusser, Mannheim, and Habermas, Ricoeur bluntly asserts that there is no more. In this sense, there is no escape from the human condition.

This does not, however, necessarily lead to an enervating skepticism or nihilism. Ricoeur questions many times whether even the Christian faith should demand more. It was the seductive siren song of modernity that caused Christians to think they could do more, to sell their soul for a mess of epistemological pottage. One of the challenges of the current postmodern situation, where most of us continue to have modernist nostalgia, is learning to live with what we have always had—but not more.

Therefore, at this point, Ricoeur makes some of his most revealing comments on epistemology, which point toward our full-fledged account of his epistemology in chapter 7. In light of the hermeneutic of suspicion that we have just seen, Ricoeur's affirmations are carefully guarded because of his conviction that all our hopes are shadowed by suspicion. We may live in the desert of criticism and fear that in it we will perish—but in our postmodern situation, we cannot avoid it or go back, only forward. Ricoeur reflects:

> There is no answer to Mannheim's paradox except to say that we must try to cure the illnesses of utopia by what is wholesome in ideology . . . and try to cure the rigidity, the petrification, of ideologies by the utopian element. It is too simple a response, though, to say that we must keep the dialectic running. My more ultimate answer is that we must let ourselves be drawn into the circle and then must try to make the circle a spiral. We cannot eliminate from a social ethics the element of risk. We wager on a certain set of values and then try to be consistent with them; verification is therefore a question of our whole life. No one can escape this. Anyone who claims to proceed in a value-free way will find nothing. . . . In a certain sense my answer is fideist, but for me it is only an avowal of honesty to admit that.[74]

73. Ibid., 177.
74. Ibid., 312.

Ricoeur then points, as did Gadamer, to the unavoidability of reliance on practical wisdom, or *phronesis.*[75] Considered judgment that has passed through the fires of criticism is the best we have—but it is what we have.

It is clear that, after this close examination of Ricoeur's hermeneutic of suspicion, we are returned to his fundamental hermeneutical arc, now enhanced by dialogue with great masters of suspicion. Even if Ricoeur appropriates them critically, he does not reject them outright. The beginning point in the arc, that of first-order expressions, is deepened by attention to the first-order life of praxis. In the second moment, there is room for Freudian analysis and Marxist ideology critique, even for their highly developed methods; but these are finally relativized by Ricoeur's rejection of any objectivist standpoint that they promise but cannot deliver. He again points, therefore, to a postcritical appropriation on the far side of criticism, one that is hardly conceivable without faith and hope, whose secular equivalent is utopia.

Biblical Prophecy and Hope

Before tying together these many strands in Ricoeur's epistemology in chapter 7, it is helpful to pause and gather up some of the implications for theology of Ricoeur's hermeneutic of suspicion, especially since, for so many Christians, the figures with whom Ricoeur largely sympathetically deals, such as Freud and Marx, are seen as the great foes of Christianity. Has he not in his own way sold his birthright for a mess of pottage? Has he not himself succumbed to the withering heat of the modern desert of criticism?

Ricoeur is careful not to "Christianize" these great enemies of Christianity, but he is not alone in seeing critical appropriation of them as salutary for a tested faith. The issue is whether suspicion is at home in or foreign to faith. To this question we can respond with Ricoeur by bidding it welcome.

The dialectic to which Ricoeur constantly appeals, of affirmation *and* critique, runs throughout scripture and Christian history. The criticism of ideology is inherent in the biblical narratives. The creation stories and the exodus give witness to an ideal that was never realized in Israel's history. The Deuteronomic History itself was a criticism of Israelite actuality. Implicit in the Deuteronomic History was an attempt to deal with the

75. Ibid., 314.

exile, which involved criticism of a theology that could make no sense of exile. The Deuteronomic theology, in turn, was assaulted by the book of Job. The prophets of course represent the clearest note of criticism, sometimes raised to a scream. Jeremiah could question the entire sacrificial system as a human construction and not divine (7:22). Amos could point to other nations as also people whom God had led to their place (9:7). When considered in conjunction with their poetically devastating criticisms of idolatry and injustice, no modern ideology critique rises to greater heights than that found in the biblical narratives. Jesus' questioning of the vested interests in religious practices of prayer and giving in the Sermon on the Mount is later focused in his barrage against the hypocrisy of the Pharisees. Paul calls for the Thessalonian church to "test everything" (1 Thess. 5:21).

The dynamic interplay of ideology and critique is also manifest throughout Christian history, from the early church, to the Constantinian establishment, to the Reformation, to believers' churches, to the Pentecostal churches, to the Two-thirds World churches of today. Criticism is thus not a foreign element to Christian faith. Particularly, the critical principle of utopia is allied with the way eschatology functions as critical principle, as in "Thy will be done on earth as it is in heaven." In fact, Ricoeur raises the question "whether all utopias are not in some sense secularized religions that are also always supported by the claim that they found a new religion."[76]

It is not surprising that Ricoeur, despite his attempt to keep his philosophy and faith separate, constantly finds recourse to religious language such as faith, hope, and eschatology. Ideological distortion would have been known to the prophets as "sin" and "evil." It is well known that the Marxist "story" is a kind of material parallel to the Christian narrative of innocence, fall, salvation, and renewed paradise. Ricoeur's understanding of ideology as a constitutive power that is necessary but constantly vulnerable to abuse fits contemporary interpretations of the Pauline "principalities and powers" as power structures that are created by God, fallen and thus part of human bondage, and in need of redemption.[77]

76. Ibid., 305.

77. Major interpreters in this area are John Howard Yoder, *The Politics of Jesus,* 2d ed. (Grand Rapids: Wm. B. Eerdmans Publishing Co., 1994); and the three-volume treatment: Walter Wink, *Naming the Powers: The Language of Power in the New Testament* (Philadelphia: Fortress Press, 1984); Walter Wink, *Unmasking the Powers: The Invisible Forces That Determine Human Existence* (Philadelphia: Fortress Press, 1986); Walter Wink, *Engaging the Powers: Discernment and Resistance in a World of Domination* (Minneapolis: Fortress Press, 1992). For a succinct treatment, see Nancey C. Murphy and George F. R. Ellis, *On the Moral Nature of the Universe: Theology, Cosmology, and Ethics,* Theology and the Sciences (Minneapolis: Fortress Press, 1996), 179–81.

Rather than viewing the withering criticisms of Freud and Marx as foreign, it is possible to see their criticisms, at least, if not their positive solutions, as aids in Christian critique. Merold Westphal in fact recommends them as Lenten readings, sharpening our awareness of sin.[78] Using Westphal's utilization of radical postmodernists as an example, Gary Percesepe characterizes in a lively way such dynamic appropriation:

> Westphal rejects postmodern assumptions, non sequiturs, fatal prejudices, and that which is offered without evidence. Out with the chaff. Or, to change the metaphor, having fired the furnace and burned off the dross, what Westphal believes he is left with is pure postmodern gold. This gold, it turns out . . . is pirated Christian gold, for the postmodernists, it turns out, are thieves and plagiarizers. Just as Marx might have learned from Amos the prophet's unmasking of religious self-interest masking economic injustice, just as Freud and Sartre are modern theologians of original sin against their will, just as Nietzsche played a prophetic role in exposing Christian virtues as nothing but flittering vices, even so Westphal gives us Foucault and Derrida in the service of God, a stunning reversal which mimics, in its way, the consistent word of Scripture, where every idol is cast down and God makes all things new.[79]

As Ricoeur cautions, this is not to baptize the critical enemies of Christianity, but it is to see their fundamental insight into human alienation and distortion as compatible, even helpful, to the Christian awareness of the universal pervasiveness of distortion and even depravity.

Ricoeur strives, however, to balance the need for an archaeology with a teleology, critique with affirmation, suspicion with retrieval. His work reflects the theological emphasis on how evil is parasitic upon the good, upon sin's subordination to creation on the one hand and redemption on the other, and upon the way fallenness is answered by redemption. Theology itself is deeply dialectical. Without Ricoeur's dialectics of ideology and utopia, affirmation and critique, we cannot understand his complex understanding of the self and the self's knowledge, to which we now turn.

78. Merold Westphal, *Suspicion and Faith: The Religious Uses of Modern Atheism* (Grand Rapids: Wm. B. Eerdmans Publishing Co., 1993).

79. Gary Percesepe, "Against Appropriation: Postmodern Programs, Claimants, Contests, Conversations," in *Postmodern Philosophy and Christian Thought*, ed. Merold Westphal, Indiana Series in the Philosophy of Religion (Bloomington: Indiana University Press, 1999), 78. I should note that Percesepe, while having great appreciation for Westphal's project, expresses reservations about Westphal's success, couched in terms of a Derridean critique that the appropriated haunts the appropriator (85).

CHAPTER SIX

Oneself as Another

One of the remarkable confluences of theology and philosophy occurred in the twentieth century when simultaneously, and seemingly separately, an emphasis on a holistic, embodied self arose in both realms. Like two mighty rivers flowing together, this dual emphasis has virtually swept away the traditional understanding of modernity that we noted, namely, dualistic intellectualism. Descartes above all separated mind and body—and the world—to such an extent that he set the problem for the remaining centuries of the second millennia, which was to try to bring them back together again. While attempts to retain dualism continue in philosophy, they represent an increasingly minority position. A third stream of support for reunification has more recently arisen from cognitive science, which continues to add evidence for the inseparability of mind and brain. From this perspective, George Lakoff and Mark Johnson outline the situation vividly, if a bit melodramatically, at the beginning of their recent book *Philosophy in the Flesh:*

> The mind is inherently embodied.
> Thought is mostly unconscious.
> Abstract concepts are largely metaphorical.
> These are three major findings of cognitive science. More than two millennia of a priori philosophical speculation about these aspects of reason are over. Because of these discoveries, philosophy can never be the same again.[1]

Astonishingly, virtually the same thing concerning embodiment could be said of theology. The irony is that the dualism that reigned in theology for almost two millennia is as suspect in theology as in philosophy and science, stemming, however, from an entirely different source. The waves

1. George Lakoff and Mark Johnson, *Philosophy in the Flesh: The Embodied Mind and Its Challenge to Western Thought* (New York: Basic Books, 1999), 3.

that shattered dualism in theology came from biblical studies, where the recovery of the Hebraic view of the self toppled the Greek and traditional view of a dualistic self.[2]

The significance of Ricoeur is that he represents the flowering of a tradition of incarnational philosophy in France that is quite consistent with the emphasis on the holistic self in biblical studies.[3] What he offers to theology is detailed elaboration of the implications of such a self. Moreover, attention to the self brings us close to the nerve center of Ricoeur's entire philosophy. All that we have looked at thus far in Ricoeur's philosophy comes to a focus in his anthropology. Because of the centrality of anthropology in Ricoeur's philosophy, in some ways he represents the modern "turn to the subject." His turning *to* the subject, however, is at the same time a turning *away* from the subject. Ricoeur's subject is not an autonomous, individualistic soul but one inseparable from the body, the world, language, and other people.

His first major work, *Freedom and Nature,* was a lengthy and detailed study of what we might call the embodied will.[4] While he returned to this theme only intermittently over the next several decades, it is clear that it functioned as a presupposition to the rest of his work. In what we have considered the capstone of his work, *Oneself as Another,* Ricoeur returns more thematically to the issue of embodiment but extends the situated nature of the self dramatically in several directions. Besides the embodied self, he regards the self as deeply intertwined with the world and with others. We take up these wider themes in order by looking at the embodied self, the narrative self, the interpersonal self, and the social self.

The Embodied Self

As we noted in the introduction, Ricoeur was influenced heavily by Gabriel Marcel, a noted phenomenologist of the embodied self, or "the

2. For one of the best recent attempts to provide such integration, and for an overview of the entire development, see Warren S. Brown, Nancey C. Murphy, and H. Newton Malony, eds., *Whatever Happened to the Soul? Scientific and Theological Portraits of Human Nature,* Theology and the Sciences (Minneapolis: Fortress Press, 1998). For earlier accounts, see, for example, Oscar Cullmann, *Immortality of the Soul; or, Resurrection of the Dead? The Witness of the New Testament* (New York: Macmillan Co., 1958); John A. T. Robinson, *The Body: A Study in Pauline Theology,* Studies in Biblical Theology 5 (Naperville, Ill.: Alec R. Allenson, 1957).

3. Erazim Kohák, the translator of *Freedom and Nature,* said that this incarnational philosophy represented a third force in French philosophy beside idealism and empiricism. See Paul Ricoeur, *Freedom and Nature: The Voluntary and the Involuntary,* trans. Erazim Kohák, Northwestern University Studies in Phenomenology & Existential Philosophy (Evanston, Ill.: Northwestern University Press, 1966), xii–xiii.

4. Ricoeur, *Freedom and Nature.*

lived body" *(le corps propre).* As Marcel says at one point, "What clearly emerges . . . is the fact that there is no distinct haven to which I can repair either outside of or within my body. Disincarnation is not practically possible and is precluded by my very structure."[5]

Ricoeur dialogues also with Jean-Paul Sartre's phenomenological reflections, which give important place to embodiment but do not finally escape a dualist position.[6] More closely, Ricoeur's *Freedom and Nature* (1950) followed and was inspired by Maurice Merleau-Ponty's *Phenomenology of Perception* (1945), which emphasized the embodied nature of perception.[7] Lakoff and Johnson particularly cite Merleau-Ponty as a philosophical backdrop for the embodied view of the self emphasized by cognitive science.[8] *Freedom and Nature* was a phenomenology of the will that can be seen as a complement to Merleau-Ponty's famous work.

This French incarnational tradition is so important for Ricoeur that it may help to provide more on Merleau-Ponty in particular, whose death in 1961 cut off someone whose interests and inclinations were leading down a path similar to Ricoeur's. Merleau-Ponty set himself against what he called the "intellectualist" tradition, meaning the Cartesian, idealist tradition, and the "empiricist" tradition. The former did not do justice to the way in which we think in and through the body. The latter did not do justice to the way in which our experience is structured from the beginning, rather than being atomistic. He saw that it is *through* our bodies that we engage the world. He said, "We are involved in the world and with others in an inextricable tangle."[9] This led to an emphasis on our situatedness, our finitude, and even the fundamental ambiguity of our experience, far from the clarity and distinctness so prized by Descartes and the Western tradition.[10] Merleau-Ponty did not see this as a liability; rather, he saw our

5. Gabriel Marcel, *Creative Fidelity,* trans. Robert Rosthal (New York: Crossroad, 1982), 20.

6. See, for example, the introduction to Jean-Paul Sartre, *The Emotions: Outline of a Theory,* trans. Bernard Frechtman (Secaucus, N.J.: Citadel Press, 1948), 1–21, titled "Psychology, Phenomenology, and Phenomenological Psychology." Ricoeur says, in Paul Ricoeur, "Intellectual Biography," trans. Kathleen Blamey, in *The Philosophy of Paul Ricoeur,* ed. Lewis Edwin Hahn Library of Living Philosophers 22 (Chicago: Open Court, 1995), 11; "Sartre's *Being and Nothingness* produced in me only a distant admiration, but no conviction: could a disciple of Gabriel Marcel assign inert things to the dimension of being and reserve only nothingness for the vibrant subject of affirmations of all sorts?"

7. Ricoeur states, "I also hoped, not without a certain naivety, to provide a counterpart in the practical sphere to Merleau-Ponty's *Phenomenology of Perception.* This great book had been a thrilling discovery in the years following my return [from captivity in WWII]." Ibid.

8. Lakoff and Johnson, *Philosophy in the Flesh,* xi.

9. Maurice Merleau-Ponty, *Phenomenology of Perception,* trans. Colin Smith, International Library of Philosophy and Scientific Method (New York: Humanities Press, 1962), 454.

10. See Albert Rabil, *Merleau-Ponty: Existentialist of the Social World* (New York: Columbia University Press, 1967), 143–53.

embodiment, like Gadamer's presuppositions, as giving us our foothold in the world, making it possible for us to be and to exist. It is, he said, "the pivot of the world."[11] In fact, he remarked in a takeoff of his longtime collaborator Sartre, who had famously said, "We are condemned to freedom," that we are "condemned to meaning."[12] Descartes's notion that we are cut off from the world and our bodies appears as an illusion, as inconceivable as the thought of a square circle.

Ricoeur took up this tradition, passed through the phenomenological tradition, of the lived body and turned it toward a phenomenology of willing. Already, however, he saw that the body cannot fully be made present to conscious thought. Like Merleau-Ponty, he uses phenomenology to go beyond phenomenology.[13]

Ricoeur analyzes willing in terms of three components, which he states thus: I decide, I move my body, I consent.[14] Another way of putting it is to say that, in willing, we choose a project; we have a certain practical capability of carrying out that project; and we have to deal with a certain impotence in carrying out that project. Each aspect involves voluntary and involuntary dimensions. In terms of deciding, Ricoeur recognizes that the role of motives brings in the bodily issues of needs and pleasures that influence motivation. In movement, he treats instincts (which he calls "preformed skills"), emotions, and habits. In terms of consent, especially, he considers what is given to us that is not voluntary. The need to consent has to do with acceptance or integration of that which we cannot control and which limits us. He examines here character traits, the unconscious, and the dynamics of biological and psychological development. He especially emphasizes how our birth and early life occur apart from our memory but have enormous impact on us.

In all these ways, Ricoeur is underscoring the dispossession of the self that we introduced in chapter 5 on the hermeneutic of suspicion. He, Merleau-Ponty, and others reject the idea that the self is an autonomous agent, fully transparent to itself. As we saw in chapter 5, Freud and Marx in particular caused a Copernican revolution in self-understanding by pointing out how influenced we are by factors of which we are unaware. Gadamer was doing something similar by making the point that we are shaped by our traditions. Ricoeur here is emphasizing what Lakoff and

11. Merleau-Ponty, *Phenomenology of Perception,* 82.

12. Ibid., xix.

13. I am referring here to Merleau-Ponty's statement "The most important lesson which the reduction teaches is the impossibility of a complete reduction" (ibid., xiv).

14. Ricoeur, *Freedom and Nature,* 6.

Johnson are saying is now commonly accepted among cognitive scientists, that is, that most of our perceiving and thinking occurs apart from conscious awareness and is inextricably tied to bodily processes:

> It is the rule of thumb among cognitive scientists that unconscious thought is 95 percent of all thought—and that may be a serious underestimate. Moreover, the 95 percent below the surface of conscious awareness shapes and structures all conscious thought. If the cognitive unconscious were not there doing this shaping, there could be no conscious thought.[15]

As they also point out, this runs against the grain of our entire Western philosophical tradition.

Ricoeur in 1950 did not have the benefit of the explosion of scientific studies into these processes, but he clearly identified the issue. Even without those studies, he pointed out how tied to our decision making are bodily givens such as temperament, emotions, needs, and habits. He thus calls for the intermingled "diagnostic" or dialectical methodology that we mentioned in the previous chapter. He puts the dimensions of the voluntary and involuntary into dialogue, much as doctors must connect their external knowledge of physical processes to a patient's self-report of what is happening.[16] This "mixed vocabulary" is not purely phenomenological, but it is a combination that gives us a better understanding of the dynamics of willing.

He does not see the involuntary as the agent of deception. Rather, it is the necessary condition of the voluntary and is integrated into what we consider as conscious action. What it does mean is that selfhood, as we have seen, is a task and not a given. We cannot start from scratch, from pure mind or thought, or from a blank slate. We start too late—consciously, that is. This approach is therefore a frontal assault on the modern and even premodern project that often assumed the clarity of the mind apart from the body, reason apart from emotions, and a conscious self apart from the unconscious.

The embodied and embedded nature of the self undergirds the entire hermeneutical project because it suggests that we ourselves are not transparent texts, whose meaning is to be read off univocally. We are more like a rich poetic text, full of allusions and depth. It is not just that others must interpret us, but we must interpret ourselves. We are as much riddles to ourselves as to others. The interactive nature of the self, with all its subterranean passages, means that the hermeneutical task will never be fin-

15. Lakoff and Johnson, *Philosophy in the Flesh,* 13.
16. Ricoeur, *Freedom and Nature,* 12–13.

ished. And we have yet to speak of how our selfhood is intricately involved with other people.

Ricoeur's approach may be clarified by relating it to the independent but similar approach of the philosopher of science Michael Polanyi.[17] Polanyi claimed that even our explicit knowledge has a tacit background that makes the foreground explicit.[18] Our knowledge thus involves bodily aspects of skill and cognition that operate without conscious thought. He said this against the idea that knowledge is completely explicit, particularly the ideal of the scientist as being wholly rational and going strictly by the facts. In terms of the Cartesian ideal, we cannot be said to know unless our knowledge is both clear and certain. Polanyi argued that this is not true of any of our knowledge. From his practice as a scientist, he was aware of the role of tacit skills in appraisal. He thus indicated aphoristically that we know more than we can tell.[19] The point is that this tacit dimension is not just a regrettable accompaniment to explicit knowledge; it is the condition of any explicit knowledge. As he starkly concluded, "A wholly explicit knowledge is unthinkable"—an idea that has itself been unthinkable in modernity.[20] His prescient insight in the 1950s has been dramatically sustained in philosophy of science since that time.[21] Whether it is knowing or willing, our body is not dispensable but integral; it does, however, give us a tacit dimension that is, in a sense, "food for thought." We can, and must, continually interpret ourselves.

In a more specific way, Ricoeur sees the complex interaction of the voluntary and involuntary moving in a certain direction. He says, "The involuntary is *for* the will and the will is *by reason* of the involuntary."[22] At the point of decision, there is not necessity. There are usually many motives. None compel. The reciprocal nature of the two Ricoeur expresses in this way: "I submit to the body which I guide."[23] The emphasis on the involuntary therefore does not make Ricoeur a behaviorist or a determinist. Freedom is real, but it is a situated and constrained freedom. Yet freedom could not exist apart from conditions of limitation. Absolute

17. Jerry Gill also connected Michael Polanyi's thought with the French emphasis on embodiment through Merleau-Ponty, in Jerry Gill, *On Knowing God: New Directions for the Future of Theology* (Philadelphia: Westminster Press, 1981), esp. 163 n. 4.

18. Michael Polanyi, *Personal Knowledge: Towards a Post-Critical Philosophy,* 2d ed. (Chicago: University of Chicago Press, 1962).

19. Ibid., 88.

20. Michael Polanyi, "The Logic of Tacit Inference" (1964), in *Knowing and Being: Essays by Michael Polanyi,* ed. Marjorie Grene (Chicago: University of Chicago Press, 1969), 144.

21. See the section on science in chapter 7.

22. Ricoeur, *Freedom and Nature,* 86.

23. Ibid., 276.

freedom is not necessarily a coherent idea. Chaos theorists point out that chance makes no sense apart from conditions of necessity. Similarly, freedom occurs within limiting conditions. The body and the world constrain; we decide, act, and consent in light of the constraints. *Constraint* may even be too negative a word. One might see the constraints as possibilities, which the expression of freedom can turn into positive actualities. One could summarize, "While nature makes freedom actual, freedom makes nature meaningful."[24] Freedom actuates within possibilities that are given.

For example, my gifts are also limitations. They enable certain possibilities for careers, but they exclude others. My finitude means that I must foreclose many of the careers that are possible, not to mention the ones that are not. I may focus on teaching and become quite good. This likely means not being so good at many other things. Trying to do some of those other things, such as writing or going on outings with the family, sometimes hinders the teaching and sometimes enhances it. Even in the focus on teaching, I have a limited capacity to read, to remember, to prepare. Yet the magic of getting through, of teaching and learning, can happen in the midst of my limitations and all the other limiting factors, such as time, attention, and interest on the part of the students. Great experiences of learning occur not despite these constraints but in and with them. The constraints make possible and in a sense define what such an experience of learning means. The point is that freedom occurs within conditions that both make it possible and limit it. Our actions in situations, as Ricoeur says, render these events meaningful. They become part of our life stories and part of the wider human story.

Such an embodied self chimes in with contemporary Christian reflection on the meanings of creation and of humanity. The finitude of the world is not seen as evil but as good. Our embodiment is not seen as a useless appendage but as the way we live out the Christian life. The emphasis now is not on the natural immortality of the soul but on the resurrection of the whole self. Thus, theologians are examining afresh the meaning of our embodiment.

As Ricoeur develops further in *Fallible Man,* our embodiment is both our grandeur and our vulnerability. We have the potential of using our freedom well, which freedom is the gift of our being-in-the-world. Our being-in-the-world, however, makes us prone to fall. Ricoeur's work here is very similar to Reinhold Niebuhr's *The Nature and Destiny of Man,* where the self as both finite and infinite is pulled in different directions,

24. The words of Erazim Kohák, trans., *Freedom and Nature,* xv.

and so the delicate balance is easily broken.[25] Embodiment per se is not evil, but it makes us prone to evil. Our fragile freedom enables us to say yes to God but also to say no. Our will easily falls into bondage, but it is a will that can respond to grace in obedience to God.

Moreover, the sense of our embodiment as integral to thought gives depth to the understanding of our human situation. For example, Ricoeur points out concerning the emotions:

> Whether in the disadapted (negative) form or in the substitutive (positive) form, emotion is lived as specific intentionality. Being afraid does not mean feeling my body shake or my heart beat; it is to experience the world as something to shun, as an impalpable threat, as a snare, as a terrifying presence.[26]

In general, in terms of being the fulfillment of creation and recovery of fallenness, the very meaning of redemption is inseparably tied to its roots in our human—all too human—immersion in this world.

The Narrative Self

Our situated passage through time means that the self is not just embodied and in the world; rather, it is also a story. Ricoeur understands humans as inherently story-shaped, and he also notes the centrality of narrative to scripture. Our finite location in time and space provides for the drama of extended and meaningful action, in other words, a plot. We emplot ourselves as we go.

Grammatical Identity

Ricoeur turns to narrative as central to selfhood in *Oneself as Another,* but only after situating the self within analytical philosophy's attempt to locate identity grammatically. In fact, he begins his study with grammatical hints. As we know, he is opposed to philosophies of the subject. For them, "the cogito is without any genuine philosophical signification unless its positing is invested with the ambition of establishing a final, ultimate foundation."[27] Along with this foundational ambition is the desire for

25. Reinhold Niebuhr, *The Nature and Destiny of Man* (New York: Charles Scribner's Sons, 1949).
26. Ricoeur, *Freedom and Nature,* 271.
27. Paul Ricoeur, *Oneself as Another,* trans. Kathleen Blamey (Chicago: University of Chicago Press, 1992), 4.

transparent possession of the self that also provides a surety against doubt. Such an ideal became too easy for someone like Nietzsche to topple, who, as Ricoeur observes, could simply say, "I doubt better than Descartes."[28] Against such an oscillation between an exalted and a shattered subject, Ricoeur calls for a "hermeneutics of the self."[29]

The turn to language in the first place is already recognition that the meaning of the self lies in part outside the self. Language is a public phenomenon in which we express ourselves, refer to ourselves, and have others refer to us. We swim in language as fish swim in the sea, but we are not the sea. Language is in a sense given to us; it does not arise from us personally. In terms of our earlier focus on Gadamer, language is both a part of the larger tradition or horizon that is given to us before we are self-aware and the background with which we approach anything. In this sense, as Gadamer and Heidegger would say, language speaks us.

Beginning with grammar, Ricoeur sees self-possession in terms of "I" but also a certain dispossesion in terms of opposition between "I" and "self" as a reflexive pronoun. Like his formula for willing, "I move my body," we can say, "I move myself," which hints furtively at an otherness in the sphere of simple action. This leads him to a second opposition, especially in French, where he is intrigued by the difference between the meaning of *même* in the sense of "same," on the one hand, and in the sense of "self" in the reflexive pronoun *soi-même,* "oneself," literally "self-same," on the other.[30] This is matched in Latin with the different terms for "identity," *idem* and *ipse.* Though English and German do not possess this equivocalicy of sameness and selfhood, it leads Ricoeur to make virtually the central theme of his book the significance of selfhood as "*ipse*-identity" rather than "*idem*-identity." The reason is that *ipse*-identity allows for identity but also for complex but positive relationships to temporal change and to the other-than-self.[31] In both cases, *idem*-identity is opposed to such relationships. "The difference between *idem* and *ipse* is nothing more than the difference between a substantial or formal identity and a narrative identity."[32] In other words, the self's changing and dynamic identity is not vitiated but validated by time and the Other.

Ricoeur thus appropriates analytical philosophy in offering a first answer to the question of identifying persons in relation to otherness. We

28. Ibid., 15.
29. Ibid., 4.
30. Ibid., 2.
31. Ibid., 3.
32. Paul Ricoeur, *Time and Narrative,* vol. 3, trans. Kathleen Blamey and David Pellauer (Chicago: University of Chicago Press, 1988), 246.

note that his complex analysis reveals his unusual willingness and ability to integrate the traditions of Anglo-American with Continental philosophy. He indicates that this is integration and not just eclecticism, because this is "the price to pay for a hermeneutics characterized by the indirect manner of positing the self."[33] Since the self is neither immediate nor forever lost, it is recovered by a detour through the mediacy of the interpretation of external signs. Analytical philosophy's linguistic analysis is, he believes, one of those byways that repays exploration.

He then takes up analytical philosophy's attempt to identify not just the person as speaking but the person as acting. The connection is that speakers are engaging in speech actions, connecting the question of "Who is speaking?" with "Who is acting?"[34] Ricoeur will characteristically find that the resources of analytical philosophy are both promising and limiting, needing recourse to narrative, which is both enriched by and yet extends analytical philosophy's attempt to deal with identity.

In linguistic analysis of the first question, Ricoeur notes that identification involves an objective and a subjective side. On the one side is the identification of properties that are rather public with a person. This relates to the traditional attempt of philosophers to identify persons by traits. For example, Michael Jordan played for the Chicago Bulls and won six National Basketball Association titles. On the other side is the logic of proper names, where precisely Michael Jordan is the one and only person who possesses these various properties. Even more subjectively, Michael Jordan can designate himself, as in an introduction: "Hello, I am Michael Jordan." Does one need the objective properties to make sense of the latter? Here is already entrée into the "strangeness" of personhood, as Ricoeur puts it.[35] Both seem necessary, but even both together are insufficient, as philosophers have long realized.[36] Virtually no criteria of identity, such as properties or memory or continuity over time, are entirely adequate, yet all the criteria are valuable. Ricoeur finds that analytical linguistic philosophy itself had to have recourse to the body in order to ascribe identity. The body reveals also the strangeness of the two dimensions of identification in grammar. One is that of the inscription of properties and the other is a subjective sense of "mineness."[37] The objective characteristics cannot do justice to the singular subjectivity of the "I," but

33. Ricoeur, *Oneself as Another,* 17.

34. Ibid.

35. Ibid., 36.

36. See Ricoeur's treatment of the paradox of personal identity in the attempts of modern philosophers since John Locke to identify persons in terms of various criteria; ibid., 125–39.

37. Ibid., 54.

neither can the "I" do without the objective. The linguistic plane points to the strangeness but does not dissolve it.

Ricoeur encounters a similar result when turning from linguistic analysis to the theory of action in analytical philosophy. It provides further resources for identifying the intertwined dimensions of the subjective and the objective but is limited by being so punctiliar that it cannot do justice to a "life" rather than an "event." It cannot deal with the issue of responsibility over time and thus an ethical self.[38] The theory of action has helped in making a distinction between "two universes of discourse": One is the difference between actions and events, the other is the difference between motives and causes. Agents engage in intentional actions that are inherently related to motives. Events are not necessarily intentional; they are more easily related to external causes.[39] As Ricoeur earlier noted, actions can be seen as texts whose motives can be interpreted, which is different from a "scientific" explanation that deals with physical causes only.

Further exploration has shown, however, that the two universes, or "language games," are not so dichotomous after all. The "diagnostic" relation that Ricoeur saw in *Freedom and Nature* and in the mixed discourse of Freud returns. Our embodiment gives rise to motives that are sometimes virtually causes. Drives, reflexes, even passions move us. The poverty of the Wittgensteinian tradition, according to Ricoeur, is that in its focus on the descriptive and observable, it loses the agent in the action.[40] It serves as a corrective to the Cartesian tradition that privileges an autonomous, disembodied ego, but it swerves to the other extreme. One may note here Ricoeur's view that a phenomenological perspective is more adequate than the descriptive analytical perspective.[41] Specifically, Ricoeur says of Donald Davidson's approach that it is an "agentless semantics of action" that "is a matter only of identity in the sense of *idem* and not of identity in the sense of *ipse,* which would be the identity of a self."[42] What is omitted is the phenomenologically mysterious sense of a self that endures and is responsible for its actions through time.

In terms of what Ricoeur calls the "ascription" of actions to an agent, the immersion of persons in history is already entailed. When one considers assigning responsibility for a historical event, one cannot transcend the entanglement of causes that extend far beyond an actor and the causal

38. Ibid., 57, 113.

39. Ibid., 61ff.

40. Ibid., 72. Ricoeur's analysis is focused on the work of Peter Strawson, Elizabeth Anscombe, and Donald Davidson.

41. Ibid., 72–73.

42. Ibid., 85, 87.

initiative of an actor. Again, a hermeneutical dimension is opened up. Ricoeur observes, "We must not be afraid to say that determining the end point where the responsibility of an agent ends is a matter of decision and not some fact to be established."[43] The mixed discourse that involves subjects who are, as Merleau-Ponty says, "inextricably entangled in the world" is something that analytical philosophy at the same time exemplifies yet obscures. In attempting to overcome the tension of the two discourses altogether, the irreducible mystery of personhood is lost. In response to this aporia or intractable mystery, Ricoeur turns to the resources of narrative here, just as he did in *The Symbolism of Evil* to deal with the incoherence of evil.

Narrative Identity

The major gap that Ricoeur saw in analytical philosophy was the self's temporality; he concludes that the self's identity is not possible without attention to history and thus narrative. The detour through analytical linguistic philosophy illuminated some of the ways in which the self finds itself by looking outside the self. An aspect of the hermeneutics of the self is a hermeneutic of our identity inscribed in language, just as is a hermeneutic of our embodiment. The result, however, is not a punctiliar object but a temporal self, where multiple aspects coalesce into a story. In other words, the self is a life.

We noted earlier, in the treatment of Ricoeur's philosophy of narrative, the centrality of narrative to his thought. At that point, we focused on narrative's indispensability in understanding the biblical narrative and faith. We highlighted principal features, such as its capacity to convey truth in an original way that is not fully translatable into philosophical or theological prose, thereby transforming the nature of theological reflection. In keeping with Ricoeur's hermeneutical arc, narrative is not only the beginning but the ending of theology. Theology cannot start without it or end without spiraling back to it. Here we draw on this broader narrative philosophy to focus on how narrative is indispensable to self-identity, quite apart from the central place that narrative has in Christianity or that it does not have, say, in Buddhism. Nevertheless, it is easy to imagine the creative symbiosis that can occur through the engagement of a fresh appreciation of the constitutive role of narrative both in the Judeo-Christian tradition and in human identity. Ricoeur, in fact, offers biblical Israel as a

43. Ibid., 107.

prime example of a community formed by its stories, because "no other people has been so overwhelmingly impassioned by the narratives it has told about itself."[44]

In any context, though, Ricoeur argues that narrative is central to human identity. In *Oneself as Another,* Ricoeur sharpens just what this means, in ways that go beyond *Freedom and Nature* and *Time and Narrative.* Since he concludes that no final determination can overcome the mystery of selfhood in the way that it combines the subjective and objective, he approaches or approximates it through narrative as a mediator.

Any attempt to deal with the temporality of the self must allow for both continuity and discontinuity. People change. Physically, we are not literally made of the same constituents as we were years before. Moreover, we change in many other ways—experiences, character, and personality. Yet we continue to speak of the same person. This continuity in discontinuity is what interests Ricoeur. He attempts to locate the balance in between the continuity that stems from character and that which stems from commitment, such as keeping one's promise.[45] He sees character as representing the virtually complete overlap of *idem* over *ipse,* whereas promise keeping represents the widest gap that does not break the continuity altogether. Narrative, he believes, is then the mediator between these two poles.[46]

Ricoeur saw character in *Freedom and Nature* as on the nature side, representing givens with which our freedom must deal, as something to which we must consent. Much later, he still sees character as providing constancy in perhaps the strongest sense, but he also notes the role of freedom in the realization of character. Character, he says, "designates the set of lasting dispositions by which a person is recognized."[47] Nevertheless, character develops over time and is in part a result of choices that lead to habits, identification with certain people, and internalized traditions. Thus, "character has a history."[48] It has a narrative. Despite character's givenness or "sedimentation," to use a good phenomenological term, it is not absolutely opposed to freedom or change. Ricoeur says it nicely: "What sedimentation has contracted, narration can redeploy."[49]

To character Ricoeur contrasts commitment. "The perseverance of character is one thing, the perseverance of faithfulness to a word that has

44. Ricoeur, *Time and Narrative,* vol. 3, 247.
45. Ricoeur, *Oneself as Another,* 118.
46. Ibid.
47. Ibid., 121.
48. Ibid., 122.
49. Ibid.

been given is something else again."[50] The validity of such continuity that may include radical discontinuity in many other ways can hardly be understood apart from narrative continuity. To recall in *Time and Narrative,* Ricoeur saw that narrative involves the configuration of a plot that yields a discordant concordance. The tension among different facts and events and between external, chronological time and experienced time is perhaps not resolved but related in a story. His issue there was how the aporias of time, exemplified classically by Augustine, are mediated by the interweaving of historiography and fiction in narrative.[51] Ricoeur says that this practical narrative response is a "synthesis of the heterogeneous."[52]

In our context, the heterogeneous has been increased—by embodiment, by language, and by action. Rather than having isolated events or disparate phenomena, one has them woven by the consistency of life commitments into a connected and meaningful story, centered on a character or characters. Much like Gadamer's idea that our preunderstandings actually enable our understanding, the objective facets of the story, as disparate as they may be, make the story possible. At the same time, they do not replace the unique way in which the heterogeneous are interpreted, or to put it in Gadamer's terms, the way in which two horizons are fused into one. We could say that narrative provides a way in which the discordances work for us, yet without their wholesale elimination.

Ricoeur further suggests that the very experience of time is not absolute. He virtually moves from philosophy to theology at this point, drawing on how Augustine set time within the context of eternity. At the beginning and end of the three volumes of *Time and Narrative,* Ricoeur turns to this theme. His point is to relativize human time and thus to relativize narrative—in this philosophically modest way, he opens the door for theological reflection on the eschatological relation of time to eternity. He acknowledges, "There comes a moment, in a work devoted to the power of narrative to elevate time to language, where we must admit that narrative is not the whole story and time can be spoken of in other ways, because, even for narrative, it remains inscrutable."[53] In the "meantime," narrative is unavoidable even if not totally concordant.[54]

50. Ibid., 123.

51. Ricoeur, *Time and Narrative,* vol. 3, 99.

52. Ricoeur, *Onself as Another,* 141.

53. Ricoeur, *Time and Narrative,* vol. 3, 272.

54. I do not think that these reflections by Ricoeur ineluctably lead to affirmation of a traditional, Augustinian "timeless" eternity, thus ruling out more contemporary notions of a God who is temporal and open to the future. What they do remind us is that divine temporality and human temporality, at least, are not symmetrical.

With all his estimation for fiction, Ricoeur recognizes the disparities between fictional narratives and the narrative of a lived life.[55] We are not absolute authors of our stories and are at best coauthors. We consequently have much less control than authors over the events that happen to us (even though authors often report that their stories have lives of their own). We have to make do with accidents, contingencies, and tragedies. Even more, our attempt to make a meaningful narrative of our own lives intersects with others who are doing the same; we are not all writing totally separate stories. Ricoeur's criticism of Alasdair MacIntyre's similar narrative approach lies here, namely, that MacIntyre does not appreciate the radical difference between authors of fiction and authors of lives.[56] Nevertheless, Ricoeur sees valid similarities and a productive relationship. Even if we are but coauthors, we naturally configure our lives. As Merleau-Ponty said, "We are condemned to meaning." We reflect on our past and try to render it a meaningful whole. What is more, as Martin Heidegger notably emphasized, we project our plot into the future—we *are* projects. We may have to rewrite continually, but we are constantly configuring. In this process, fiction writers and tellers of stories offer us material and help. They offer possible imaginative variations for us to try out. As we saw in chapter 2 on Ricoeur's hermeneutical arc, they offer possible worlds in which we might live. Ricoeur says, "As the literary analysis of autobiography confirms, the story of a life continues to be refigured by all the truthful or fictive stories a subject tells about himself or herself. This refiguration makes this life itself a cloth woven of stories told."[57] The act of appropriating fiction is an especially creative fusion of horizons, which points again to the deeply hermeneutical nature of Ricoeur's entire enterprise. The paradigmatic model of the interpretation of a text extends to what it means to be a self; and from there, obviously, to everything else, since what is a world without its being a world for a self?

While the element of discordance in life stories is inherently greater than in fiction, fiction, too, has a way of intensifying discordance. It can explore the loss of self just as easily as the construction of self. Ricoeur cites the example of Robert Musil in *The Man without Qualities* as a literary figure who says, "I am nothing."[58] Ricoeur wishes to take the existential sense of a loss of meaning and the dissolution of the self extremely seriously. He nevertheless points out that even in such "nights of personal identity," a

55. Ricoeur, *Oneself as Another*, 158–63.
56. Ibid. Ricoeur develops this point in dialogue with MacIntyre.
57. Ricoeur, *Time and Narrative*, vol. 3, 246.
58. Ricoeur, *Oneself as Another*, 149, 166.

certain "apprehension of the self" remains, relating it to the dark night of the soul in religious conversion experiences.[59] He asks, "But who is *I* when the subject says that it is nothing?"[60] Firmer grasp of the I is possible, he believes, on the other side of the existential and literary night of the self, by balancing it with the promising self. The self's commitment to something provides a kind of self-constancy that also provides an answer to the question of identity. As Ricoeur suggests, the taking of a stand in saying, "Here I am," is a way of answering "who I am." The dynamic of responsibility "marks a halt in the wandering that may well result from the self-confrontation with a multitude of models for action and life, some of which go so far as to paralyze the capacity for firm action."[61] Ricoeur directs attention to the fictional component of this ethical side of identity. Despite the suspension of disbelief by which we enter the literary world, we do not necessarily cast out a moral dimension. Ricoeur says, "In the unreal sphere of fiction we never tire of exploring new ways of evaluating actions and characters. The thought experiments we conduct in the great laboratory of the imaginary are also explorations in the realm of good and evil."[62] The ensuing "fragile concordance" between character and commitment is also a gift of the imagination as we construct a narrative identity. It is, however, a modest identity, which Ricoeur contrasts with the "Stoic pride of rigid self-consistency."[63] It is neither the inflated self of the Enlightenment nor the dissolved self of poststructuralism; it is a hermeneutical self who, in religious terms, is fragile enough to be haunted by sin and substantial enough to be redeemable by grace.

Ethical Identity

Ricoeur expands this ethical dimension by taking up the Aristotelian emphasis on the good as being the ethical aim. Action is not just singular but involves an aim that, on an individual basis, constitutes a "life plan" or project. Ricoeur offers a significant and creative "little ethic" that situates the deontological tradition of Kant that focuses on the *right* within the Aristotelian tradition that focuses on the *good*.[64] Similar to MacIntyre, Ricoeur sees a complex interrelationship between the good at which we aim and the practices that get us there.[65] Internal to such practices are

59. Ibid., 166–67.
60. Ibid., 166.
61. Ibid., 167.
62. Ibid., 164.
63. Ibid., 168.
64. Ibid., 170. See for the larger development the whole of studies 7–9 of this book.
65. Ibid., 176.

necessary virtues of excellence. For example, being a doctor involves standards and rules that constitute being a good doctor. Our lives, however, are composed of many practices that may involve our roles at work, as a spouse, as a parent, as an amateur musician or athlete, as a citizen, and as a Christian in a church.

In narration, the issue of norms and precepts arises from these being embedded in the practices constitutive of a life. Narrative therefore also helps, in Ricoeur's eyes, to bridge the gap between the "is" and the "ought."[66] In the teleological context of seeking the good, Ricoeur believes, we place the moral norms in a deontological context that requires the right. In this way, Ricoeur distinguishes between ethics and morality. Ethics has to do with what is required for the good life. Morality has to do with the right thing to do. Rather than choosing one instead of the other, Ricoeur sets the deontological within the teleological, the right within the good. As we see below, the abstract formalism of the deontologically obligatory requires ethical substance. The ethical is purified and extended, however, by passing through "the sieve of the norm."[67] When the universal comes into conflict and perplexity, though, it must again have recourse to the practical judgment rooted in the ethical aim of a good life. Narrative is required to bring these various dimensions into a whole.

Despite this attractive mediating and integrating facility of narrative, Ricoeur sees neither in fiction nor in life the elimination of discordance and tension. Thus he still regards the narrative of a life as ongoing and incomplete. Although narrative identity is a significant step beyond attempts of analytical philosophy to deal with the puzzles of personhood,[68] Ricoeur does not see it as dissolving them completely. Ricoeur may be seen to move from puzzles to mystery. Ricoeur expresses this relationship in another way: The mystery of personhood is not capable of being resolved *speculatively,* which means in a Cartesian, objectivist sense; it can, however, be put to work productively or *practically.*[69] Ricoeur escapes the dualism and skepticism of the Kantian provenance of this distinction between the speculative and the practical by seeing the narrative configuration as a genuine advance in understanding. In his mentor Marcel's terms, personhood is a mystery and not a problem. Mysteries can be understood better but never wholly resolved.

66. Ibid., 170.

67. Ibid.

68. See Ricoeur's extended treatment of Derek Parfit's concern with such puzzles that lead Parfit, in a sense, to give up on the issue; ibid., 129–39.

69. Ibid., 147.

Ricoeur raises here the kind of knowing involved at this point, namely, attestation, which we develop further in the next chapter. Attestation is precisely the kind of postmodern affirmation we have already described, which lies between objectivism and relativism. It is modeled on Aristotle's practical wisdom, which concerns the way we make ethical decisions that relate the larger good and the specific circumstance. It is a considered judgment, based on evidence and reasons, but that cannot be objectively proven. It is a testimony backed by one's life, but one made without the solace of certainty. It is, moreover, not best expressed in the paradigmatically logical, propositional form of modernity but better expressed in narrative form. Narrative thus is a form of attestation. The hermeneutic of the self is an interpretation, but of the most serious nature, for it is the interpretation of one's life.

Ricoeur draws on attestation as central to two other dynamics of the narrative identity of the self. First, attestation is identified with the conscience, where an interpretation is given to us of our existence and what we are to do.[70] Ricoeur connects it with Heidegger's view of conscience *(Gewissen)* as the call *(Ruf)* to the self to be authentic.[71] Despite the fact that conscience falls prey to suspicion as "that place par excellence in which illusions about oneself are intimately bound up with the veracity of attestation," it remains central to selfhood.[72] This interior voice, however, represents in a way another kind of otherness, much like the body, so close to us and sometimes so far. Not, in Ricoeur's view, having the moral neutrality of Heidegger's conception, it is still where the self hears the call to an ethical aim. It is also where the self, having traversed the field of moral injunctions and come to moral choice in situation, expresses a conviction: "Here I stand! *I cannot do otherwise.*"[73] It expresses intention as well as limitation, willingness as well as consent. Seemingly from beyond, one is called to be and act as oneself—surely, as Ricoeur says, "an original form of the dialectic between selfhood and otherness."[74] In Ricoeur's lectures that were not published with *Oneself as Another,* he connects this call of conscience with the call of God.[75] As a philosopher, however, he cannot go so far:

70. Ibid., 309.
71. Ibid., 350.
72. Ibid., 341.
73. Ibid., 352.
74. Ibid., 341.
75. Paul Ricoeur, "The Summoned Subject in the School of the Narratives of the Prophetic Vocation," trans. David Pellauer, in *Figuring the Sacred: Religion, Narrative, and Imagination,* ed. Mark I. Wallace (Minneapolis: Fortress Press, 1995), 262–75.

> Perhaps the philosopher as philosopher has to admit that one does not know and cannot say whether this Other, the source of the injunction, is another person whom I can look in the face or who can stare at me, or my ancestors for whom there is no representation, to so great extent does my debt to them constitute my very self, or God—living God, absent God—or an empty place. With this aporia of the Other, philosophical discourse comes to an end.[76]

The second dynamic between attestation and the self lies in Ricoeur's longtime fascination with Spinoza's idea of desire, *conatus,* as central to the self.[77] Conscience attests to our *desire* to live well. Ricoeur's philosophical anthropology is a philosophy of the will, of action, of desire. His view of consciousness as a task reflects his view of Spinoza's willing desire over Descartes's thinking being. The self's desire is initiated not by possession but by dispossession through all the forms of otherness.

The Interpersonal Self

Like narrative, attestation synthesizes the heterogeneous. Ricoeur is not finished with the heterogeneous with his discussion of narrative, because he has not yet opened up one of the most significant dimensions of the self, which has been seen traditionally as the contrary to the self: namely, other selves. Narrative is a mediator. It mediates the sameness of character with temporal change. Yet Ricoeur also says that it mediates this form of continuity with the continuity of keeping one's word and with the ethical aim of a good life. The practices that are thus involved are inconceivable apart from others, for their norms precede us and arise in the interpersonal world.[78] Doctors and scientists, for example, are trained in an already existing social practice. Thus, it should be clear that, on Ricoeur's terms, we cannot conceive of the self apart from turning to the Other.

Modern philosophy has struggled with intersubjectivity. The Cartesian legacy dispensed with an embodied and a social self. Insofar as others were considered, they were reduced to the Same, not the Other. They, too, were regarded as having universal reason, at least potentially unencumbered by bodies and prejudices, and atomistically disconnected from one another. Ricoeur points out that much political philosophy presupposes "a subject,

76. Ricoeur, *Oneself as Another,* 355.
77. Ibid., 315.
78. Ibid., 176.

complete and already fully endowed with rights before entering into society."[79] Such a subject can, in principle, bow out of the social nexus largely intact. Ricoeur responds that "this hypothesis of a subject of law, constituted prior to any societal bond, can be refuted only by striking at its roots."[80] The basic blow is against the idea that a subject apart from the social bond is an illusion.

Already in language, as Wittgensteinian philosophy emphasizes, and in practices, selfhood is public. We interpret and understand ourselves in language, in ideas, and in narratives that arise from others and are offered to us. The narratives that are offered to us to explore possible ways of being in the world come initially from others. Before we are old enough to be self-conscious, we already possess language, traditions, and a narrative identity. As Ricoeur points out in general terms, reflection cannot start from absolute beginnings. It arrives too late. This means that we cannot start from scratch but also that we need not. The gift from others is that we have a self who has an identity and tools with which to reflect. Ricoeur's view correlates with insights of developmental psychology that understand human identity as necessarily bound up, in children, with interactions with parents and others. If we are deprived of such interactions, we may have stunted or malformed selves, as we are reminded in tragic tales of abuse and isolation. Such stories remind us of our entanglement not just in the world, as Merleau-Ponty says, but with one another.

Postmodern thought in general rejects a disconnected and atomistic view of the self but sometimes goes so far as to lose the self in its sociality. Ricoeur offers a view of the self who is inherently intersubjective but who nonetheless maintains responsibility. Again, like Gadamer's "prejudices," the factors that in modernity threatened the self—in this case, other people—are in Ricoeur's thought also conditions of positive possibility.

The identity of the self as a promiser also presupposes other people. It is possible to promise oneself, but the paradigmatic case is making a promise to others. We make a claim, so to speak, as to whom we will be to others. Ricoeur draws on Marcel at this point: "It is to the other that I wish to be faithful. To this fidelity, Gabriel Marcel gives the beautiful name of *disponibilité* (availablility, disposability)."[81]

We see again how inescapable the ethical dimension is and how quickly and subtly it arises when contemplating the self. Emmanuel Levinas has

79. Ibid., 181.
80. Ibid.
81. Ibid., 268.

prominently argued for the primacy of the ethical over the metaphysical in the way that the "face of the other" raises a primordial injunction to respond.[82] Ricoeur is skeptical of the ethical one-sidedness of Levinas and so balances it with an equally primordial sense of solicitousness toward the other. Drawing on Aristotle's treatment of friendship, Ricoeur develops the primitive sense in which we are lacking by ourselves and develop esteem, commitments, and a life plan aimed at the good with others.[83]

In one sense, Ricoeur argues that Levinas is correct in that the face of the Other offers us a basic experience of one who "forbids murder and commands justice."[84] However we might respond, this is a universal in human life to which we must answer. By itself, however, it is too disjunctive. Part of the power of the "face" is the sympathy that arises from solicitude for the other. In one sense, solicitude includes friendship as relations of esteem and mutual recognition of equals, participating together in projects impossible apart from collaboration. One might say, great authors require great readers and great teachers require great students. The Other cannot be collapsed into the self as in a narcissistic personality, lest the benefit or good be lost. It must arise from another center of being than myself. What I need is the relationship to another, not myself. Ricoeur explains one of the dynamics of this reciprocity in the following way:

> It is in experiencing the irreparable loss of the loved other that we learn, through the transfer of the other onto ourselves, the irreplaceable character of our own life. It is first for the other that I am irreplaceable. In this sense, solicitude responds to the other's esteem for me. But if this response were not in a certain manner spontaneous, how could solicitude not be reduced to dreary duty?[85]

Without regarding others as myself, there is little meaning in my own esteem. " 'As myself' means that you too are capable of starting something in the world, of acting for a reason, or hierarchizing your priorities, of evaluating the ends of your actions, and having done this, of holding yourself in esteem as I hold myself in esteem."[86]

Ricoeur adds to friendship what he calls "perhaps the supreme test of solicitude," namely, the solicitude for suffering. Ricoeur's understanding

82. Emmanuel Levinas, *Totality and Infinity: An Essay on Exteriority,* trans. Alphonso Lingis, Duquesne Studies: Philosophical Series 24 (Pittsburgh: Duquesne University Press, 1969); Emmanuel Levinas, *Otherwise than Being, or Beyond Essence,* trans. Alphonso Lingis, Martinus Nijhoff Philosophy Texts 3 (The Hague: Martinus Nijhoff, 1981).

83. Ricoeur, *Oneself as Another,* 181ff.

84. Ibid., 189.

85. Ibid., 193.

86. Ibid.

of the embodied will recognizes the dimension of consent, that is, freedom occurs within limits. In a sense, we always *suffer* the things that constrain or limit our action. Our action in an intersubjective world is also one where we act in relationship with others. This may be mutually beneficial, as in friendship and collaborative work. It may tragically, however, involve domination, cruelty, and the infliction of pain. Ricoeur thus does not at all imagine that the intersubjective world is always realized in positive friendship and response to the injunction of the Other. From the outset, he has been concerned not only with the neutral sense of human power to act but with how it goes wrong in evil, the movement from fallibility to fault. As a result, a fundamental human experience is that of suffering oneself and also encountering the suffering Other. The Other calls me to respect; the Other also calls me at times to compassion. Then we express or repress it, but our response shapes our identity. Our capacity to respond is part of our humanity. Such feelings of sympathy are not peripheral or contingent but essential. Unlike Kant and much modern philosophy, we do not act apart from feeling but with it, raising again the embodied nature of our being.

As the sufferer, we feel that we need friends. We feel the lack in ourselves of what the other can give. We ourselves have little to give but are not thereby entirely destitute. Ricoeur expresses powerfully:

> For from the suffering other there comes a giving that is no longer drawn from the power of acting and existing but precisely from weakness itself. This is perhaps the supreme test of solicitude, when unequal power finds compensation in an authentic reciprocity in exchange, which, in the hour of agony, finds refuge in the shared whisper of voice or the feeble embrace of clasped hands.[87]

We find here perhaps the tragic echo of Ricoeur's experience of the suicide of his son, who had helped with the editing of *Oneself as Another* and to whom he dedicated the section on tragic action. Ricoeur's sense of a fallible and fragile self interlaces with his sense of the inherent suffering and tragedy in the world. Far from reason being able to rise above life's tragedies, knowledge is rooted in a tragic wisdom of the suffering self who inescapably suffers with others. The chastened nature of Ricoeur's notion of knowledge that is not certainty but conviction or testimony can scarcely be understood apart from his anthropology that includes not only our embodiment and our intersubjectivity but also the wisdom that stems from tragic suffering. Ricoeur reflects:

87. Ibid., 191.

> By refusing to contribute a "solution" to the conflicts made insoluble by fiction, tragedy, after having disoriented the gaze, condemns the person of praxis to reorient action, at his or her own risk, in the sense of a practical wisdom in situation that best *responds* to tragic wisdom. This response . . . makes conviction the haven beyond catharsis.[88]

With Kant, however, and in light of the perversion of esteem in domination and violence, Ricoeur sees the need for the good to pass into universal norms, the desirable into the moral "ought." At this level, the counterpart of *esteem* in the ethical aim is *respect* in the moral norm.[89] The model for this transition is strikingly the Golden Rule, "Do unto others as you would have them do unto you," or the negative version, "Do not do unto your neighbor what you would hate him to do to you."[90] The demand in the Golden Rule, with its implicit indignation at injustice, leads to the absolute prohibition "Thou shalt not." The intimacy of the Golden Rule also, however, protects the Kantian universal respect from losing the particularity and plurality of persons in their situations in a homogeneous sameness. Against the infamous Kantian prohibition never to tell a lie, even when the persecutor is knocking at the door of the refugee whom you are hiding, the moral within the more inclusive ethical allows for the exceptional good to be done—even when it means dissimulating to turn away the threat of violence and death.

The Social Self

Yet one more dimension must be added to Ricoeur's exploration of oneself as another, namely, the social or institutional other that is also as inscribed in our identities as our bodies, our language, our friends, and our enemies. Ricoeur sees the addition of a "third," so to speak, beyond our personal relations to others, as bringing in the institutional and judicial realm. Literally, we could not exist as isolated selves or in one-on-one relationships, for we could never have emerged as a species and as children. The horizon and traditions that we spoke of at the beginning arise in communities that endure over time. We are born into them as much as we are born into a particular family. When we reflect on the meaning of our lives, we reflect with the aid of the legacy that they have given us, even as we might modify or reject them. The larger communities and institu-

88. Ibid., 247.
89. Ibid., 171.
90. Ibid., 219.

tions that shape us bring, according to Ricoeur, a distinctive dimension all their own.

Ricoeur expresses as his basic thesis that the life project of persons is "aiming at the 'good life' with and for others, in just institutions."[91] We have already elaborated the meaning of this pithy thesis except for the last phrase, "in just institutions." The institutional dimension raises the issue of justice. As Ricoeur says, "The other is also other than the 'you.' Correlatively, justice extends further than face-to-face encounters."[92] Human life certainly now includes far more people than we can encounter and is more complex than dialogical or interpersonal relations. This distance or anonymity elicits a certain objective nature of justice that cannot be reduced to familial or friendship relations. Perhaps we might be inclined to see this as negative. Ricoeur characteristically accepts it as phenomenological description and then explores its strengths and weaknesses. Without going into all the details of Ricoeur's political or judicial philosophy, we can indicate its basic direction.

The positive nature of this dimension is that it offers the prospect of living together or "action in concert" in an equitable and fair way. At the same time, it raises, through a hermeneutic of suspicion, issues of power, domination, and violence. In short, justice is possible and injustice is possible. In the religious sphere, no one can read the Hebrew Bible without noting the centrality of the drama revolving around justice and injustice. The significance of living out faith in the church is also at issue. As soon as we talk about faith, we presuppose the traditions and institutions in which faith is embedded and in which we express faith. As in the notorious problems of the Corinthian church with which Paul dealt, issues of respect, distribution, and judgment arise. As soon as there are many human beings, we have the issues of institutions and justice. Central to the desire to live well is the desire to live well *together.*

When a plurality is involved, relationships of distance occur. Ricoeur believes that the sense of justice arises first out of our sense of injustice, that is, out of our indignation at what we perceive to be unfair. The institution replies to the fragility of the interpersonal that may allow for simple vengeance or the exercise of dominative power in reaction to such indignation. It provides a way to reach for equity and fairness in distributing the goods in a society or group where recourse to dialogical, personal relationships is not possible. In a larger way, it recognizes Moses' problem in the wilderness, when his father-in-law, Jethro, told him that he could

91. Ibid., 172.
92. Ibid., 194.

not mediate personally all the problems of all whom he had led out of Egypt.

Ricoeur again creatively reconciles the teleological and deontological traditions in setting the conditions of justice in the context of the good. Threading his way between the intense philosophical discussions that have polarized these approaches, he sees that the vision of the good life that arises from a tradition and is adjudged by practical wisdom to be the good sets the basic conditions for setting out the obligatory and the requisite. In extensive reflection on John Rawls's political theory, which represents the liberal deontological tradition, Ricoeur argues that Rawls's notion of the "original position" cannot be neutral. Rawls initially supposed that by thinking of ourselves in a situation before we knew what position we would have in a society, we could reach agreement on how best to arrange the society equitably. For example, we would not necessarily want to eliminate the possibility of using natural talents and hard work to succeed more than others and thus have absolute equality, but since we might not be very gifted, we would want to have some freedoms and benefits easily accessible to the least able. The problem is that those in the original position already presuppose modern democratic values and have a sense of self, with its various needs and desires, that is not necessarily universal in all respects. As even Rawls came to concede, one cannot have an original situation without some presuppositions, which is the kind of emphasis that is basic to Gadamer's and Ricoeur's hermeneutical philosophy. Ricoeur consequently argues that we cannot dispense with a sense of the good that then shapes our sense of the just. Within the sphere of the just, however, we may have virtually unqualified obligations. In the biblical context, we see that the Ten Commandments are apodictic commands, but their very formulation begins with the supposition of their coming from the God who led Israel out of Egypt and purposed for that people not slavery but freedom in a land of their own. Within this narrative context of the good the deontological obligatory can be placed. Ricoeur thus offers a fascinating example of his own hermeneutical method of appropriation in attempting to bring together liberal and communitarian adversaries. Bernard Dauenhauer, after an extensive study of Ricoeur's political thought, concludes, "Ricoeur's third way between liberalism and communitarianism is a substantial contribution to the theoretical debates about democracy."[93]

The upshot for Ricoeur's anthropology is that a level of rather impersonal institutions and law is integrated into the formation of the self. One

93. Bernard P. Dauenhauer, *Paul Ricoeur: The Promise and Risk of Politics,* Twentieth-Century Political Thinkers (Lanham, Md.: Rowman & Littlefield Publishers, 1998), 318.

might conclude that the unencumbered self of the Enlightenment is now too encumbered—with the body, with the world, with language, with other people, and with institutional society. Yet this picture of the self, after the failure of the Enlightenment project, represents an attractive realism. It is a chastened view of the self in some ways, but it is an enriched view in other ways. Ricoeur sees in it both promise and peril. By itself, the self with all its encumbrances is rich in potential. He also, however, is well aware of the fallibility and fault of all these dimensions of human beings. A Frenchman who lost his father in World War I, who was himself a prisoner of war in World War II, and who suffered through the student riots of 1968 is not being pessimistic but realistic when he reminds us of the fragility of our lives and our institutions. In this he shares the deconstructive tendencies of much postmodernism. Where he differs in many respects is in discerning what we might call a postcritical or postdeconstructive hope in the good and the just. He earlier wrote that in the desert of criticism, we yearn to be called again. His efforts in recent years have increasingly moved toward expressing the viability of responding to such a call. Far from giving up on the good and the just, he has increasingly devoted himself to their affirmation and clarification. He has not given up on practical wisdom, but he realizes that it is equally a tragic wisdom.

The Self and Theology

Ricoeur's entire philosophical project can be regarded as an anthropology. It represents a truly postmodern view of the self, rich in range and nuance. What is striking is the confluence of the philosophical themes with movements in theology. Theologians have largely rejected, too, the dualistic and individualistic self of modernity, cut off from its rootedness in the world. They see in this shift a recovery of a more biblical, Hebraic sense of the self as inherently embodied, interpersonal, and social. Besides being congruent with this shift, Ricoeur's anthropology is compatible with two other striking theological themes of the twentieth century.

One is the Barthian insight into the meaning of the image of God in Genesis as social.[94] One of the liabilities of that rich theological concept is

94. Karl Barth, *Church Dogmatics,* ed. G. W. Bromiley and T. F. Torrance, vol. 3.1: *The Doctrine of Creation,* trans. J. W. Edwards, O. Bussey, and Harold Knight (Edinburgh: T. & T. Clark, 1958), 184ff.; David Cairns, *The Image of God in Man,* rev. ed., Fontana Library of Theology and Philosophy (London: Collins, 1973).

that Genesis 1 does not define the meaning of the image. In the absence of explicit description, tradition, under heavy Hellenistic influence, has understood it as reason or the mind, in an individualistic and mental way. Barth, however, emphasized the contextual clue in the text that the statement about being created in the image of God is immediately followed by "male and female he created them." From that prompt, he and others have emphasized that the image of God is our relational capacity toward others and to God. With the general understanding of the Hebraic sense of a holistic, embodied self, this gives an understanding of the self that is remarkably similar to the kind of emphasis made by philosophers like Ricoeur.

A second and related theological emphasis is a recovery of the social view of the Trinity, which has been more dominant in Eastern theology than in Western. The West has tended to model the Trinity after an individual, the East after a union of persons. As Jürgen Moltmann in particular has argued, this has influenced the West toward individualism and toward domination by a hierarchical superior.[95] While still recognizing the majesty of God, the social Trinity, he argues, connotes the basic values of sociality, sharing, and mutuality. Again, the result is an interpersonal and social view of the self.

Theologians cannot just adopt Ricoeur's anthropology as it is, because to this point he omits another dimension of the self as another, the other being God or the spiritual dimension. Nevertheless, he moved in that direction himself in the lectures he did not publish in *Oneself as Another*. In them, he speaks of a "mandated self" or a "summoned self," where the call of God comes through the conscience.[96] Despite his protestations that his philosophy is separate from his theology, it is clear that his anthropological reflections are consistent with his deep Christian faith. He provides only hints, however, of how to relate his anthropology in more detail. It is also possible that one may appropriate his work in different directions, in accordance with the principle of the surplus of meaning. Yet it does provide a resource, rich in detail and rich in implication, for theologians who have moved in the same direction. Beyond vague affirmations of a holistic, narrative, and social self, Ricoeur contributes to theologians a way to elaborate these views that may match the great traditional theological anthropologies based on quite different views of the self.

95. Jürgen Moltmann, *The Trinity and the Kingdom: The Doctrine of God* (New York: Harper & Row, 1981).

96. Ricoeur, "Summoned Subject."

We take up again questions of how to relate philosophy and theology in a postmodern context in the conclusion. With the resources now at our disposal, however, we must turn our attention to questions at the heart of the postmodern turn: How do we know? If we have a different view of the self, how do we know it to be true? How can we claim it to be true? How sure can we be? Can we even make such claims? And how do they differ from modernity's claims? The answer to these questions is deeply related to the nature of the self that we have just explored and to the nature of hermeneutics that we earlier developed. What does all this entail for epistemology and truth? It is striking that one of the most direct cross-fertilizations between Ricoeur's philosophical and religious reflections occurs right at this point, coalescing in *Oneself as Another* as a way of dealing with how one decides on the good and the just in terms of testimony or attestation.

CHAPTER SEVEN

Truth and Attestation

Up to this point, we have seen how Ricoeur's philosophy engages in various ways the threefold contemporary context of postmodernity, pluralism, and praxis. Besides the basic affiliation that his hermeneutical paradigm has with theology, his hermeneutical model addresses the interpretative turn in postmodernity. His awareness of the conflict of interpretations and the role of the other in self-identity addresses pluralism. His fundamental understanding of the self as a willing agent who is also ineradicably political addresses praxis. There is one missing piece, however, which is crucial in completing the puzzle, namely, epistemology. The postmodern revolution is, if anything, an epistemological revolution, and major components of the change involve the challenges of pluralism and how knowing is inseparable from doing. With our fuller understanding of Ricoeur's hermeneutical model, along with his hermeneutical view of the self, we have the means to elaborate his hermeneutical epistemology and how it addresses these issues. In this way, we can gain a vantage point from which to envisage anew the relationship of reason to faith and philosophy to theology, which will occupy us most explicitly in the conclusion.

When it comes to epistemology, Ricoeur recognizes that the prime challenge is the modern spirit of skepticism and criticism. Our treatment of his hermeneutic of suspicion reveals that he not only has concern to respond to this dimension of our time, he makes a contribution to it. He is aware, however, that such focus raises a question of the possibility of the affirmation of truth. He muses in the concluding chapters of his lectures on the Marxist tradition, "This process of suspicion which started several centuries ago has already changed us. We are more cautious about our beliefs, sometimes even to the point of lacking courage; we profess to be only critical and not committed. I would say that people are now more paralyzed than blind."[1]

In a time of such criticism, he also notes that the human quest for meaning will not be stilled. In this context, he offers one of his reflections that continues to beguile:

> In the very age in which our language is becoming more precise, more univocal, more technical, better suited to those integral formalizations that are called precisely "symbolic" logic . . . —it is in this age of discourse that we wish to recharge language, start again from the *fullness* of language. But this too is a gift from "modernity." For we moderns are men of philolology, of exegesis, of phenomenology, of psychoanalysis, of the analysis of language. The same age develops the possibility of emptying language and the possibility of filling it anew. It is therefore no yearning for a sunken Atlantis that urges us on but the hope of a re-creation of language. Beyond the wastelands of thought, we seek to be challenged anew.[2]

What we address in this chapter is how Ricoeur takes up this challenge in terms of epistemology, following his pathway through caution to courage. In the process, we attempt, by taking our cue from Ricoeur, to address the challenging and vexatious nature of a postmodern epistemology, particularly in relation to science, that does not succumb to relativism.

The Wounded *Cogito*

We begin with his criticism of modernity, catching up some of the points he has already made. In general, Ricoeur is clearly postmodern in his trenchant criticism of modernity, but we also consider "remnants" of modernity that continued, at least for a time, in his thought.

As we have noted, Ricoeur's basic hermeneutical approach is opposed to the modern assumption of an absolute beginning and an absolute ending. Both Ricoeur and Gadamer, in their hermeneutical philosophies, question the capacity to set aside presuppositions and arrive at a Cartesian new beginning, uninfluenced by tradition, the passions, or opinion. The

1. Paul Ricoeur, *Lectures on Ideology and Utopia,* ed. George H. Taylor (New York: Columbia University Press, 1986), 313.

2. Paul Ricoeur, "The Hermeneutics of Symbols and Philosophical Reflection: I," trans. Denis Savage, in *The Conflict of Interpretations,* ed. Don Ihde, Northwestern University Studies in Phenomenology & Existential Philosophy (Evanston, Ill.: Northwestern University Press, 1974), 288.

previous treatment of Marx and Freud reveals that for Ricoeur, the Cartesian *cogito*'s pretension to objectivism is a will-o'-the-wisp, a chimera that has lured us for nearly four centuries but is in the process of dissolution. The result is not necessarily jubilation, as Friedrich Nietzsche saw in his parable of the madman who proclaimed the death of God, but initially a "wounded *cogito.*" Nietzsche expressed his dismay in terms of the absence of God. More precisely, this is the loss of what is considered "onto-theology," the grounding of our philosophical knowledge in the secure knowledge of God. Nietzsche's madman cries out:

> All of us are his murderers! But how did we do this? How could we drink up the sea? Who gave us the sponge to wipe away the enire horizon? What were we doing when we unchained this earth from its sun? Whither is it moving now? Whither are we moving? Away from all suns? Are we not plunging continually? Backward, sideward, forward, in all directions? Is there still any up or down? Are we not straying as through an infinite nothing? Do we not feel the breath of empty space? Has it not become colder?[3]

Our Nietzschean consternation stems in part from a sense of finitude and brokenness that precludes absolute knowledge. It stems also in part from the initial shock that arises when the heightened hopes of modernity to overcome such limitations are shattered.

Apocalyptic notes resound through the philosophers of the modern era, who warn darkly of the fate of a humankind that has not achieved certain and grounded knowledge but who also offer epistemological salvation in ever-renewed edifices of thought. René Descartes's rigorous thinking was preceded by nightmares and followed by a jubilant and grateful pilgrimage to offer tribute to the shrine of Our Lady of Lareto.[4] David Hume confessed to despair in his skeptical questionings that could only be resolved by recourse to everyday activities, such as dining or playing backgammon.[5] Late in life, Immanuel Kant was awakened from his dogmatic slumber by Hume's skeptical reflections to an unrivaled philosophical effort to establish thought for the first time on solid ground.[6] Edmund Husserl similarly spoke of himself as a Moses who would himself not enter

3. Friedrich Nietzsche, *The Gay Science,* trans. Walter Kaufmann (New York: Vintage Books, 1974), par. 125.

4. Norman Kemp Smith, *New Studies in the Philosophy of Descartes: Descartes as Pioneer* (London: Macmillan & Co., 1952), 33; T. Z. Lavine, *From Socrates to Sartre: The Philosophic Quest* (New York and Toronto: Bantam Books, 1984), 87.

5. David Hume, *A Treatise on Human Nature,* ed. L. A. Selby-Bigge (1888; reprint, Oxford: Clarendon Press, 1967), 1.4.7, p. 269.

6. See his preface to the 2d ed., Immanuel Kant, *Critique of Pure Reason,* trans. Max Müller (Garden City, N.Y.: Anchor Books, 1966), esp. xxxii–xxxiii.

the promised land but who had finally laid the foundation on which subsequent generations could build securely.[7] During World War I, the young Wittgenstein found refuge from thoughts of suicide, death, and madness in a pristine philosophical structure that he thought for the first time set philosophy on solid foundations—and then promptly quit philosophy.[8]

As one easily notices, the metaphor of a foundation is laced throughout their language. As we observed in the introduction, Alvin Plantinga traces the foundational metaphor through the history of Western thought but sees it as especially crucial in the modern period, when the alternative appeal to knowledge on the basis of religious authority had been rejected. This "classical foundationalism," as Plantinga terms it, not only means that our knowledge is structured like a building but also calls for the foundations to be incorrigible or certain. The breakdown of this foundationalist paradigm initially leads to a kind of epistemological shock because, as Richard Bernstein noted, the alternative seems to be only relativism.[9]

Ricoeur is well aware that a common response to the breakdown of modernity is a sense of loss and even of humiliation. We continue to yearn for what has vanished, just as we try to remember a dream that is quickly dissipating in the light of day. As I noted in the introduction, the challenge is to find an alternative when we have rejected modernity's cravings for clarity and certainty. What do we do when the prizes of a subject transparent to itself and an object clearly conceived have both been lost?

What we have instead is a subject already immersed in life, in which starting points come too late for absolute beginnings and in which the object is so entangled in the subject that absolute knowledge in history cannot be attained. Both subject and object are socially constructed, but not in a conscious or clearly comprehensible way. This is why the self is hermeneutical, a text that must be deciphered.

Ricoeur expresses the changed situation but also the hope beyond it in the following passage:

> Perhaps one must have experienced the deception that accompanies the idea of a presuppositionless philosophy to enter sympathetically into the problematic we are going to evoke. In contrast to philosophies concerned with

7. Edmund Husserl, *Ideas: General Introduction to Pure Phenomenology,* trans. W. R. Boyce Gibson (New York: Collier Books, 1962), 21.

8. Ludwig Wittgenstein, *Tractatus Logico-Philosophicus,* trans. D. F. Pears and B. F. McGuinness (London: Routledge & Kegan Paul, 1961), preface. See, for an account of the wider context, Ray Monk, *Ludwig Wittgenstein: The Duty of Genius* (New York: Free Press, 1990), chaps. 6–7, esp. 137–38. Of course, Wittgenstein took up philosophy again, beginning another major movement.

9. Richard J. Bernstein, *Beyond Objectivism and Relativism: Science, Hermeneutics, and Praxis* (Philadelphia: University of Pennsylvania Press, 1985).

> starting points, a meditation on symbols starts from the fullness of language and of meaning already there; it begins from within language which has already taken place and in which everything in a certain sense has already been said; it wants to be thought, not presuppositionless, but in and with all its presuppositions. Its first problem is not how to get started but, from the midst of speech, to recollect itself.[10]

What is also expressed in this passage of a quarter-century ago is the way in which the search for truth beyond the wounded *cogito* is set in a linguistic mode that is irreducibly hermeneutical. We can see the significance of this shift by putting it in the context of Ricoeur's hermeneutical arc.

Hermeneutics as Epistemology

Hope arises beyond the simple modern dilemma of objectivism and relativism when one yields the presumed necessity of an absolute starting point. The special insight of Gadamer and Ricoeur in their hermeneutical philosophies is a kind of gestalt switch: The immersion in history and in tradition is not a disadvantage but an advantage. Rather than being a barrier to knowledge, presuppositions are requisite. This is the sense of Gadamer's trenchant criticism of the Enlightenment "prejudice against prejudice."

It is perhaps easier to see at this point the significance of Ricoeur's hermeneutical arc for a postmodern epistemology. It challenges modern epistemologies at every point. The very fact that the *first understanding* is not the moment of critique, nor a moment of doubt, nor a moment of presuppositionless, objective sight, marks it off from modernity. Critical reflection, the second moment, is significantly based on a first, holistic understanding of a text or event or experience. The point is that we can never completely bracket our presuppositions, which in part enable our understanding, but must work with them. We are situated beings who never transcend our historical situation but who can continually enlarge our horizons. Rather than being a total impediment, such historical location gives us a foothold, so to speak, for understanding. We can call this an "incarnational" epistemology because it is rooted in our embodiment and our total situation, understood in the full-fledged sense described in the previous chapter. The incarnational dimension of Ricoeur's thought means that it always involves a fusion of horizons, not a simple leaving behind of our horizon to a God's-eye point of view or to a pristine first-

10. Ricoeur, "Hermeneutics of Symbols I," 287f.

century point of view. Rather, *we* are always brought into the equation. With all the limitations of which moderns are too painfully aware, this situation is not something wholly to deplore but something in part to celebrate.

A further aspect of the lack of "clarity and distinctness" is that beliefs or ideas have a fluidity of meaning that allows for different emphases in different contexts. Perhaps the later Wittgenstein expressed this better than has Ricoeur with his insight that words rarely have precise meanings but usually have some clear paradigmatic or prototypical cases, along with "rough" or "ragged" edges.[11] In Wittgenstein's thought, this is related to the fact that beliefs are embedded and get their meaning in the context of the practices in which they are used.[12] Ricoeur does not express the idea quite this way, but it is compatible with his general emphasis on action that is already symbolically mediated. After all, he began his philosophical project as a philosophy of the will, which led him to the inextricable connection of human action, language, and knowledge.

Another factor behind this hermeneutical play of meaning is Ricoeur's emphasis on figurative language. Symbol, metaphor, and story are irreducible aspects of any large-scale claim to meaning, including science. Both understanding and evaluation involve a grasp of figurative language. Crude reduction of analogical to univocal language is as much a distortion of meaning as is language that is too vague. Norman Perrin underscored this difference in terms of the kingdom of God, whose "tensive," metaphorical meaning has often been unduly flattened into some literal identification of the kingdom of God with a particular historical manifestation.[13] As we have pointed out, sometimes a metaphor or story is best explained not by a prosaic explanation but by another metaphor or another story. The resultant yield in meaning nevertheless precludes the precision so coveted by modernity.

What makes the arc post-*modern,* that is, including a dimension of modernity, is the *critical element.* It is thus not a return to premodernity, which, to be sure, had its critical elements, but it recognizes that we live after the Enlightenment; after the development of historical understanding; after the discovery of other cultures that are not inferior, just different; after the development of modern science, which may not be as exact

11. Ludwig Wittgenstein, *Philosophical Investigations,* trans. G. E. M. Anscombe, 3d ed. (New York: Macmillan Co., 1958), par. 71; Ludwig Wittgenstein, *Culture and Value,* trans. Peter Winch, ed. G. H. von Wright (Chicago: University of Chicago Press, 1980), 45.

12. See, for example, Wittgenstein, *Philosophical Investigations,* pars. 7, 23, 107.

13. Norman Perrin, *Jesus and the Language of the Kingdom: Symbol and Metaphor in New Testament Interpretation* (Philadelphia: Fortress Press, 1976), chap. 2.

as people hoped but which has offered us a dramatically different picture of the universe; and after the development of modern psychology, which, as Ricoeur pointed out, has dissolved the illusion of a sovereign consciousness. If we are to be naïve, it must be a postcritical naïveté that has appropriated these critical changes into our understanding. The critical dimension can be ignored only at our peril, because the suppressed tends, in an almost Freudian manner, to reappear unconsciously, for example, in the way in which much conservative theology has consciously repudiated modernity but has also adopted modern assumptions uncritically at very deep levels.

What makes Ricoeur's epistemology *post*-modern is that the critical dimension is set within limits. It cannot start itself, as we have seen; nor can it reach its desired objectivist ends. Despite the utilization of critical methods and rigorous reflection that, given certain assumptions, can often result in precise and widely agreed-upon conclusions, even in the humanities, we can never exhaust the surplus of meaning on the one hand and the conflict of interpretations on the other. Our knowledge is always fallible in the sense that it can be challenged, usually most dramatically by others in a quite different context. Within a culture or a more particular "research program," we usually live within widely shared agreements, but in a pluralistic world, our views are somewhere subject to challenge.

In an ecclesial context, a community of faith shares deep agreement internally but may have sharp divergence as the circle widens. This may range from disagreements between groups in a local church, to disagreements between local churches or presbyteries in a denomination, to disagreement between broad denominational traditions. The disagreements, however, should not occlude our recognition of the agreements that exist.

Critical reflection deploying developed methodologies has its place, but it is not the starting or ending point. It points beyond itself to a *postcritical appropriation* that is in turn testable. Since appropriation has to do with what we do, the test is not simply theoretical but practical, giving a pragmatic flavor to Ricoeur's epistemology.

Ricoeur's emphasis on appropriation means that not only is there no objective starting point, but there is no objective ending point. The variety that results in a surplus of meaning pushes the hermeneutical arc into a spiral in which reflection is tested by returning to the original text or context that gave it rise, again and again. A historian might return to the U.S. Civil War, a literary critic to *The Brothers Karamazov,* a film critic to *Life Is Beautiful,* a theologian to the Gospels, even a physicist to theories of subatomic phenomena. Final, definitive interpretations are difficult to find. This rules out for Ricoeur not only foundationalism but also a Hegelian absolute synthesis at the end.

More specifically, Ricoeur accepts, to a certain extent, Kantian strictures on knowledge. Because of the human role in the construction of knowledge, Kant thought we could not describe things-in-themselves or a transempirical reality such as God. Ricoeur is not strictly Kantian and sees reason for affirmations beyond what Kant would allow, but he is as negative as Kant in claiming absolute knowledge. While he favors Hegel's more historical and dialectical treatment of knowledge over Kant's, he rejects the Hegelian claim to absolute knowledge and thus makes his noted claim to be a "post-Hegelian Kantian."[14]

In a genuine sense, Ricoeur's hermeneutical arc points "beyond objectivism and relativism." No foundation, no method, and no higher synthesis can escape our hermeneutical situation, but this need not lead to skepticism and despair. It allows for a conviction of truth that is not controlled by foundations or methods but also not without reasons or grounds. This is a truth that is not grounded on Cartesian or positivist method, but it is also a truth that is not naive but critical. How is this possible? And what, more specifically, is the nature of Ricoeur's idea of an alternative claim to knowledge?

Attestation

Ricoeur states clearly in *Oneself as Another* his desire to elude both horns of the modern dilemma as he develops a view of the self as historical and social, calling this incarnational epistemology one of "attestation." It is a testimony to the truth that involves conviction and reasons but does not rely on Cartesian objectivism. As he puts it:

> To my mind, attestation defines the sort of certainty that hermeneutics may claim, not only with respect to the epistemic exaltation of the cogito in Descartes, but also with respect to its humiliation in Nietzsche and its

14. Paul Ricoeur, "Freedom in the Light of Hope," trans. Robert Sweeney, in *Essays on Biblical Interpretation,* ed. Lewis S. Mudge (Philadelphia: Fortress Press, 1980), 166–67. Pamela Anderson explores in great detail Ricoeur's appropriation of Kant in her valuable work: Pamela Sue Anderson, *Ricoeur and Kant: Philosophy of the Will,* AAR Studies in Religion 66 (Atlanta: Scholars Press, 1993). She, however, thinks Ricoeur points to a transcendence of Kant but is not ultimately successful. My own reading of Ricoeur, while I agree that his notion of attestation can be further developed, sees Ricoeur in several ways pointing to a legitimate post-Kantianism that revises Kant's strictures in epistemology and his deontology in ethics. Anderson does not regard *Oneself as Another* as responding to her objections (129 n. 35), but perhaps Ricoeur's later *The Just* helps. See Paul Ricoeur, *The Just* (Chicago: University of Chicago Press, 2000).

> successors. Attestation may appear to require less than one and more than the other.[15]

He similarly states, "As credence without any guarantee, but also as trust greater than any suspicion, the hermeneutics of the self can claim to hold itself at an equal distance from the cogito exalted by Descartes and from the cogito that Nietzsche proclaimed forfeit."[16]

How did Ricoeur arrive at the idea of attestation?

A Hermeneutics of Testimony

As we have seen, Ricoeur suspected from the outset the modernist ambition of a completely rational, self-possessed truth. He saw that truth could sometimes be expressed only in symbols, which in turn could not be fully explicated. His work on Freud and Marx underscored the suspicion of false consciousness and ideology that haunts any human assertion, pockmarked with dissimulations of power that are largely unconscious and unknown, thereby all the more powerful. These limitations also caused him early to see that human claims to truth are proffered more by hope than by sight, thus setting epistemology within the religious context of eschatology. That is, we can never see from a God's-eye point of view in this life but can hope that we will be vindicated in our claims in the future, possibly the religious eschatological future.[17]

These rather vague suggestions came to a focus first in a religious context, in which Ricoeur desired to relate a philosophical "hermeneutics of testimony" to the biblical notion of "witness."[18] He begins with a familiar rejection of absolute knowledge of the absolute but wishes to retain, unlike some philosophers, some grasp of the absolute. In light of Ricoeur's

15. Paul Ricoeur, *Oneself as Another,* trans. Kathleen Blamey (Chicago: University of Chicago Press, 1992), 21.

16. Ibid., 23.

17. Paul Ricoeur, *History and Truth,* trans. Charles A. Kelbley, Northwestern University Studies in Phenomenology & Existential Philosophy (Evanston, Ill.: Northwestern University Press, 1965), 54–55; Paul Ricoeur, *The Symbolism of Evil,* trans. Emerson Buchanan, Religious Perspectives 17 (New York: Harper & Row, 1967), 357.

18. Paul Ricoeur, "The Hermeneutics of Testimony," trans. David Stewart and Charles E. Reagan, in *Essays on Biblical Interpretation,* ed. Mudge, 119–54. He was working off the thought of one of his great influences, Jean Nabert, who in a 1966 book had dealt with the metaphysics of testimony and the hermeneutics of the absolute. Ricoeur had raised the issue of testimony in *The Symbolism of Evil* and even earlier in his work on Marcel and Jaspers. See, for helpful discussion, Loretta Dornisch, *Faith and Philosophy in the Writings of Paul Ricoeur,* Problems in Contemporary Philosophy 29 (Lewiston, N.Y.: Edwin Mellen Press, 1990), 99–100.

general approach, he is open to an experience of the absolute that is not yet comprehensive. He affirms, consistent with his early thought, that such an experience is usually first expressed symbolically—which gives rise to thought. What is surprising at this point is that he thinks symbols are lacking apart from some affirmation that concretizes them. In other words, apart from a witness, someone to embody the symbols and something about which the witness testifies, symbols lack "historic density."[19]

He then turns to a general notion of testimony. First, testimony involves what he calls a "quasi-empirical" claim to have experienced something—a claim, however, that is already hermeneutical, already interpreted. Second, it involves a "quasi-juridical" dimension in the way in which a witness usually is involved in a trial, where his or her testimony must be evaluated. One's testimony must be judged, and such judgment is usually not exact or methodically controlled. It concerns, as Ricoeur says of it and of hermeneutical judgment in general, "not the necessary but the probable."[20] Third, beyond its probable nature, testimony runs the risk of false testimony. This raises the specter of not just being wrong but being deceived. Due to this threat, we see the historical connection between the witness and the martyr. Witnesses must back their beliefs. Commitment does not guarantee the veracity of a belief, but lack of commitment undermines it.[21] "Testimony is also the engagement of a pure heart and an engagement to the death."[22] Thus we have what we might call a "quasi-martyrial" dimension.

Ricoeur then turns to connect this "profane" context for testimony to a biblical context. He sees that the biblical or "sacred" meaning is quite different in significant ways, but it retains contact with the profane. The location of testimony in the prophets brings out the idea of a witness as someone who has been sent. Ricoeur observes, "What separates this new meaning of testimony from all its uses in ordinary language is that the testimony does not belong to the witness. It proceeds from an absolute initiative as to its origin and its content."[23]

Ricoeur sees that all three profane senses are preserved. The sense of martyrial backing, even unto death, is the most obvious. The juridical sense of a trial continues, as the prophets often take over the form of a legal dispute in their prophecy. Ricoeur further points out that the

19. Ricoeur, "Hermeneutics of Testimony," 122.
20. Ibid., 126.
21. Ibid., 129.
22. Ibid., 130.
23. Ibid., 131.

empirical dimension is preserved in the prophet's experience, but it is also grounded in the biblical historical narrative. Ricoeur says:

> The conjunction of the prophetic moment, "I am the Lord," and the historical moment, "It is I, the Lord your God, who has led you out of the land of Egypt and out of the house of bondage" (Exodus 20:2)—is as fundamental as the conjunction of the prophetic moment and the juridical moment.[24]

Ricoeur notes that these dimensions continue from the "prophetic discourse" of the Old Testament into the "evangelical discourse" of the New Testament.[25] What happens in this biblical movement from the Old Testament to the New is an intense interiorization of the notion. Finally, the prime witness is God the Holy Spirit testifying in one's heart, in other words, the "internal testimony of the Holy Spirit" so important to Calvin.[26] Ricoeur insists, however, that the link to exterior history and signs remains crucial: "Testimony-confession cannot be separated from testimony-narration without the risk of turning toward gnosticism."[27]

On this basis of examination of the profane and sacred uses of testimony, Ricoeur raises the question of how these meanings relate to a philosophical affirmation of the absolute. The huge problem since Gotthold Lessing, who pointed to the "ditch" between the contingency of history and absolute truth, is one that Ricoeur recognizes at the outset: "An immense obstacle seems to close off the horizon of the response: do we have the right to invest a moment of history with an absolute character?"[28] In other words, is a "philosophy of testimony" possible? Ricoeur answers that it is, but only as a "philosophy of interpretation" or of hermeneutics.

Ricoeur offers a rather complicated account of the philosophical approach, but for our purposes, only a few issues are paramount.

1. One issue is that the focus is on interpreting the testimony given by another. This has a two-sided aspect. There is the side of interpreting the testimony of another and also the side of relating it to oneself, that is, the issue of appropriation. From one angle, he is dealing with the fusion of horizons. From another, he is assuming his hermeneutical arc. He does not mention the hermeneutical arc in this context, but one can see how it

24. Ibid., 133.

25. Ibid., 134.

26. Ibid., 138. See John Calvin, *Calvin: Institutes of the Christian Religion,* trans. Ford Lewis Battles, ed. John T. McNeill, The Library of Christian Classics 20 (Philadelphia: Westminster Press, 1960), 1.7.4.

27. Ricoeur, "Hermeneutics of Testimony," 139.

28. Ibid., 142.

applies. The first understanding grasps testimony, followed by the second moment, critical analysis; finally, one personally appropriates it in a second understanding.

2. A second issue is the classical philosophical concern for the absolute, for Being, for the truth taken as a whole. In a religious context, one would speak of God. Hence, the testimony of others to their encounter with the Absolute must be adjudged. As well, one's own evaluation of the truth of another involves one's judgment of oneself in relation to the Absolute, which Ricoeur, following Jean Nabert, refers to obliquely as one's "criteriology of the divine." Ricoeur summarizes, "Thus the hermeneutics of testimony arises in the confluence of two exegeses—the exegesis of historic testimony of the absolute and the self in the criteriology of the divine."[29]

3. A third issue is that in engaging the horizon of the other, Ricoeur points out that it involves all three facets of testimony that we have seen run through the common and religious uses of the term. There is the *empirical* side of manifestation, where something is given to be interpreted. In the midst of history, Ricoeur says, "the absolute declares itself here and now."[30] He asserts, not uncontroversially in the context of modern philosophy, that something of reality is given to us. This gets us going by beginning the hermenetical spiral. Otherwise, "a hermeneutics without testimony is condemned to an infinite regress in a perspectivism with neither beginning nor end."[31] At the same time, the testimony does not only lie there passively to be interpreted; it calls for an interpretation. Its appearance in history cries out for critical analysis. In the testimony, as Ricoeur puts it, "there is no separation between the Jesus of history and the Christ of faith."[32]

In hearing the testimony, however, we must assess it, thus calling for the *juridical* moment. In assessment, "a split is sketched, a split which is not the ruin of testimony but an endless mediation on the divided immediacy."[33] Ricoeur indicates that this chain of interpretation was begun by the early church in their myriad titles for Christ.[34] An event and its meaning cannot be divorced; rather, interpretation is a natural consequence of their integral dialectic. The claim to truth calls for contestation, which involves the judgment of "things seen and things said."[35] Ricoeur says,

29. Ibid.
30. Ibid., 144.
31. Ibid.
32. Ibid., 145.
33. Ibid.
34. Ibid.
35. Ibid., 146.

"Hermeneutics arises there a second time: no manifestation of the absolute without the crisis of false testimony, without the decision which distinguishes between sign and idol."[36]

The juridical is followed by the *martyrial.* The truth of the Absolute's manifestation is evaluated in part in terms of the disciple's commitment to it. Ricoeur meditates:

> The testimony of Christ is his works, his suffering, and the testimony of the disciple is, analogously, his suffering. A strange hermeneutic circle is set in motion; the circle of Manifestation and of Suffering. The martyr proves nothing, we say, but a truth which is not strong enough to lead a man to sacrifice lacks proof.[37]

4. Fourth, parallel to this horizon of the other is the issue of one's own horizon. The appropriation of an "original affirmation" of the Absolute, as Nabert and Ricoeur call it, involves one's assessment of one's own understanding of the Absolute or the divine. This, too, is a hermeneutic. Why? Ricoeur answers, "There is no unitary intuition, no absolute knowledge, in which consciousness would grasp both consciousness of the absolute and consciousness of itself. The moment of awareness can only be broken up and dispersed in the predicates of the divine."[38] The hermeneutics of the self must pass the same tests as the hermeneutics of history. Ricoeur asks, "Is it not the same trial which, little by little, proves to be the trial of testimony and the trial of the predicates of the divine?"[39] Here we revisit Ricoeur's insistence on the postmodern dispossession of the self. Selfhood is a task, not a given. Ricoeur and Nabert speak here of the dynamic of losing one's self in order to find it: "The criteriology of the divine corresponds to the greatest divestment of which human consciousness is capable in order to affirm an order freed from the limitations from which no human existence can deliver itself."[40]

The knowledge thus attained is not Hegel's absolute knowledge or the positivist's scientific ideal of complete verification or the phenomenologist's apodictic certainty.[41] It is a knowledge marked by humility, in fact, a double hermeneutical humility, chastened by the hermeneutics of history

36. Ibid.
37. Ibid.
38. Ibid., 147.
39. Ibid., 148.
40. Ibid., 147f.
41. Ibid., 149–50. Ricoeur refers to Hegel and to scientific verification. I added the apodicticity sought by Husserl because Ricoeur refers to its impossibility elsewhere. Also, I qualified science as positivist again because most philosophers of science would not nowadays accept Ricoeur's characterization. See below.

and of the self.[42] Ricoeur acknowledges that this is a kind of probable knowledge that should not be downplayed. He asserts, "To attest is of a different order than to verify in the sense of logical empiricism."[43] In realizing (as we develop below) that the logical-positivist notion of knowledge is discredited and at best subject to this prior hermeneutical knowledge, Ricoeur was making a more significant point than he understood at the time. This hermeneutical knowledge of probability, risk, and suffering lies at the heart of all of our knowledge.

At this point, Ricoeur sees the relation between the testimony to the absolute and our assessment of it as the relation between religion and philosophy, faith and reason. Philosophy, he also says, can never be adequate to the testimony. Their difference, he says, "prevents us from subsuming, in Hegelian fashion, religious representations to the concept."[44] This is a point made clearer by Ricoeur's treatment elsewhere of the manifestation of religious expressions primarily in symbol and narrative, which can never be wholly reduced to univocal language. The inability of philosophy to attain Cartesian clarity and distinctness or absolute foundations marks the inherent humility of philosophy before testimony in general and religion in particular. Thus, Ricoeur sees a dialectical connection between general hermeneutics and biblical hermeneutics. "Nothing," he says, "allows us to derive the specific features of religious language . . . from the general characteristic of the poetic function."[45] Ricoeur concludes provocatively, "The mutual promotion of reason and faith, in their difference, is the last word for a finite consciousness."[46]

42. Ibid., 149.
43. Ibid., 150.
44. Ibid., 153.
45. Paul Ricoeur, "Toward a Hermeneutic of the Idea of Revelation," trans. David Pellauer, in *Essays on Biblical Interpretation,* ed. Mudge, 104. This point makes Vanhoozer's criticism of Ricoeur puzzling, namely, "Ricoeur is trying to establish a universal theory of interpretation within which the Bible is to be understood." See Kevin J. Vanhoozer, *Biblical Narrative in the Philosophy of Paul Ricoeur: A Study in Hermeneutics and Theology* (Cambridge: Cambridge University Press, 1990), 156. It seems that Ricoeur is being very careful to avoid just that problem. James Fodor applauds Ricoeur's making this distinction, which is not usually recognized by those amenable to the Yale school interpretation. See James Fodor, *Christian Hermeneutics: Paul Ricoeur and the Refiguring of Theology* (Oxford: Clarendon Press, 1995), 246, 303–4. Yet Fodor still wonders whether Ricoeur does justice to the concrete, ecclesial location (334). It is not clear, however, whether any philosophy, including Wittgenstein's with its emphasis on concreteness, or "rough ground," can do more than indicate that religious language has commonalities with language in general but must be considered in its specificity, which often shatters the commonalities—which is something that Ricoeur does. The development of Ricoeur in terms of a Christian philosophy such as Alvin Plantinga's, which I elaborate in the conclusion, may help clarify the troubling connections between philosophy and theology in any thinker.
46. Ricoeur, "Hermeneutics of Testimony," 153.

By this time, more questions than answers have likely been raised. Ricoeur assumes the stark difference in this essay that he usually maintains between philosophy and religion, yet in the process brings them so close together that they cannot be fully separated. The implication of his reasoning is that there is no philosophy without original "religious" testimony. Testimony, like symbols, gives rise to thought. Thought has its necessary place, but it cannot supersede the testimony. The modern philosophical ideal is humbled by the inescapability of testimony and its expression in symbol and narrative. As Kevin Vanhoozer puts it:

> Indeed, the image of the philosopher with cupped hands—or better, open ears—is especially appropriate for describing the humble spirit of Ricoeur's philosophy that only begins with a revelation from poetic texts.[47]

Philosophy cannot transcend the trial of hermeneutics because it must attend to the absolute in its ambiguous manifestation in history and to the self in its dispossesion. Philosophy cannot, therefore, transcend the humbled reasoning that Ricoeur calls here testimony or attestation.

We must look at Ricoeur's further development before showing how we can untie some of these knots. What is important to see is how he raises early the issue of testimony in a religious context. It then drops into the background, until it reappears at the center of his epistemology a quarter of a century later. What we have to consider, then, is how it is integrated with its original religious provenance. What is also important is to see how he moves to the dynamic of unavoidable personal judgment. The symbol or testimony may give rise to thought, but the individual must judge its meaning. We will see that there is no escaping this personal risk, which Ricoeur also sets here in the context of trial, commitment, and suffering. Ricoeur later hearkens back to the sense in which our knowledge calls for suffering, then in the context of a general epistemology. Ricoeur's philosophy and his religion could not finally be kept asunder, a division that in the end is more of a modern than a postmodern ideal.

The Body, the Emotions, and the Imagination

Before turning to Ricoeur's later development of attestation in the sense of a general rather than religious epistemology, we need to add a few more ingredients from his various sorties into the subject of epistemology. Par-

47. Vanhoozer, *Biblical Narrative,* 275.

ticularly, his emphasis on the role of the body, the emotions, and the imagination forms an important backdrop to his general theory of knowledge.

Drawing on Ricoeur's anthropology from the previous chapter, we know that *Freedom and Nature* primarily treated the will, but it is clear that many of the same dynamics would apply to knowing. He elaborated in that work the integral role of the body in willing, and particularly the mediation of the emotions.

Ricoeur has not developed these ideas in terms of epistemology as much as he could have, given that the importance of the body and the emotions to knowing has been strengthened more and more since the time of that book.[48] Still, his anthropology points to an embodied epistemology. Contrary to the philosophical tradition that has seen the body and emotions as threats and hindrances to knowing, contemporary epistemology is aware that our thinking is incarnate, that is, it is a bodily action, however it is finally explained in terms of a qualified dualism or holism. Apart from the body and the emotions functioning properly, thinking is hindered. It is still possible that emotions can carry us away, as Ricoeur points out, but the alternative is not a dualism that stoically suppresses the emotions but a holism that attempts to work productively with them. As the existentialist tradition has often emphasized, sometimes we have the best insight when we are most passionate, not least.

One aspect of our embodied nature that Ricoeur does develop further is the interplay of the feelings and the imagination. In fact, Vanhoozer concludes his study of Ricoeur by saying, "Ricoeur does not proclaim the Gospel. Rather, like John the Baptist, Ricoeur serves the Gospel by baptizing our imaginations, philosophically preparing the way for the Word."[49] The imagination combines the feelings and thought in creative ways. Mark Johnson has pointed out that we have oscillated between strict control of the imagination, as in Kant's first critique, and its anarchy in the Romantics.[50] Johnson and Ricoeur point to a use of the imagination,

48. For a critical example of how Ricoeur could have, perhaps should have, gone further, see Helen M. Buss, "Women's Memoirs and the Embodied Imagination: The Gendering of Genre That Makes History and Literature Nervous," in *Paul Ricoeur and Narrative: Context and Contestation,* ed. Morny Joy (Calgary: University of Calgary Press, 1997), 87-96.

49. Vanhoozer, *Biblical Narrative in the Philosophy of Paul Ricoeur,* 288. Garrett Green similarly understands the imagination to be the key to reconceiving theology and scripture. Interestingly, he is a theologian who works primarily out of the Yale school tradition, but he speaks approvingly of Ricoeur's work on the imagination and metaphor. See, for example, Garrett Green, *Imagining God: Theology and the Religious Imagination* (San Francisco: Harper & Row, 1989), 127, 140. As a Yale theologian, it is striking that he does not believe that the appropriation of a general understanding of the imagination in theology violates the ad hoc principle of apologetics (5).

50. Mark Johnson, *The Body in the Mind: The Bodily Basis of Meaning, Imagination, and Reason* (Chicago: University of Chicago Press, 1987).

involving the body and the feelings, as rule governed but not rule dominated. Their idea is similar to Ricoeur's understanding of metaphor as creative and irreducible but not out of control. Metaphor, of course, is an activity of the imagination and, Ricoeur argues, of the feelings.[51] The picturing activity is such an embodied act that it includes in its projecting of a world the feelings, obviously giving depth to what one might take as an overly rational enterprise. In fact, it is doubtful that the understanding of a projected world is possible apart from this "feelingful" understanding. Ricoeur appeals here also to Heidegger's indications that "moods" disclose our situatedness or being-in-the world.[52] Ricoeur speaks similarly in *Freedom and Nature:* "Affectivity is still a mode of thought in its widest sense. To feel is still to think, though feeling no longer represents objectivity, but rather reveals existence."[53] The contrast between objectivity and existence has been broken down since *Freedom and Nature,* but the connection of affectivity to thought, radical at the time, is on target. Johnson, an erstwhile student of Ricoeur, develops the understanding of "the body in the mind" further than Ricoeur, but he does so consistent with Ricoeur. Cognitive studies will likely illuminate further the importance of the body, similar to the way in which Damaso Garcia has shown through brain studies how persons cannot think apart from feelings.[54]

The significance of this aspect of Ricoeur's thought is further to see how his notion of thought is situated and incarnate, shaped by influences that cannot wholly be made clear and distinct. The hermeneutical surplus of meaning is in part rooted in our immersion in the body.

Attestation and Phronetic Thinking

It is time to draw together a number of strands of Ricoeur's thought to capture his central epistemological focus. First, in his analysis of the self, he concluded that self-knowledge is not a given but a goal; it is a task that

51. Paul Ricoeur, "The Metaphorical Process as Cognition, Imagination, and Feeling," in *Philosophical Perspectives on Metaphor,* ed. Mark Johnson (Minneapolis: University of Minnesota Press, 1981), 228–47.

52. Ibid., 245–46. See Martin Heidegger, *Being and Time,* trans. John Macquarrie and Edward Robinson (New York: Harper & Row, 1962), 172–79.

53. Paul Ricoeur, *Freedom and Nature: The Voluntary and the Involuntary,* trans. Erazim Kohák, Northwestern University Studies in Phenomenology & Existential Philosophy (Evanston, Ill.: Northwestern University Press, 1966), 86.

54. See, for example, Damaso Garcia, *Descartes' Error: Emotion, Reason, and the Human Brain* (New York: G. P. Putnam's Sons, 1994). For another philosophical account of the importance of feelings in cognition, see William J. Wainwright, *Reason and the Heart: A Prolegomenon to a Critique of Passional Reason* (Ithaca, N.Y.: Cornell University Press, 1995).

is found by the detour through signs scattered around us. The result is narrative-in-the-making, where we continue to interpret, revise, and develop the plot of our lives in conjunction with the happenings of our lives. Such self-knowledge is not exact or finished; it fits the nature of hermeneutical knowledge that is not out of control but also not precise. It is in the context of such self-knowledge that Ricoeur, in *Oneself as Another,* develops the idea of attestation, calling it a "hermeneutics of the self." As such, it lies between the poles of objectivism and relativism that afflict modernity. As he puts it, it lies between "the epistemic exaltation of the cogito in Descartes" and "its humiliation in Nietzsche."[55]

The dynamics of attestation, as a hermeneutics of the self, fit perfectly his general notion of the hermeneutical arc, which involves knowledge that does not begin itself. It is interpreted and includes a dimension of analytical critique but also a postcritical dimension of application. Attestation is not totally clear, always faces the restriction of suspicion, and allows for the expansion of a surplus of meaning. It never escapes the conflict of interpretation but is a risk, backed by one's life, looking forward to vindication in hope. Since the hermeneutical arc itself was an extension of the basic paradigm of the interpretation of a text to general epistemology, we have here a confluence of the basic hermeneutical model and its expansion into self-understanding and general understanding.

We must add here the way in which Ricoeur originally developed a hermeneutics of testimony in terms of a philosophical affirmation of the absolute or of reality. Whereas Continental philosophy tends to use terms such as *the Absolute* or *Being,* the Anglo-American tradition might speak of a philosophical outlook on life or a worldview. Such knowledge follows hermeneutical dynamics, with a special emphasis on the significance of personal commitment or backing. Ricoeur sees that we cannot avoid some outlook on life, but it is not knowledge that can be guaranteed by some method or foundation, à la the modernist ethos; rather, it is a risk we must take that we back by our lives.

Ricoeur shows in *Lectures on Ideology and Utopia* how, in the modern period, criticism makes us falter. What is consequently needed is the commitment enabled by a hermeneutics of testimony closely related to the religious sphere that he was developing at about the same time. Ricoeur's neglect to pull all these strings together himself makes our task of interpreting his thought more difficult, but it is not difficult to grasp the

55. Ricoeur, *Oneself as Another,* 21.

connection. At this point, in Ricoeur's terminology, we are following the *Sache* of his thought and are not as worried about how he might have put these together. There is cogency in seeing the commitment in the hermeneutics of testimony as a commensurate answer to the risk and possible failure of nerve that accompanies the suspicion of critique.

In his *Lectures on Ideology and Utopia,* Ricoeur also suggested that our truth claims might even be considered fideism, such is their fragility before the withering heat of criticism.[56] He was alluding here to the element of risk and to how we cannot prove what we believe in an objective manner. Interestingly, in another essay on ideology written at roughly the same time, Ricoeur distances himself from fideism. In light of the pervasive threat of ideology, he asks, "How can we take a decision which is not a mere toss of the dice, a logical bid for power, a movement of pure fideism?"[57] In answer, he appeals to "a viable solution" that he sees in his "hermeneutics of historical understanding."[58] He further qualifies, "This knowledge cannot become total. It is condemned to remain partial, fragmentary, insular knowledge."[59] From the perspective of modernity, this lack of an objective decision procedure does imply relativism and thus fideism. A postmodern perspective, however, hinges on another alternative, namely, that of judgments based on evidence and arguments that nevertheless underdetermine conclusions. This is where we can do no other than make our best judgment, but it is "a viable solution." As Ricoeur rightly says in *Lectures,* "We wager on a certain set of values and then try to be consistent with them; verification is therefore a question of our whole life. No one can escape this."[60] Stanley Hauerwas expresses well the significance of the turn to witness or testimony in the Christian context:

> What we must understand is that witness is necessary because we are so storied. If the gospel were a truth that could be known in general, then there would be no necessity to witness. All that would be necessary would be to confirm people in what they already know. If the gospel were about general human experience that is unavoidable, then there would be no necessity of being confronted by anyone as odd as a Christian. But because the story

56. Ricoeur, *Lectures on Ideology and Utopia,* 312.

57. Paul Ricoeur, "Science and Ideology," in *Hermeneutics and the Human Sciences: Essays on Language, Action, and Interpretation,* ed. John B. Thompson (Cambridge: Cambridge University Press, 1981), 241.

58. Ibid., 242–43.

59. Ibid., 245.

60. Ricoeur, *Lectures on Ideology and Utopia,* 312.

> we tell of God is the story of the life and death of Jesus of Nazareth, then the only way to know that story is through witness.[61]

As Jeffrey Stout has pointed out, such risk need not be cause for despair. In fact, we generally share wide agreements that our disagreements tend to overshadow. We usually are able to go on in argumentation. Where we run into dead ends, we often find other means to go on. In politics in the United States, we live (however grudgingly) with the results of votes. In religion, we have freedom of religion. We continue to live out our faith and try to persuade; if we are unsuccessful, we proceed with those who agree enough to walk together. In science such disagreements occur as well, for example, in cosmology concerning the singularity that began the universe or concerning the validity of string theory. Scientists find other areas in which they agree and continue working in those areas where they disagree in hopes that they might eventually reach agreement. The lines have thus become far more blurred between science and religion. Of course, often enough disagreements devolve into violence and coercion. This is a fact of the world in which we live and can be seen in the light of a doctrine of sin. So far, no philosophical or religious view, while perhaps explaining the reality, has been able to change it. In the meantime, we are left with Ricoeur's verdict, with the responsibility of making hermeneutical judgments that we must back with our lives.

Ricoeur's transcendence of fideism is clear in his hermeneutical arc, where the role of criticism is a necessary stage. Similarly, in the hermeneutics of testimony he points to the element of evidence and arguments that give something for testimony and then undergo the trial of testimony. As in explicit court trials, conclusions are often not certain; they are based on the preponderance of evidence and finally on the considered judgments of a jury, whose judgment may still be suspect to large numbers of the citizenry, as in the O. J. Simpson trial.

With metaphor and narrative often figuring into one's knowledge claim, judgments cannot always be deemed exact or precise. We may rather function with Jerry Gill's "principle of sufficient precision."[62] With Wittgenstein again, we see that our concepts have ragged edges; they are

61. Stanley Hauerwas, *After Christendom: How the Church Is to Behave if Freedom, Justice, and a Christian Nation Are Bad Ideas* (Nashville: Abingdon Press, 1991), 149. This is surprising agreement, since many would see Hauerwas as far apart from Ricoeur. In actuality, they make many of the same points; Hauerwas tends to make them, however, much more pungently and provocatively—but also in a less qualified and careful manner.

62. Jerry Gill, *On Knowing God: New Directions for the Future of Theology* (Philadelphia: Westminster Press, 1981), 83–86. See the reference to Gill in the inroduction.

often not exact—but they are exact enough to fulfill their function.[63] Ricoeur and Wittgenstein agree that more precision is often impossible. What Wittgenstein and Gill bring out, which elucidates Ricoeur's point, is that more precision is often unnecessary and even undesirable. Wittgenstein's example is of standing in the street and giving directions by pointing someone to go "stand roughly there."[64] Is it necessary or desirable to specify to the hundredths of an inch? In a similar vein, the elucidation that a metaphor can provide—say, the kingdom of God embedded within Jesus' parables—may be enough.

The import of the postmodern paradigm change is that the role of indeterminacy and vagueness is not necessarily a problem to lament or to overcome. It may in fact be key to human cognition, just as presuppositions are necessary in order even to ask questions and to be able to recognize an answer. As is evident in the hermeneutical arc, there is a place for method and for the accuracy often involved in method. In the philosophical tradition, this precision was seen as the ideal that ruled out imprecision. In this postmodern perspective, the precision is actually predicated on the relatively imprecise background. In other words, if there is enough agreement on the background assumptions and premises, great exactitude is possible, as in mathematics. The problem, as "Gödel's theorem" demonstrated even in relation to mathematics, is that no system can be completely proven internally but must rely on external assumptions.[65] In the end, these assumptions are based on what we are calling hermeneutical judgments, which cannot be finally proven in a universal, objective way. In this respect, all knowledge has an irreducibly hermeneutical flavor that cannot be eradicated. We can nevertheless see a degree of certainty in mathematics and sometimes in the sciences. As I have already intimated, it is possible in religion, too, if there is widespread agreement within a group. Calvinists can agree on the interpretation of passages on election; Arminians can agree, too, but on a different interpretation. Pentecostals can agree exactly on the interpretation of the "tongues" passages in Acts, but their interpretation will differ from those of other groups. In philosophy, Kantians can agree precisely on some things but will differ from Hegelians, and so on. Jean-François Lyotard, who wrote perhaps the major manifesto of postmodernism, referred to this phenomenon as "local deter-

63. Wittgenstein, *Philosophical Investigations,* par. 71.

64. Ibid.

65. For a helpful discussion, see John Polkinghorne, *Science and Creation: The Search for Understanding,* New Science Library (Boston: Shambhala, 1988), 82.

minism" or certainty "in patches."[66] Thus, seen from the inside, a group's language can often appear quite literal and realistic; seen from the outside, it will appear to be much more perspectival and interpretive. What makes a group's consciousness postmodern is its recognition of how it may appear to those on the outside.[67]

The significance of this turn to *hermeneutical* rather than *theoretical* knowledge as basic was alluded to in chapter 1, concerning Gadamer in connection with his reversal of the Aristotelian evaluation of "practical wisdom," or *phronesis.* Aristotle was more balanced than Plato in seeing that some areas of life cannot be reduced to the clear and demonstrable knowledge that he saw in mathematics. In the area of ethics and politics, we attain the most precision we can, but it is one of practical wisdom. In the end, one cannot supersede the judgments of a good person in answering the question, What is the good in a specific situation? No method or rule can substitute for personal judgment. Both Gadamer and Ricoeur see in Aristotle's *phronesis* a category that is similar to their notion of hermeneutical judgment. Aristotle nevertheless retained the notion of knowledge per se for things that could be demonstrated, for his notion of theoretical knowledge, wisdom, and science. Thus, *phronesis* was subordinate to demonstrated and certain knowledge. Gadamer turns Aristotle upside down by making *phronesis* the basis for the latter. Gadamer is here consistent with the way in which mathematics has been relativized and shown to be inherently incomplete. Much of the history of philosophy has been based on the mathematical model, along with its apparent certainty and proof, which Aristotle in the end also followed. Gadamer's shift is quite revolutionary. Ricoeur follows Gadamer in putting a great deal of emphasis on *phronesis* and in seeing it as a model of his hermeneutical notion of knowledge. While he sometimes continues to place the hard sciences in a privileged position, inconsistent both with his own general philosophy and with contemporary philosophy of science, the import of his

66. Jean-François Lyotard, *The Postmodern Condition: A Report on Knowledge,* trans. Geoff Bennington and Frian Massumi, Theory and History of Literature 10 (Minneapolis: University of Minnesota Press, 1984), xxiv. The full quotation is: "There are many different language games—a heterogeneity of elements. They only give rise to institutions in patches—local determinism." The context indicates that his reference to "institutions" involves the security or "certainty" that is possible within language games.

67. Garrett Green suggests a similar idea in terms of the imagination: "Seen from outside the world of the narrative itself . . . the 'as' governs. . . . Seen from within that imagined world, . . . the 'is' governs" (*Imagining God,* 142–43). Green explicitly connects this postcritical perspective with Ricoeur on p. 140.

thought as a whole is the same as Gadamer's: The nature of thought is thoroughly "phronetic."

Following Ricoeur's appropriation of *phronesis* further refines our understanding of his epistemology. Ricoeur in fact calls his approach "phronetic" judgment in his latest work *The Just.*[68] It is not surprising that he turns to this terminology in the context of political philosophy, but what is significant is that he is thinking here of the kind of hermeneutical judgment that he has developed throughout his work. Evidence for that conclusion stems from the fact that "phronetic" judgment shares the dynamics of and also appears parallel to attestation in *Oneself as Another.*

It is odd, however, that Ricoeur has not added much detail to his Aristotelian appropriation of the idea of epistemic virtues that enable one to know and make good judgments.[69] The idea of epistemic practices with associated virtues is prominent in the Yale postliberal theology and in the work of MacIntyre, which is a hermeneutical, narrative approach quite similar to Ricoeur's.[70] The emphasis in these approaches is on skills and virtues that cannot usually be made wholly explicit but that are necessary to the explicit knowledge that we possess. From a similar perspective of philosophy of science, as we have seen, Michael Polanyi claims that even our explicit knowledge has a tacit background that make the foreground possible.[71] Our knowledge thus involves bodily aspects of skill and cognition that operate without conscious thought. As we also saw, Lakoff and Johnson, from the perspective of cognitive studies, have recently pointed out that this tacit dimension means that our knowledge depends in great part on unconscious processes, going on behind the scenes.[72] Much of this background processing, they have further shown, occurs in terms of metaphorical schemas rather than precise univocal linkages.[73] All this is very consistent with Ricoeur's approach, with its inclusion of the body, of

68. Ricoeur, *The Just,* xxii.

69. An exception is his article: Paul Ricoeur, "The Erosion of Tolerance and the Resistance of the Intolerable," in *Tolerance between Intolerance and the Intolerable,* ed. Paul Ricoeur, Diogeres Library (Providence, R.I.: Bergahn Books, 1996), 189–201.

70. See MacIntyre's idea of "tradition-constituted enquiry" in Alasdair C. MacIntyre, *Whose Justice? Which Rationality?* (Notre Dame: University of Notre Dame Press, 1988), 383. For development of his approach, especially his emphasis on practices, as applied to religious faith and ethics, see Nancey C. Murphy, Brad J. Kallenberg, and Mark Thiessen Nation, eds., *Virtues and Practices in the Christian Tradition: Christian Ethics after MacIntyre* (Harrisburg, Pa.: Trinity Press International, 1997).

71. Michael Polanyi, *Personal Knowledge: Towards a Post-Critical Philosophy,* 2d ed. (Chicago: University of Chicago Press, 1962).

72. George Lakoff and Mark Johnson, *Philosophy in the Flesh: The Embodied Mind and Its Challenge to Western Thought* (New York: Basic Books, 1999).

73. Ibid. See also Johnson, *Body in the Mind.*

skills, and of the unconscious, but is relatively undeveloped in his later work. Ricoeur's thought is strengthened, in my view, by development in the direction of these other thinkers.

As is evident, many are the facets of such a hermeneutical epistemology. In essentials, it can be set in contrast to the main features of a modernist epistemology. It is not based on the goal of certainty, clarity, or absolute foundations. It does not presuppose a dualistic intellectualism but rather an embodied, holistic self. It includes claims to the truth but not claims that can be absolutely verified by method or by a foundation. It does not lead to relativism or fideism because the claims are based on evidence and reasons that can appeal to others. Like discussion of the meaning of a text, the text limits or constrains the possibilities, and interpretations of the text are based on the text and reasoning about it. Not just anything goes, even though there is the reality of the more negative conflict of interpretations as well as the more positive surplus of meaning. To this basic nature we add attention to a few more aspects.

Reference to Reality

One of the criticisms of postmodernity is that it is relativistic, bearing no relation to reality. The crass version is "Everyone is entitled to their own opinion, for no opinion is better than any other." It would be difficult to find any major postmodern thinker holding that view, but some, such as Derrida and Rorty, question the viability of truth language. And a serious philosopher of science such as Robert Klee could off-handedly comment about a philosopher of science that she "seems basically uninterested in truth, as indeed any genuine postmodernist would be."[74] The actuality is that many postmodernists are concerned about truth, but in a different mode or paradigm. It should be apparent by now that Ricoeur is no objectivist, but he is also disinclined to give up reference to the real. Sometimes Ricoeur's use of the language of truth and reference strikes some as implying direct access to an external, unmediated reality, but this is to assume that the modernist paradigm is the only possible paradigm. Again, according to a modernist, if one is not a relativist, one must be an objectivist. As James DiCenso points out, however, "Clearly, Ricoeur is not accepting a rigid dichotomy that imposes a choice between positing human access to

74. Robert Klee, *Introduction to the Philosophy of Science: Cutting Nature at Its Seams* (Oxford and New York: Oxford University Press, 1997), 99.

'things as such' or positing closed linguistic universes incapable of self-transcending referential functions."[75] What he does do, in my view, is point to a more genuine postmodern paradigm change, where reality is referenced in the light of our situated, finite, historical perspective. It is a stance that is impossible in the modernist paradigm, but it makes sense in another paradigm and has the virtue of diminishing the specter of relativism that haunts the objectivism of modernity. Seyla Benhabib's notion of a situated universality describes it well.[76] We can make a claim to a truth for all, but it is one that is conditioned by our framework. Apart from our framework, the claim might not even make any sense. Fusions of horizons are possible, however, albeit sometimes with extreme difficulty. There is no guarantee that everyone will be convinced of a particular view, but that is the human situation. The Enlightenment assumption of one universal rationality, where truths would be self-evident to any rational mind, was never realized and is farther from reach than ever. In fact, in light of our explorations, no such thing could exist. Agreement is often possible, but it does not come about because people have divorced themselves from their traditions and assumptions and attained to a presuppositionless objectivity. Rather, it occurs *through* them, not *around* them.

The reference to truth or to reality will always be mediated through our traditions, presuppositions, and culture. It will always be a perspectival picture that is capable of being reshaped. In some respects, many people will be able to agree on very basic human experiences and findings, such as the sun being a yellow orb in the sky or even that the brain consists of two lobes or that the atom is divisible. Even so, some peoples historically would have interpreted the "sun" very differently than a hot ball of gas. People now accept that the earth moves around the sun, although many even in the West have not come to accept evolution or the multibillion-year age of the universe. In some ways, one has to enter the West or something of the modern scientific mind-set in order to see the point and to be convinced. A Hindu who thinks all empirical reality is *maya,* or illusion, might have a very different perspective. It is Gadamer's point that often only in the encounter with the Other, from very different cultures, do we realize how particular and perspectival our own views are. Despite the fact that all our beliefs are colored, we may have what Polanyi called "universal intent," that is, we intend that our beliefs, given our context, should be

75. James DiCenso, *Hermeneutics and the Disclosure of Truth: A Study in the Work of Heidegger, Gadamer, and Ricoeur* (Charlottesville: University Press of Virginia, 1990), 127.

76. Seyla Benhabib, *Situating the Self: Gender, Community, and Postmodernism in Contemporary Ethics* (New York: Routledge, 1992), 3.

convincing and true for anyone.[77] This might entail that someone else must enter our world to some extent even to understand, much less appraise, our point of view.

Stout gives the example of the moral disapprobation of slavery as an example of a truth claim from this postmodern standpoint.[78] We know that slavery has not always been condemned, and its prohibition throughout the West is of recent origin. That does not mean, though, that we think it was "good" or "right" then but not now. Our "intent" is that slavery has always been wrong.

Ricoeur obviously affirms that most, if not all, of our truth claims are hermeneutically conditioned; they are risks and even wagers that cannot be ultimately verified in an objective way. At the same time, he is critical of those who stop short of reference. He pushes beyond the meaning of a text, for example, appreciating what New Critics and structuralists might say about the world of the text, but he is adamant that the text projects a referential world. Ricoeur claims that despite the denial of literal meaning on one level, the indirect reference of figurative language "constitutes the primordial reference to the extent that it suggests, reveals, unconceals . . . the deep structures of reality to which we are related as mortals who are born into this world and who *dwell* in it for a while."[79] In other words, such language makes an imaginative truth claim, which we may or may not affirm. If we do affirm it, it is a creative fusion of horizons that goes beyond the text to be appropriated creatively in our lives and in our new context.

Ricoeur as a Continental philosopher talks in terms of reality, Being, and the Absolute. A parallel in the Anglo-American context, although Ricoeur does not make the connection, is the idea of "critical realism" in philosophy and in science.[80] Rather than our views being pictures, mirrors, or representations of reality, they are "something like" reality filtered through our perspectival lenses. This view is clearly post-Kantian in seeing that knowledge is always constructed, but it also maintains on the other side a stronger claim than Kant's that our views are commensurate in some

77. Polanyi, *Personal Knowledge,* 37, 145.

78. Jeffrey Stout, *Ethics after Babel: The Languages of Morals and Their Discontents* (Boston: Beacon Press, 1988), 21–22.

79. Ricoeur, "Metaphorical Process," 240.

80. For the scientific discussion, see Ian G. Barbour, *Religion and Science: Historical and Contemporary Issues,* rev. ed. (San Francisco: HarperSanFrancisco, 1997), 117–20; Janet Martin Soskice, *Metaphor and Religious Language* (Oxford: Clarendon Press, 1985), chaps. 7–8; Arthur Peacocke, *Intimations of Reality: Critical Realism in Science and Religion* (Greencastle, Ind.: Depauw University Press, 1984). See also, for a similar approach from a different perspective, Johnson, *Body in the Mind,* chap. 8.

way with reality. In fact, this view denies that there is some objective reality apart from a human perspective that tests our view; rather, any view will be a human perspectival view. We can do no better—but we can do this much.[81] We are left again in the hermeneutical situation, where a text does not allow for just any reading at all, but it is a field of possible readings that allow both warrants and disagreements.

This is a significant point in that even in the scientific field, as we see below, a major alternative is that the hard sciences tell us nothing about reality but only about what is practically effective for us. Ricoeur points toward a reality claim, but one that is probably more imaginatively mediated than even most critical realists. His is a configured, hermeneutical realism that is chastened and liable to diverse interpretations and suspicion, but a realism nonetheless. It represents a paradigmatically new approach to issues such as truth, reality, and objectivity. Rather than throwing out the terms, which in a sense is a modern move, it reframes them. In a postmodern situation, one may have the possibility, though admittedly not the necessity, of reconfiguring these terms. They simply will not mean the same things as they did in a modern framework. A situated universality and a perspectival objectivity make sense in a postmodern but not a modern framework. Similarly, reference to the real that is hermeneutical through and through, involving truth claims mediated by metaphor and narrative, makes sense in a postmodern but not a modern framework.

Furthermore, if such a hermeneutical view is firmly in place in contemporary science, it certainly has affinity with the Christian tradition's reserve in taking God-talk as literally descriptive. Rather, God is generally understood as transcending any thorough description in univocal language; our language about God is most commonly seen as analogical or symbolic in a way that cannot be reduced. The denial of any meaning at all, however, is also usually rejected.[82] The result is that we have some indirect and imprecise understanding.

With respect to God-talk, we can say that we understand God to a certain extent but not completely. Ricoeur's hermeneutical realism allows for

81. Janet Soskice puts it even in terms of science: "The scientific realist's argument is that the success of science means that its practitioners must assume not only that the world, its structures, and relations exist independently of our theorizing but also that our theorizing provides us with access to these structures, limited and revisable as that access may be at any given time." See Soskice, *Metaphor and Religious Language,* 122.

82. See my account in Dan R. Stiver, *The Philosophy of Religious Language: Sign, Symbol, and Story* (Cambridge: Blackwell, 1996), chap. 2, for the three main traditions on religious language in Christianity.

our reticence concerning language's capacity to describe God but sees this reserve as perhaps the most extreme case of the way in which language depicts reality in general.

Despite Ricoeur's strong claims to reference to the real and the true, he is sometimes criticized as lacking a strong referent, particularly in religion. This appears to be due to his tendency to speak of understanding the world in terms of self-understanding, raising the suspicion that he has not escaped his existentialist background. Kevin Vanhoozer thinks that Ricoeur improves on Rudolf Bultmann's existentialist theology but does not escape his reduction of the meaning of the gospel to a changed subjective self-understanding.[83] William Placher, a Yale school theologian, defends Ricoeur in some ways against the criticisms from the Yale school, but he, too, after consideration of Ricoeur's views of the reference of religious language, concludes that Ricoeur's answer would only "interpret the biblical narrative texts as about possibilities for human existence."[84] To these critics, Ricoeur intimates that what is important is what we think and not necessarily the way the world is. In other words, they interpret him as essentially Bultmannian, where we may live and act as if there were a God or as if a certain kind of world existed, but the important thing is not the reality of the referent but our existential attitude. He thus comes off as too subjective and individualistic.

The problem is that Ricoeur has insistently rejected such approaches for the same reasons, namely, that they are too subjective and individualistic. In an important preface to the French translation of one of Bultmann's books, Ricoeur expresses both appreciation and criticism.[85] He particularly subordinates the existential and philosophical dimension to the encounter of the theologian with God as the object of faith (indicating that he thinks it is a misunderstanding of Bultmann to read him as using "God" as only a name for authentic personal existence).[86] He chides Bultmann, however, for moving too quickly to the moment of decision and not doing justice to the objectivity of language and the way in which

83. Vanhoozer, *Biblical Narrative,* 141, 159, 181, 236, 251.

84. William Placher, "Paul Ricoeur and Postliberal Theology: A Conflict of Interpretations," *Modern Theology* 4 (1987): 49.

85. Paul Ricoeur, "Preface to Bultmann," trans. Peter McCormick, in *Essays on Biblical Interpretation,* ed. Mudge, 49–72.

86. Ricoeur says, "To be sure, there is no authorization for saying that God for Bultmann is only another name for authentic existence. Nothing in Bultmann seems to authorize any kind of a 'Christian atheism,' in which Christ would be the symbol of an existence devoted to others. For Bultmann as for Luther, justification by faith comes from an other than the self, from an other who grants me what he commands of me" (Ibid., 69–70). The context indicates that Ricoeur would similarly be quite opposed to such an interpretation of his own views.

Being comes into language.[87] In another essay around the same time (1968), Ricoeur contrasts his own "eschatological" view with Bultmann's type of existential approach in the following way:

> The distance is further widened between an eschatological interpretation of freedom and an existential interpretation which contracts it within the experience of present, interior, subjective decision. Freedom in the light of hope of resurrection has a personal expression, certainly, but, even more, a communitarian, historical, and political expression in the dimension of the expectation of universal resurrection.[88]

Ricoeur sees himself finding a third way between the existentialist approach that overemphasizes the subject and the structuralist approach that eliminates the subject, in the process affirming truth claims beyond what either movement generally supports. He says, "If there is no objective meaning, then the text no longer says anything at all; without existential appropriation, what the text does say is no longer living speech. The task of the theory of interpretation is to combine in a single process these two moments of comprehension."[89]

Vanhoozer is also concerned that Ricoeur does not do justice to the particular way in which faith arises. Is it generated, so to speak, simply by the texts, or does it require an act of the Holy Spirit? Vanhoozer concludes:

> While Ricoeur is remarkably successful in providing a philosophical approximation for many biblical ideas (e.g., revelation, resurrection, creation, the fall, justification by faith), his hermeneutical philosophy lacks an adequate approximation for the Christian teaching about the Holy Spirit. To suggest that the work of the Holy Spirit has its approximation in the phenomenon of imaginative appropriation is, in my opinion, to miss the whole point of the Gospels, namely, that it is only thanks to a divine initiative of deed and word that the power of the possibility of resurrection freedom becomes ours.[90]

87. Ibid., 68–69. Against the suggestion that Ricoeur places all the weight of reality on ideality of the word event, he says, "It [the meaning of the text] presupposes also that the word itself belongs to the being who addresses himself to my existence" (70). At another place, Ricoeur similarly says, "What in theological language is called 'faith' is constituted, in the strongest sense of this term, by the new being that is the 'thing' of the text. By recognizing the hermeneutical constitution of biblical faith in this way, we resist, as far as this is possible, the psychologizing reduction of faith." See Paul Ricoeur, "Philosophical and Biblical Hermeneutics," trans. Kathleen Blamey and John B. Thompson, in *From Text to Action: Essays in Hermeneutics, II,* Northwestern University Studies in Phenomenology & Existential Philosophy (Evanston, Ill.: Northwestern University Press, 1991), 99.

88. Ricoeur, "Freedom in the Light of Hope," 164.

89. Ricoeur, "Preface to Bultmann," 69.

90. Vanhoozer, *Biblical Narrative,* 278.

While I have indicated that Ricoeur's philosophical framework allows for a diversity of theological approaches, Ricoeur himself puts emphasis on how scripture references the reality of God and how the Holy Spirit elicits testimony.[91] This is a far cry from a noncognitive approach to religion, and it goes beyond universal experiences belonging to everyone.[92] Ricoeur certainly sees all truth as appropriated by subjects, but, as we have noted, this does not mean that it is necessarily produced by subjects themselves apart from historical encounters, even encounters with God. His hermeneutics of testimony insists on the viability of a historical foundation for testimony.[93] Ricoeur takes great care not to reduce that which is beyond the self, preeminently God, to a possession of the self. In this sense, he does not shy away at all from saying that when God is encountered, the encounter is mediated *by* the imagination, but this does not mean that the meaning of God *is* the imagination—or even that texts about God are produced solely by the imagination. I agree with Mark Wallace's conclusions at this point that ambiguity may arise because Ricoeur at times emphasizes all three dimensions of the reality of reference to God. Sometimes he emphasizes the human dimension, at other times

91. Interestingly, Ricoeur at one point says, "The testimony that the witness has in himself is nothing other than the testimony of the Holy Spirit" ("Hermeneutics of Testimony," 138). Cf. Ricoeur, "Toward a Hermeneutic of the Idea of Revelation," 93. At one point Ricoeur explicitly limits his hermeneutics, saying, "The thematics of faith eludes hermeneutics and attests to the fact that the latter has neither the first nor the last word." See Ricoeur, *From Text to Action,* 99. See also the section on "the call of conscience and the call of God" in the conclusion to see how Ricoeur emphasizes the place for response not just to self or to a text but to the summons of God.

92. For instance, Ricoeur at one point criticizes "Greek Christologies" precisely because "they have made the Incarnation the temporal manifestation of eternal being and the eternal present, thus hiding the principal meaning, namely, that the God of the promise, the God of Abraham, Isaac, and Jacob, has approached, has been revealed as He who is coming for all" ("Freedom in the Light of Hope," 159).

93. For another example, Ricoeur says, "Where a 'history' of liberation can be related, a prophetic 'meaning' can be not only confessed but attested. It is not possible to testify *for* a meeting without testifying *that* something has happened which signifies this meeting. The conjunction of the prophetic moment, 'I am the Lord,' and the historical moment, 'It is I, the Lord your God, who has led you out of the land of Egypt and out of the house of bondage' (Exodus 20:2)—is as fundamental as the conjunction of the prophetic moment and the juridical moment. A tension is thus created between confession of faith and narration of things seen, at the heart of which is renewed the ever-present tension between the judgment of a judge, who decides without having seen, and the narration of the witness who has seen. There is therefore no witness of the absolute who is not a witness of historic signs, no confessor of absolute meaning who is not a narrator of the acts of deliverance." See Ricoeur, "Hermeneutics of Testimony," 133–34. It would not be necessary to quote at such length if the interpretation of Ricoeur as denying historicity and truth claims were not so common, as among many representatives of the Yale school. Given Ricoeur's many explicit texts that reject such a subjectivistic hermeneutic, it is puzzling why such an interpretation persists. Note also Charles Scalise's defense of Ricoeur's attention to history over against Brevard Child's view that Ricoeur is unhistorical: Charles J. Scalise, *Hermeneutics as Theological Prolegomena: A Canonical Approach,* Studies in American Biblical Hermeneutics 8 (Macon, Ga.: Mercer University Press, 1994), 72.

the imaginative world, and at other times God.[94] All three are involved in any attestation of God. Confusion arises when any one of the three is taken to the exclusion of the others. Considering Ricoeur's work as a whole, I thus regard a more historical and objective reading of Ricoeur's religious views as more tenable.

What I emphasize, however, is that quite apart from disagreements concerning Ricoeur's particular religious perspective, his philosophy more unambiguously allows for robust historical and ontological truth claims. My focus, then, is not on the particular way Ricoeur himself extends his philosophy into theology but on the way his philosophy supports multiple extensions. It is evident that Ricoeur has not developed a theology with the same thoroughness that he has developed his philosophy. His religious pronouncements are consequently open to a variety of interpretations. His philosophical perspective, conversely, is clear on the validity of historical and ontological truth claims. I maintain that his philosophical epistemology of attestation is thus open to a more conservative theological perspective, such as Vanhoozer's, as well as a more liberal one, such as David Tracy's.[95] In fact, it is striking that an evangelical such as Van-

94. Mark I. Wallace, *The Second Naiveté: Barth, Ricoeur, and the New Yale Theology,* Studies in American Biblical Hermeneutics (Macon, Ga.: Mercer University Press, 1990), 100.

95. I think it has been unfortunate that Tracy (as well as Langdon Gilkey and Hans Küng) with his notion of faith as "re-presentation," has so often been taken as the theological exponent of Ricoeur's views. For example, Vanhoozer tends to move seamlessly to Tracy when he is expositing Ricoeur. See Vanhoozer, *Biblical Narrative,* 166. A specific point arises where Ricoeur distinguishes religions of manifestation, which would be tribal religions of the sacred as studied by Mircea Eliade, and religions of proclamation, which include the Western religions of Judaism, Islam, and Christianity. Ricoeur as a Protestant Christian tends toward the "proclamation" type but, unsurprisingly, desires a "mediation" between the two. See Paul Ricoeur, "Manifestation and Proclamation," trans. David Pellauer, in *Figuring the Sacred: Religion, Narrative, and Imagination,* ed. Mark I. Wallace (Minneapolis: Fortress Press, 1995), 63. Tracy takes up Ricoeur's hint that there are elements of both in Christianity and distinguishes between manifestation (Roman Catholic) and proclamation models (Protestant) within Christianity, which is a different project from Ricoeur's. See David Tracy, *The Analogical Imagination: Christian Theology and the Culture of Pluralism* (New York: Crossroad, 1981). Vanhoozer deals with Tracy's usage rather than Ricoeur's and places Ricoeur on the manifestation side. The problem is that Christianity as a historical faith does not even fit Ricoeur's notion of a clearly manifestational religion. The end result of conflating these projects, I believe, is to miss Ricoeur's emphasis on historical revelation, which he has developed in several places. To complicate things further, Tracy himself has moved from a more modernist position in *Blessed Rage for Order,* where he receives most of the criticism from Ricoeur's critics, to a more postmodern position in *Plurality and Ambiguity.* See David Tracy, *Blessed Rage for Order: The New Pluralism in Theology,* The Seabury Library of Contemporary Theology (New York: Seabury Press, 1979); David Tracy, *Plurality and Ambiguity: Hermeneutics, Religion, Hope* (San Francisco: Harper & Row, 1987). Obviously, they were colleagues together at the University of Chicago, and Tracy has been influenced by Ricoeur. The point is, however, that Tracy represents one possible appropriation of Ricoeur, and not necessarily the best because of Tracy's ambivalence about objective truth claims that can be backed only by philosophy. As I point out in the conclusion, a number of evangelical theologians also are quite consistent with Ricoeur's philosophical framework—including Vanhoozer, in my judgment! Ultimately, Vanhoozer thinks Ricoeur, if interpreted in his best light (which he terms the "right-wing view"), is consistent

hoozer can find Ricoeur's philosophy so congenial in the many categories that he mentions. Whatever Ricoeur's particular theological view, his understanding of human beings as those who can attest to historical events and encounters with God makes room, I believe, for Vanhoozer's kind of emphasis on the initiative of the Holy Spirit.[96] Ricoeur's listening philosophy, which must receive before it can give, conceives of the human as someone who, in Karl Rahner's words, is a potential "hearer of the Word."[97] When and if that happens, the result is not predetermined. Because such a revelation is disclosive and redescriptive, it most naturally gravitates to the appropriate language of metaphor and narrative—but metaphor and narrative do not necessarily produce it or exhaust it on their own. They can potentially convey its meaning to a certain extent but cannot wholly warrant it. In the end, as in Ricoeur's general epistemology, one cannot prove but can only attest.

What Ricoeur is in fact offering, I believe, is a postmodern approach to faith that does not set faith over against reason, subjectivity over against objectivity, experience over against history, or imagination over against God's mighty acts. Rather, he reconceives all these relations in a nondualistic way that avoids the modernist dilemmas.

The Other

A related issue important in postmodernity is that of intersubjectivity. *Oneself as Another* brings out what we just saw in Ricoeur's earlier thought,

with his own approach (Vanhoozer, *Biblical Narrative,* 286). As Vanhoozer himself says, "Indeed I have already suggested that Ricoeur's own prescriptions for mediating history and fiction and preserving the realism of the event are a sufficient cure for the occasional lapses in hermeneutic equilibrium" (286).

96. Interestingly, Vanhoozer says, "I think Ricoeur would be truer to his own principles if he allowed the historian to testify to certain deeds as well as values that have universal significance for the human condition (*Biblical Narattive,* 281–82). Exactly. Even though Vanhoozer considers Ricoeur's *theological* perspective to be more one of affirming values, he seems to recognize that Ricoeur's *philosophy* allows for and in fact is perhaps "truer" to the affirmation of deeds. This is why it is extremely important to distinguish Ricoeur's philosophical framework from his particular religious appropriation of it, something Ricoeur himself is always careful to do. In the conclusion, I take up again the nuanced character that the relationship of philosophy and theology must have in a postmodern context.

97. Karl Rahner, *Hearers of the Word,* trans. Michael Richards (Montreal: Palm Publishers, 1969). Ricoeur's language need not be taken in the sense of a natural possibility that can be fulfilled apart from historical, divine initiative. Rahner's conception is that the potentiality of hearing the Word of God is itself an act of grace. Similar also is the language of Emil Brunner, who sees a formal "image of God" in our possibilities of hearing that can be fulfilled by the "material image." Of course, a view that sees the image of God as being obliterated or completely lost, as sometimes John Calvin and Karl Barth are interpreted as saying, would not be consistent with such a view. At this point, though, such an extreme view is probably not defensible in either Calvin or Barth, much less biblically. See, for a good discussion, David Cairns, *The Image of God in Man,* rev. ed., Fontana Library of Theology and Philosophy (London: Collins, 1973).

namely, that we are not selves in splendid isolation but our being a self includes a "communitarian" dimension. Modern psychology reveals that the development of a sense of self is impossible apart from a social world. Far from Descartes's idea that we could begin by doubting the existence of an external world and other people, we are, as Martin Heidegger expressed, ineradicably beings-in-the-world, meaning that Cartesian doubt can never get started. Moreover, our being-in-the-world includes our being-with-others; we thus live in a "with-world." In general, postmoderns have insisted on a situated self that is inherently social, as opposed to the isolated and unencumbered self of modernity, and Ricoeur explicates this shift with more thoroughness than most.

Ricoeur and other philosophers, such as Wittgenstein, have also noted that the presence of language in which we might express doubt is already an aspect of the public world in which we exist. We could not even engage in Cartesian doubt about the existence of others apart from the presence of others in the language of our very thoughts. In making truth claims, too, we back our claims in the presence of others, recognizing a certain moral obligation in that backing in the face of the Other. As we saw in the previous chapter, responsibility arises further in the presence of a third element that gives rise to institutions, responsibility, and law, in which we also have our being. Human being is inherently socially situated, and so is epistemology, with all its gifts and risks. We learn from others, testify to others, appeal to the judgment of others, and sometimes suffer their violence in response to our testimony.

Modernist arguments tend to be seen as starting from one place and proceeding in one way. Postmodernist arguments presuppose a social world where the starting point depends on the other. Where one begins depends on the contingent places of agreement. Much may be skipped with one person; little can be presupposed with one another. The art of discussion is therefore based in part on finding the places of agreement, which may differ from one context to another. Lest this seem too odd, imagine beginning a conversation with a Buddhist in Thailand, or a Muslim in Iran, or a Western skeptic (who truly doubts you exist). Then think about discussing the fine points of one of your views with a colleague who shares your approach in great detail. Rorty expresses the difference in saying that, in postmodernity, we are looking to build not a bridge for everyone to come to our island but causeways to connect our islands.[98] The Gadamerian fusion of horizons is obviously at work here.

98. Richard Rorty, *Objectivity, Relativism, and Truth,* Philosophical Papers 1 (Cambridge and New York: Cambridge University Press, 1991), 14, 38, 216, 221.

Wager and Hope

Numerous times we have encountered Ricoeur's idea that a knowledge claim, particularly of an interpretation of a text or of a philosophical view of reality, is a wager and runs the risk of being wrong. This perhaps sounds skeptical or fideistic. It does not sound like someone who affirms references to reality and philosophical truth, and even religious truth. It is, however, a central and consistent part of Ricoeur's thinking about truth claims, so it repays special attention. This is a place where Ricoeur's philosophical, literary, and religious reflection come together, for he says basically the same thing concerning knowledge in general, literary interpretation, and religious knowledge.

One of the first combinations of the philosophical and religious realms comes early in an essay that attests our beliefs rest on eschatological hope. The image of "the Last Day" functions as a limit to "the pretension of philosophies of history to express the coherent meaning of all that has passed and all that is to come."[99] As "a total meaning which is thought but not known," it is a reminder that "the last word therefore is not uttered anywhere."[100] He follows this specifically with the idea of wagering on the truth in *The Symbolism of Evil,* in the context of his discussion of a postcritical naïveté.[101] As he developed his postcritical notion in terms of a hermeneutical arc, recall that he thought the arc begins with a guess or a wager at the meaning of a passage that is tested by criticism and then appropriated in a postcritical understanding. From what we have seen, the postcritical understanding does not altogether leave the element of risk behind; it does not mean a risk-free affirmation of certainty but a reference claim to truth that continues in the hermeneutical spiral to run the risk of critical testing. In an essay on science and ideology, Ricoeur says:

> From the whole of this meditation it follows that the critique of ideology is a task which must always be begun, but which in principle can never be completed. Knowledge is always in the process of tearing itself away from ideology, but ideology always remains the grid, the code of interpretation.[102]

Despite the fact that we may take for granted much of our knowledge and never raise serious skeptical doubts about it, it is nevertheless the case that we can never leave the hermeneutical arc or spiral behind. Just as our

99. Ricoeur, *History and Truth,* 12.
100. Ibid.
101. Ricoeur, *Symbolism of Evil,* 355–57.
102. Ricoeur, "Science and Ideology," 245.

postcritical conclusions cannot leave the text behind but must return again and again to be tested in its light, our beliefs are tested by both our experiences and critical methods. Our beliefs therefore are historical and form part of our ongoing narrative. They may be reaffirmed, rejected, or more likely modified or transformed, but they are set in ever new chapters of our lives.

Ricoeur in his religious writings relates this to the dynamic of hope, which he then connects with all our knowledge. All of it is even "eschatological," to use his earlier term. His postmodern perspective accepts for the most part Kantian strictures on totalizing and absolute knowledge, but he retains the demand for an affirmation of totality or of truth that is in Kant. As he says, "A philosophy of limits which is at the same a practical demand for totalization—this, to my mind, is the philosophical response to the kerygma of hope, the closest philosophical approximation to freedom in the light of hope."[103] Philosophy, he maintains, cannot substitute for a religious affirmation of the truth. It can, however, deal with the limits of knowledge that make room for and also encourage religious affirmation.

As we have seen, Ricoeur goes beyond this strict separation between religion and philosophy at numerous points to speak of all knowledge claims as, in a sense, based on what is given to thought—thought can never start itself. Reflection always begins too late. And reflection cannot arrive at Hegelian absolute knowledge. Ricoeur goes beyond Kant in asserting imaginative, referential claims to reality that are reasonable but not demonstrable. His recognition of the historical, perspectival nature of such claims is the Hegelian element that makes his view a post-Hegelian Kantianism. In this life, we are encouraged not to succumb to the despairing spirit of skepticism but to make affirmations of truth. These are in a sense wagers, however, in which we can say, "I hope that I am within the bounds of truth."[104] We hope that the future and perhaps even the eschaton will bear us out. In the meantime, we live in risk and in hope. This is why truth claims are a kind of testimony that we back with our lives, even our sacrifices and suffering.

This is in part the case because, in the face of finitude and fault, our truth claims and our actions occur in the midst of ideology, oppression, and evil. Our attestations must be made in hope "in spite of." Ricoeur actually expresses his discussion of philosophical freedom and hope in the Christian context thus: "It is the meaning of my existence in the light of

103. Ricoeur, "Freedom in the Light of Hope," 167.
104. Ricoeur, *History and Truth,* 54; Ricoeur, "Erosion of Tolerance," 194.

the Resurrection."[105] He says that he is won over by Jürgen Moltmann's eschatological theology that affirms a theology of promise against one of presence.[106] The promise of Christian hope relates psychologically, he says, to a "passion for the possible," which arises from our productive imagination in the ways we have discussed, such as metaphor, emplotment, and utopia. It relates ethically to a mission that should not be understood in existential terms, in terms of the individual in the eternal present, but with "communitarian, political, and even cosmic implications."[107]

The twofold dynamic of the Christian hope is hope "in spite of," offering "how much more."[108] These Pauline ideas reflect first the recognition that the good news always occurs in light of the bad news. They reflect the intermingling of finitude, fallibility, and fault. In Kantian terms, "the 'postulate' of freedom must henceforth cross through, not only the night of knowing, with its crisis of the transcendental illusion, but also the night of power, with its crisis of radical evil. Real freedom can spring up only as hope beyond the speculative and practical Good Friday."[109] With this recognition, however, comes the affirmation of hope in spite of these realities. "Henceforth," Ricoeur says, "all hope will carry the same sign of discontinuity, between what is heading toward death and what denies death."[110] In another place, he speaks of faith that must pass through the test of atheism.[111] Hope persists "in spite of" the negative. It is an affirmation, an affirmation of "how much more."

Here is reflected his criticism of the Heideggerian analysis that we are basically beings-toward-death. As important as that reality is, it is also met by the reality of hope, of possibility, of much more. To deny this is also to deny reality, as much as to deny death. Ricoeur says more fully:

> This logic of surplus and excess is as much the folly of the Cross as it is the wisdom of the Resurrection. This wisdom is expressed in an *economy of superabundance,* which we must decipher in daily life, in work and in leisure, in politics and in universal history. To be free is to sense and to know that one belongs to this economy, to be "at home" in this economy. The "in spite of," which holds us ready for disappointment, is only the reverse, the dark side, of the joyous "how much more" by which freedom feels itself, knows

105. Ricoeur, "Freedom in the Light of Hope," 159.
106. Ibid., 157–59.
107. Ibid., 162.
108. Ibid., 163.
109. Ibid., 178.
110. Ibid., 163.
111. Paul Ricoeur, "Religion, Atheism, and Faith," trans. Denis Savage, in *The Conflict of Interpretations,* ed. Ihde, 440–67.

> itself, wills to conspire with the aspiration of the whole of creation for redemption.[112]

It is difficult to maintain the clean separation between philosophy and religion in this passage. Ricoeur himself confesses at this point, "Nowhere are we closer to the Christian kerygma: hope is hope of resurrection, resurrection from the dead."[113] As we "decipher" this wisdom in all our lives, it is not clear how it can be kept separate from our epistemological hopes as well as from other hopes. Ricoeur says in this essay, in a takeoff of the Augustinan "faith seeking understanding" tradition, "I hope in order to understand."[114] As we have seen, Ricoeur sees our epistemological beliefs as based on what is given to us from life and as held in the risk of hope. On the one hand, certainly Ricoeur is correct to underscore the fact that philosophy cannot prove religious faith and is not equivalent to religious faith. On the other hand, a Christian could argue that our epistemological hopes are ultimately set within an eschatological context, a context that the Christian philosopher, at least, can recognize. In Ricoeur's concern to overcome modernity, he may tip his hand too much to the limits of philosophy. In the process, he maintains a distance between the two that is neither possible nor what he actually accomplishes. In fact, Ricoeur anticipates the discussion of the economy of "the gift" in contemporary philosophical discussion, upon which his religious discussion directly bears.[115] A quarter of a century after Ricoeur's essay from where we now stand, it looks odd for him to place his discussion of the gift completely on the side of religion and not see its significance for philosophy. This reveals, however, the difficulty of being consistent in a time of turmoil and transition. The mark of the postmodern is that it arises from the modern. Perhaps only later generations will see the distinctions clearly.

We take up again the tension in Ricoeur's distinction between philosophy and theology in the conclusion, but this is the place to consider another area where there is a remnant, so to speak, of modernity in Ricoeur's thought, revealing him to be working through the treacherous terrain in the transition to postmodernity, namely, his treatment of science.

112. Ricoeur, "Freedom in the Light of Hope," 164.

113. Ibid., 178–79.

114. Ibid., 166.

115. For contemporary discussion, see John D. Caputo and Michael J. Scanlon, eds., *God, the Gift, and Postmodernism,* The Indiana Series in the Philosophy of Religion (Bloomington: Indiana University Press, 1999). For example, Ricoeur says, "Kant has no place for a concept of gift, which is a category of the Sacred." See Paul Ricoeur, "Freedom in the Light of Hope," *Essays on Biblical Interpretation,* trans. Robert Sweeney, ed. Mudge, 176.

Science and Attestation

We have noted at several points how Ricoeur seems to appeal to what we might call a pre-Kuhnian understanding of science (in honor of Thomas Kuhn's hermeneutical turn in the 1960s, seeing the sciences as interpretive and shaped by history and context much like the humanities). Kuhn has been followed in large part by contemporary philosophy of science. Mary Hesse points out that the characteristics that were formerly ascribed to the humanities over against science are now applied to science.[116] This again refers to the way in which science is situated in history, is constructed, involves the imagination along with metaphorical models, is socially embedded, and is affected by power and ideology.

A major part of the impetus for postmodernism has thus come from the changes in science itself, for it was perceived to be the paragon of objective knowledge. Like a Trojan horse, hermeneutics was found to be endemic to the practice of science, thus radically changing our understanding. If objective knowledge could not be found in science and mathematics, so the plot line runs, then it simply cannot be found. Rather than throw out the idea of knowledge and truth altogether, some postmoderns have responded by saying, "So much the worse of our theories of knowledge. They should be adapted to fit our practice rather than vice versa."

In light of these changes, Ricoeur's references to science's model of verification as objective in contrast to other forms of knowing is jarring. It is perhaps not surprising, for it is difficult in a time of transition to make a wholesale change all at once. Gadamer, too, is a transitional figure who sometimes lapses into objectivist language dissonant with his own thought. Let us look specifically at some places where Ricoeur, too, appeals to a model of science that is inconsistent with his own larger views.

One place is in terms of the moment of explanation in his hermeneutical arc, developed in the 1970s. For Ricoeur, explanation provides the objective dimension of the text. "Guess and validation," Ricoeur says, "are in a sense circularly related as subjective and objective approaches to the text.[117] Note that Ricoeur says here that this validation is not verification

116. Mary Hesse, *Revolutions and Reconstructions in the Philosophy of Science* (Bloomington: Indiana University Press, 1980), 169–72.

117. Paul Ricoeur, "The Model of the Text: Meaningful Action Considered as a Text," in *Hermeneutics and the Human Sciences*, ed. Thompson, 212f.

or falsification in the sense of the natural sciences. He believes that the best one can do is use a logic of probability where the outcome is always in terms of a better reading as compared with another.[118] Such a probabilistic approach, Ricoeur maintains, nevertheless "gives a firm basis for a science of the individual deserving the name of science."[119] Despite the fact that he is less certain about the outcome than in the case of empirical verification in the natural sciences, Ricoeur's concern is an attempt to ground interpretation in an objective method, thus justifying its claim to "scientific" status. Ricoeur makes a twofold modernist mistake. First, he contrasts the probabilistic nature of hermeneutical knowing with the objective methods of the hard sciences, a contrast that cannot be sustained. Second, he attempts to construct a methodology as close to such an objective conceived science as possible. While we have seen that method has a place and is important, the overall gist of Ricoeur's thought is similar to Gadamer's: Method cannot secure objectivity apart from assumptions that are hermeneutically grounded. Ricoeur is setting the natural sciences off in a compartment immune to hermeneutics, similar to the Diltheyan split that he is trying to overcome in this very context. He is clearly presupposing here an objectivist, pre-Kuhnian view of the natural sciences that is a model of an objective science to which the social and human sciences must try to correspond.

Ricoeur's concern to provide an objective foundation is particularly apparent when he appeals to structuralist methods as having a certain priority.[120] Structuralism, he believes, is appropriate because it does not represent the imposition of a method foreign to the social sciences.[121] What it nevertheless does provide is a radically impersonal, formal "algebra of constitutive units."[122] When he comes to the third stage of the hermeneutical arc, a second understanding, this objective foundation prevents appropriation from being merely psychological and subjective.[123]

Susan Hekman, in her analysis of the crisis of sociology of knowledge, points out that Ricoeur lapses at this point into the foundationalist paradigm that, in her opinion, has created the crisis.[124] In Ricoeur's extension of the model of textual hermeneutics to social action, he calls for a scien-

118. Ibid., 212–13.
119. Ibid., 212.
120. Ibid., 216.
121. Ibid.
122. Ibid., 217.
123. Ibid., 219.
124. Susan J. Hekman, *Hermeneutics and the Sociology of Knowledge* (Notre Dame: University of Notre Dame Press, 1986), 141–44.

tific analysis of social events as part of the moment of explanation. This objective, method-based analysis, he claims, warrants the social sciences being justifiably called "science." Hekman concludes, "By continuing the search for a model of objectivity appropriate to the social sciences, he retains the notion that objectivity is the ideal toward which knowledge in both the natural and social sciences should strive."[125] Ricoeur, of course, still appeals for holistic appropriation in a second understanding, but this does not represent, according to him, the "scientific" moment of the hermeneutical arc. David Couzens Hoy also charges that Ricoeur's employment of this linear "arc" model implies a foundationalist model and undermines his original starting point of a hermeneutical circle.[126] Despite these early criticisms, Ricoeur has never clearly modified or clarified this view of science in terms of his wider thought. Even in his later political thought, he sometimes connects *phronesis* only with ethics and politics, in a way consistent with Aristotle but not consistent with contemporary philosophy of science.

It seems to me that this problem is not difficult to repair. Following the way in which Ricoeur has intimated a general hermeneutical epistemology, we simply carry that process out in a consistent way. Similar to other philosophers of science, we then can acknowledge the greater objectivity of the hard sciences—but only in a relative sense. The reason for the greater objectivity is that the hard sciences abstract from the more complex dimensions of life. Even with respect to the material world, the rise of chaos theory has brought attention to the fact that classical sciences have arbitrarily limited themselves to closed systems—often with great success, to be sure, but in contrast to the overwhelming fact that most of life occurs in open systems. In the end, the distinctions between the spheres of knowledge, as Polanyi emphasized, are relative distinctions, not absolute as Ricoeur sometimes suggests. The irony is that Ricoeur's

125. Ibid., 144. Cf. this statement: "Ricoeur's concern is not merely to show the relevance of hermeneutics for the social sciences but also to establish the 'objectivity' of analysis in these disciplines. He argues that if the social sciences are to be classed as sciences then, first, the data of these sciences must be objectified and, secondly, the logic of analysis employed must conform to the standards of scientific method [pre-Kuhnian]. In short Ricoeur implicitly accepts the model of knowledge embodied in the scientific method and attempts, in effect, to fit the social sciences into that model. Although Ricoeur argues that the model of objectivity sought in the social sciences differs from that of the natural sciences, there is no doubt that objectivity is his goal" (144).

126. David Couzens Hoy, *The Critical Circle: Literature, History, and Philosophical Hermeneutics* (Berkeley: University of California Press, 1978), 89–92. He says, for example, "Ricoeur's structuralist hermeneutics seeks to avoid psychologism and arbitrariness by making the appropriation dependent on a scientific, structuralist, strictly intrinsic explication of the text. But apparently the effort has forced Ricoeur into a dogmatic belief in method, into the illusion of an objective *beginning* for interpretation. His attempt to reconcile the method of structuralism with philosophical hermeneutics conflicts with the spirit of Heidegger's and Gadamer's ontological hermeneutics" (89).

hermeneutical epistemology is quite consistent with the latest understanding of the hard sciences; his project is greatly strengthened and is more consistent when the anachronistic references to the sciences of strict verification are removed.

In the end, we arrive at a significant postmodern conception of reason that also responds at a deep level to the issues of pluralism and praxis. As such, this epistemology not only makes room for theologians to dialogue with science on stronger ground, which, in an age so dominated by science, is no small matter; but it is also crucial in reconceiving the relationship between philosophy and theology and between faith and reason.[127] Ricoeur's incarnational and intersubjective epistemology, rooted in both risk and hope, obviously brings reason closer to faith. It is on this basis that we turn further to rethink the relationship between theology and philosophy on the basis of Ricoeur's thought.

127. See Nancey C. Murphy, *Theology in the Age of Scientific Reasoning,* Cornell Studies in the Philosophy of Religion (Ithaca, N.Y.: Cornell University Press, 1990); Nancey C. Murphy and George F. R. Ellis, *On the Moral Nature of the Universe: Theology, Cosmology, and Ethics,* Theology and the Sciences (Minneapolis: Fortress Press, 1996), for extensive consideration of the possibilities for new integration of postmodern science and postmodern theology.

CONCLUSION

Theology and Philosophy

Ricoeur has been concerned about faith and philosophy from the beginning, but he has not particularly dealt with theology, focusing more on the first-order sources of theology—scripture, reason, and experience. Here, after our extensive consideration of his philosophy and some of its possibilities for theological appropriation, we are able to focus on the dialogue between Ricoeur's philosophy and theology, often taking Ricoeur's own cue as a guide. We also look at his ideas about how faith and reason relate, how his anthropology relates to the Judeo-Christian sense of a "summoned self," and how the authority of scripture might be reconceived in light of his work. In light of these explorations, we then consider how philosophy and theology in general can be related in a postmodern context. In this case, as in the previous chapter, we sometimes have to pit Ricoeur against Ricoeur in a certain sense, because he often separates the two in ways that are more modern than postmodern.

Faith and Reason

To return to an initial look at the situation of faith and reason in the Western tradition, it is deeply marked by dualism. Going back to Plato, faith or opinion has been sharply marked off from knowledge. The philosophical tradition long before modernity has been dominated by an epistemological model of mathematical certainty. As we have seen, the quest for certainty has continued to dominate modernity. Faith could hardly live up to such high standards. Generally, it has been seen as such a different entity, as in Plato, that it is hardly reconcilable with reason. Faith has sometimes been opposed to reason, as in Tertullian's famous question

"What has Athens to do with Jerusalem?"[1] Reason has also been opposed to faith, as among the Deists, who used the criterion of universal reason to evaluate all faith claims. More integrated variations on the theme, such as reason preceding faith (Aquinas) or faith preceding reason (Augustine), also end up with endless aporias. As Augustine saw, how can reason stand alone apart from faith assumptions? Conversely, how can one simply accept faith assumptions without a significant critical component? Much like the unsuccessful effort to reconnect mind and body after Descartes, it is difficult to reconnect faith and reason when they have been so thoroughly divorced.

Apart from some ventures into making faith as rational as any Enlightenment science, faith has generally been seen as more venturesome and less defensible. Sometimes this element of risk has been so prominent that faith lapses into fideism, as in a Kierkegaardian leap or a Bultmannian existential claim to authenticity. Frustration at these unsatisfactory options that tend to collapse faith into what is now an indefensible view of reason or to eradicate reason altogether in favor of voluntarist commitment is behind the postmodern turn in theology. In terms of the mind-body dilemma, much work has been done within the new paradigm. Such a move has hardly begun, however, with respect to the faith-reason dilemma.

It is in the face of this two-millennia perplexity that we have need of a paradigmatic shift in relating faith and reason. The first step is similar to the one Heidegger took in overcoming Descartes, namely, humans are already in the world and need not try to get there. The Cartesian answer is based on a misguided question of connecting two totally disparate entities or substances. In this sense, it has taken several centuries to question the question. Much is still left to explore after taking this step and reframing the question, as witnessed by the works of Heidegger, Merleau-Ponty, Ricoeur, and many others, but the work can hardly begin when it is has veered off so far in the wrong direction. With respect to faith and reason, similarly, there seems little "reason" to separate them so sharply in the first place. Ricoeur's epistemology is a good example of why they can be brought closer together.

With a paradigmatic reformulation of knowing, as in Ricoeur, we have a picture of knowledge that is not based on extremes of certainty and clarity. It is not individualistic but based on persons-in-community. It is not

1. Tertullian, *Proscription of Heretics,* trans. Peter Holmes, The Ante-Nicene Fathers 3 (1957), sec. 7.

classically foundational but rooted in horizons of tradition, narratives, practices, and habits. It involves evidence, to be sure, but is finally a risk and a wager, backed by personal commitment.

Our religious beliefs, while not the same as our other beliefs, can be seen to share many of the same dynamics. Religious beliefs follow the dynamics of the hermeneutical arc. Our beliefs are not constructed out of thin air but are given to us for thought and usually have some degree of warrant. They pass through reflection to some extent and are affirmed in hope. No escape from the risk and historical situation of our affirmations is possible. But this historical situatedness and embodiedness are also what makes knowledge possible. To desire otherwise is to seek nonhuman knowledge.

As we have seen at certain points, Ricoeur's thought itself sometimes contains "remants of modernity" by making sharp distinctions between scientific knowledge and faith. The general tenor of his thought, along with noting contemporary understanding of the nature of science, dispels such disparaging divisions. The result is that our thinking becomes all of one piece. Reason is not then something separable from faith but is integrated into faith. Perhaps our language fails us, for when we use separate terms such as *faith* and *reason,* it conveys that they are entirely separate things. In this case, it is a good example of reification, or what Wittgenstein called the "bewitchment of language."[2] Our language leads us to make distinctions that are not there.

At the same time, we cannot reduce all reason into a flat sameness. This, too, would fly against the sense of pluralism and difference in Ricoeur. The second step in a postmodern view of faith and reason is, after bringing them together, to distinguish the reason in faith from other kinds of reason. Reason takes on different looks in all the different ways it is employed. Physics is not psychology. Law is not literature. Chemistry is not physics. Philosophy is not religion—but more on that later. Similar dynamics apply to all areas of knowing, but there are relative differences. In some areas, the role of rigid methodology works better and looms larger; in other areas, the role of considered, practical judgment dominates. What Ricoeur has shown is that there is a place for all these dynamics in all areas of knowledge. The distinctions are not absolute, as they often are presented in the Western tradition, but relative.

Certainly, theologians would maintain that the realm of faith is distinctive, perhaps placing more strain on the commonality than in any

2. Ludwig Wittgenstein, *Philosophical Investigations,* trans. G. E. M. Anscombe, 3d ed. (New York: Macmillan Co., 1958), par. 109.

other case. Ricoeur also makes this affirmation. It is not a case of having a ready-made epistemology into which everything else fits. Rather, similarities exist between different areas. Perhaps Wittgenstein's notion of a "family resemblance" rather than an essential sameness conveys the idea.[3] In the case of faith, the role of mystery, of risk, and of interpretive judgment is greater than in perhaps any other area. In this case, if we may cautiously put it so, the "object" of knowledge is so unique and transcendent, say the theologians, that all our knowledge is tentative. Even in the Christian tradition, Aquinas regarded all our language about God as analogical, and Calvin conceived it in terms of significant accommodation. Understanding God puts tremendous pressure on our cognitive and linguistic capabilities, to say the least.

Theologians also generally make the claim, however, a tremendous claim in itself, that God has revealed God's self to us and that we have some grasp (knowledge) of God.[4] In the Western religions, this grasp of God is mediated supremely through sacred scripture. It is not surprising, then, that a general epistemology modeled on the interpretation of texts has some relevance to the "knowledge" of God arising from "religions of the Book," which involves interpretation of texts. The promising import of hermeneutical philosophy is precisely that it is a general epistemology that arises virtually from within the faith context. Until the postmodern turn, however, such an attempt to reconceive all knowing on this basis could not get off the ground. The religious and philosophical communities, therefore, were condemned to unite what they had to perceive as disparate. The illusion was that nonreligious knowing could be certain, precise, objective, and so on. The irony is that faith has generally, apart from some notable exceptions, been conceived more accurately, that is, as not fitting the objectivist paradigm. What has happened is that as this modern paradigm has been shattered for knowledge in general, it has come uncannily to resemble religious "knowing." At this point, we are all, more or less, playing in the same ballpark.

Religious faith—or more precisely, Christian faith—however, has its own distinctiveness. As trusting and committed acknowledgment of a God who is encountered spiritually, it is not identical to anything else. Its very claim to spiritual awareness is fraught with risk and difficulty, compared to the methods of the hard sciences that artificially, but appropri-

3. Ibid., par. 67.

4. The mystical tradition is a notable exception, but mystics deny concepts in a sense to make room for the most intimate encounter of all. See, for treatment of this "negative way" in religious language and how it is difficult to sustain with consistency, Dan R. Stiver, *The Philosophy of Religious Language: Sign, Symbol, and Story* (Cambridge: Blackwell, 1996), 16–20.

ately, bracket out such dimensions. At the same time, its claim to ultimacy at the level of basic presuppositions for all of our lives and thinking gives it a centrality and importance that is unrivaled. The relational dimensions of trust and fidelity to "Abba" place it in the sphere of all the interpersonal forms of knowing, but the spiritual and ultimate dimensions again give it a unique importance. This is captured in Jesus' parable of the treasure hidden in the field (Matt. 13:44). When we find it, we go and sell all that we have to buy it; such is its supreme value. One of the major contemporary understandings of religion sees it as inevitably connected to ultimacy, what Paul Tillich calls our "ultimate concern," having to do with our being and nonbeing.[5] Ricoeur similarly sees religious faith relating to the boundaries and limits of our lives and thus to our limit questions.

Still, we claim in a sense to "know" this, namely, to know that God is supremely worthy, or better, to know the God who is supremely worthy. On a modernist basis, it is almost impossible to make such a claim to knowledge. There is room, at least, in the kind of postmodern epistemology that we have envisaged, legitimately to use the word *know* in this context. It is much like Ricoeur's predilection for referring to Aristotle's manifold sense of "being."[6] Many times, Ricoeur indicates the irreducible plurality in being that gives rise to the surplus of meaning. There is also a manifold sense of knowing that does not thereby remove all sense of continuity in the use of the word.

Does this mean that faith, due to its relation to ultimacy, has now a privileged status? Have the roles now been so far reversed that all other forms of knowing must bend the knee to faith? In a sense, theologians would say yes. In the commitment of faith, the First Commandment is true: "You shall have no other gods before me." This does not, however, restore theology to her medieval role as the queen of the sciences.[7] In the public arena, the risk is not removed. No external, objectivist epistemological platform can guarantee such a claim as faith makes. It is finally a *human* claim, for all of its importance. It is a claim to belief in God but not itself a claim from a God's-eye point of view. Its incarnational status as a human, situated, embodied claim should not diminish it in a Christian context, surely. Rather than being embarrassed about the fragility of faith, as has often been the case in reaction to the hegemony of a

5. Paul Tillich, *Systematic Theology* (Chicago: University of Chicago Press, 1951), 14.

6. For example, Paul Ricoeur, *Oneself as Another*, trans. Kathleen Blamey (Chicago: University of Chicago Press, 1992), 20.

7. An interesting and bold attempt, however, to place theology in that role anew in a postmodern context is in Nancey C. Murphy and George F. R. Ellis, *On the Moral Nature of the Universe: Theology, Cosmology, and Ethics,* Theology and the Sciences (Minneapolis: Fortress Press, 1996).

modernist epistemology, we can identify a hermeneutical situation as an aspect of the goodness of creation. It is of a piece with our incarnation, but is not this how God best came to us?

With mention of creation, however, faith is not off the hook, because we know the rest of the story. Along with affirmation of creation—an affirmation that theologians have sometimes been tempted not to make in light of fallenness—we claim the brokenness and downright evil of the *cogito,* estranged from God as is all the rest of creation. In fact, faith itself is clearly vulnerable to the conflict of interpretation and certainly to the power plays of ideology. Ricoeur points out that the greatest danger of ideology perhaps lies in religion because the stakes are so high and the investment so great.[8]

The third step, then, in developing a postmodern view of faith and reason is to recognize that the risk of distortion is highest when the influence is the greatest, which is to say that faith represents the greatest danger just as it represents the greatest good. This is why some of the greatest evils have been done in the name of God, a risk to which Jesus seemed particularly attuned. Langdon Gilkey, a colleague of Ricoeur's for many years at the University of Chicago, especially discerns the ambiguous nature of religious faith. It is capable at the same time of the greatest blessing and the greatest curse.[9]

The Call of Conscience and the Call of God

With a better idea of the possibilities and limitations for a postmodern integration of faith and reason, we need to look at Ricoeur's own suggestions for relating them. In his work on parables, Ricoeur points out his agreement with the general understanding of religion as dealing with our "ultimate concern" or our "limit-experiences."[10] Drawing on the work of Ian Ramsey, he notes that religious statements relate a total commitment to a universal significance. The excessive and transgressive nature of parables, along with their counterparts in other genres, is necessary to relate

8. Paul Ricoeur, "Freedom in the Light of Hope," trans. Robert Sweeney, in *Essays on Biblical Interpretation,* ed. Lewis S. Mudge (Philadelphia: Fortress Press, 1980), 179.

9. For example, see Langdon Gilkey, "Introduction: A Retrospective Glance at My Work," in *The Whirlwind in Culture: New Frontiers in Theology,* ed. Donald W. Musser and Joseph L. Price (Bloomington, Ind.: Meyer-Stone Books, 1988), 29.

10. See above, chapter 4. The specific reference is to Paul Ricoeur, "Biblical Hermeneutics," *Semeia* 4 (1975): 123–45. Ricoeur appeals to Karl Jaspers, Paul Tillich, and Bernard Lonergan as well as Ian Ramsey.

and mediate such experiences, much more so than descriptive, prosaic language. He is speaking in general terms but is obviously thinking particularly of Jewish-Christian religious experience.

In an essay on the religious call of God that was originally a part of his Gifford Lectures but published separately, Ricoeur rejoins this discussion and gives further distinctives of the nature of religious faith, again with focus on the Jewish-Christian milieu. He offers not only an appropriation of his anthropology from a faith perspective but insight into the relationship between a philosophical and a religious perspective. The essay is titled "The Summoned Subject in the School of the Narratives of the Prophetic Vocation."[11] He desires in it to relate his philosophical understanding of the conscience as a "call" to conscience as God's "call."

In doing so, he makes several qualifications. As he says, "I do not want to insinuate that the self, formed and informed by biblical paradigms, crowns the self of our philosophical hermeneutics."[12] In other words, one does not move easily and simply from a general philosophical view of the self to a religious view of the self, as if the latter were the only implication of the former or even as if the latter were one natural extension of the former among others. Nor is it the case that the Christian view is somehow proven or warranted by the philosophical view. As Ricoeur says:

> This would to be to betray our unambiguous affirmation that the mode of Christian life is a wage [wager; *sic*] and a destiny, and those who take it up are not led by their confession either to assume a defensive position or to presume a superiority in relation to every other form of life, because we lack criteria of comparison capable of dividing among rival claims.[13]

Ricoeur's customary caution at this point concerning the relationship between philosophy and theology is well taken. From the experience of the Christian call, we can critically reflect (the second moment of the hermeneutical arc) and find "a certain congruence" or an "approximation" between a hermeneutical anthropology and a Christian calling, between human conscience and Christian conscience. The lines of connection are not laid out beforehand but are there to be discovered, and if discovered, they may be helpful in leading to a larger, postcritical (the third moment) understanding of both. This conception, perhaps surprisingly, aligns

11. Paul Ricoeur, "The Summoned Subject in the School of the Narratives of the Prophetic Vocation," trans. David Pellauer, in *Figuring the Sacred: Religion, Narrative, and Imagination,* ed. Mark I. Wallace (Minneapolis: Fortress Press, 1995), 262–75.

12. Ibid., 262.

13. Ibid., 263.

Ricoeur's view with the postliberal idea of an ad hoc correlation between theology and philosophy.

Ricoeur first points out that the Judeo-Christian notion of what he calls a "summoned self" already "diametrically opposes itself to the philosophical hubris of a self that absolutely names itself."[14] Not just any philosophical anthropology is congruent. In fact, the biblical self is one that is relational, particularly in relation to God, and in its dependence on God is certainly not autonomous, transparent, or foundational, as in much of modern thought. It is perfectly legitimate, then, for a Christian to look for connections where they can be found, and the implication is that certain postmodern anthropologies, with their emphasis on relationality, mystery, and dependence, will be a better match. Of course, in this case, Ricoeur is relating his own religious view, which he understands to be representative of the biblical tradition, to his own philosophical anthropology.

In a three-step process, Ricoeur then connects the prophetic call, the call to be like Christ, and the call of the "inner teacher," the Holy Spirit, to the testimony of conscience. First, the prophets, he believes, provide the "absolutely original paradigm" of the summoned or "responding" self.[15] The prophet is called and commissioned. The call comes *to* the prophet as it tears the prophet *from* his or her surroundings, previous vocation, and previous experience. The dialogic ego in this case is decentered at a radical level.[16] The prophet is commissioned then to go *back* to the people. The prophet may resist and the people may reject, revealing a way in which a relational and social self may be alienated and estranged. Ricoeur says of this dialectic, "The call isolates; the commission binds."[17] The prophet nevertheless has not only the commission but the promise of the presence of God. Moreover, it is not just a three-way relationship of God, the prophet, and the people. The call presupposes also a tradition, in this case the Law, the Torah, which has been transgressed. The people are also called—to God and to faithfulness to the Torah. The problem is that such a call always involves an interpretation, perhaps a new interpretation. Embedded deeply in the prophetic call experience in the Hebrew Bible is thus, in familiar Ricoeurian terms, the conflict of interpretations, growing out of the surplus of meaning. The call experience is then put into writ-

14. Ibid., 262. This later article perhaps corrects what I think is a misleading implication of "Biblical Hermeneutics" that religious language refers only to human experience and not to the God who inspires and calls it forth. Note the discussion of reference in the previous chapter.

15. Ibid., 263–64.

16. Ibid., 265.

17. Ibid., 266.

ing, which gives rise to a history of interpretation. Ricoeur aptly says, "This enterprise was made possible by the passage . . . of the prophetic word from a *Sitz-im-Leben* to a *Sitz-im-Word* [*Wort*; *sic*]."[18]

Second, Ricoeur identifies the call to Christlikeness in the New Testament as the counterpart of the "mandated self" of the Hebrew Bible.[19] He then appropriates Augustine's notion of the Holy Spirit as the "inner teacher" of the soul as a further interiorization of the call of God. In this case, Ricoeur sees the Platonic background to Augustine's thought as not a hindrance but a help. In this tradition, the teacher does not dump the truth into the bare receptacle of the student, as in the empiricist tradition; rather, "it is the inner person that discovers the truth in oneself, simply aided by the teacher."[20] While this is not wholly adequate in itself, it points to how the discovery of the truth by the Christian is not a heteronomous activity, imposed from the outside upon an incapable and unwilling subject.

Third, Ricoeur turns to conscience as "the most internalized expression of the responding self," as the way heteronomy is transcended.[21] Drawing on the Pauline view of a universal conscience that bears witness to justification by faith, Ricoeur says, "Conscience is thus the anthropological presupposition without which 'justification by faith' would remain an event marked by a radical extrinsicness."[22] This seems to be a simple synthesis at this point, but in the end, Ricoeur see a more complex relationship. Ricoeur explains in an illuminating way:

> In fact, it is already an interpretation we find in Paul when he gives "justification by faith" as the key to his message. He in no way claims to identify the conscience common to all human beings and the justification by faith that takes place through the confession of Jesus as Christ. There, it is regarding this articulation that we need to reflect further, between a conscience in which, in the spirit of the Enlightenment, we have discovered autonomy, and a confession of faith in which, in the spirit of hermeneutics, we have discovered a mediate and symbolic structure. This articulation of the autonomy of conscience and the symbolics of faith constitutes, I believe, the modern condition of the "summoned self." The Christian is someone who discerns "conformity to the image of Christ" in the call of conscience. This discernment is an interpretation. And this interpretation is the outcome of a struggle for veracity and intellectual honesty. A "synthesis" is not given and

18. Ibid., 267.
19. Ibid.
20. Ibid., 269.
21. Ibid., 271.
22. Ibid., 272.

> never attained between the verdict of conscience and the christomorphism of faith.[23]

The interpretation of faith is therefore not simply an account of what all human beings possess. It is a claim of universal intent, to be sure, but it remains an offer, a risk, and a hope that Christians make "in good conscience."

Philosophy and Theology

Ricoeur's careful and cautious distinction between common conscience and the Christian claim to be called by an inner voice is a helpful one. It does not reduce everything to one universal type, but it respects the pluralism in experience and in spheres of knowing. In this sense, it respects the difference between philosophy that is concerned with the universally human and theology that is concerned with the specifically Christian. In general, Ricoeur's notion of philosophy as at best being able to "approximate" affirmations of theology is a promising model. It allows for a relationship that is one of neither absolute domination nor absolute distinction.

At other points, however, we have seen that Ricoeur's division between philosophy and theology goes too far and appears to be a remnant of modernity more than an exploration into postmodernity. These two aspects of his thought can better be seen by comparison with two other major approaches to this question on the contemporary scene.

In one case, as indicated in chapter 1, I am convinced that the basic approach of the Yale school of theology is on track, even if they sometimes shade too far in the direction of theology "going it alone," without the aid of any other discipline. This extreme view, I pointed out, is belied by the practice of their leading representatives, who borrow liberally from other disciplines. At best, they suggest that the relationship between philosophy and theology is what they call ad hoc apologetics. That is, theology has its own integrity and should not be dominated by another approach, whether it be philosophy, sociology, psychology, or physics. Theology is enhanced, however, by drawing on other disciplines in a critical way. This not only makes contact with a wider audience and thus furthers the public and apologetic aspects of theology, but it also can illuminate theology itself.

23. Ibid., 274.

For instance, note how Hans Frei draws on literary theory and George Lindbeck draws on Wittgenstein and Geertz. Such "interweaving," to use one of Ricoeur's favorite terms, is probably unavoidable and in the end is advisable. As I argued in connection with Gadamer against the Yale school, a fusion of horizons is inescapable. The question is how critically it is done. As the Yale theologians, drawing especially on their particular interpretation of Karl Barth, point out, it must be done with care, for it is always risky. Who is able to tell for sure at the moment whether the fusion of the contemporary horizon with the biblical horizon represents gain or loss? This is one of those places where we attest to what we believe is the truth with hope that "we will continue to be in the truth." It is also the place where we remind ourselves, particularly in a postmodern setting, that we are not autonomous, individual theologians but theologize for the church and in the light of critical dialogue with the church. In a sense, the theologian is wise to heed the critical response of those outside the church as well as those in the church.

In terms of the ad hoc relation between philosophy and theology, Ricoeur does well. Some from the Yale perspective have sharply accused Ricoeur of capitulating to philosophy, which is not surprising since Ricoeur is primarily a philosopher. As I and others have shown, Ricoeur's approach is far from what Lindbeck called the universal "expressive" approach of Schleiermacher and is actually quite similar to the way in which they make their own linkages with other disciplines.[24] He is very careful to distinguish philosophical from theological conclusions and to avoid the kind of foundational tendencies of much modern theology to ground theology in philosophy. In this he is consistently postmodern. The problem is, ironically, that he is actually too careful, which will best be seen by comparing him with the call for a Christian philosophy by Alvin Plantinga.

Plantinga's appeal for a Christian philosophy represents a major force on the contemporary scene. His seminal critique of what he calls "classical" foundationalism, to which I have referred several times, is as devastating and influential as any.[25] He particularly focuses on the foundationalist claims to incorrigible and indubitable beginning points,

24. A good example of someone in the Yale tradition who connects theology in an ad hoc way with a general understanding of the imagination in a manner consistent with Ricoeur is Garrett Green, *Imagining God: Theology and the Religious Imagination* (San Francisco: Harper & Row, 1989).

25. Alvin Plantinga, "Reason and Belief in God," in *Faith and Rationality: Reason and Belief in God,* ed. Alvin Plantinga and Nicholas Wolterstorff (Notre Dame: University of Notre Dame Press, 1983).

showing that no one has yet been able to find them. His critique of philosophical attempts at foundationalism is equally applicable to theological attempts at foundationalism, which Ron Thiemann and Nancey Murphy have explored.[26] Though conservative theologically, Plantinga's approach differs from the conservative attempts to emulate in the theological context the foundationalism in the philosophical context. In reaction to his own experience of doing philosophy in a modern context that supposes a universal, neutral perspective, Plantinga and others founded the Society of Christian Philosophers, which at one point was the fastest-growing professional society in the United States and has expanded to four regions. This society represents a sea change in the general climate of philosophy, where, as Plantinga pointed, if one happened to be a person of faith, one tended to hide it or be a bit embarrassed about it. Certainly it was not something one would let influence one's philosophizing in any way. Against this view, in an important presidential address in 1984 to the Society of Christian Philosophers, he argued, in a way that sounds much like Gadamer, that every philosopher brings his or her prephilosophical assumptions to the philosophical task.[27] Philosophy does not create out of whole cloth, but as Ricoeur argues, it reflects on experiences, traditions, and ideas already present. No absolute foundations can be found. Rather, one draws on all one's resources and beliefs in philosophical reflection, including one's faith or nonfaith. Plantinga says:

> Philosophy is in large part a clarification, systematization, articulation, relating and deepening of pre-philosophical opinion. We come to philosophy with a range of opinions about the world and humankind and the place of the latter in the former; and in philosophy we think about these matters, systematically articulate our views, put together and relate our views on diverse topics, and deepen our views by finding unexpected interconnections and by discovering and answering unanticipated questions. Of course we may come to change our minds by virtue of philosophical endeavor; we may discover incompatibilities or other infelicities. But we come to philosophy with pre-philosophical opinions; we can do no other. And the point is: the Christian has as much right to his pre-philosophical opinions as others have to theirs.[28]

26. Ronald F. Thiemann, *Revelation and Theology: The Gospel as Narrated Promise* (Notre Dame: University of Notre Dame Press, 1985); Nancey C. Murphy, *Beyond Liberalism and Fundamentalism: How Modern and Postmodern Philosophy Set the Theological Agenda,* Rockwell Lecture Series (Valley Forge, Pa.: Trinity Press International, 1996).

27. Alvin Plantinga, "Advice to Christian Philosophers," *Faith and Philosophy* 1, 3 (July 1984): 253–71.

28. Ibid., 268.

As he showed rather easily, major philosophers are influenced by their own religious or nonreligious assumptions. There is nothing wrong with this; indeed, this is what we should do. What we should not do, however, is pretend that we are not influenced by some of our deepest beliefs, which depth pertains to religious beliefs by their very nature. This is to suppose that we can be Enlightenment minds without presuppositions and interests.

Of course, these varying presuppositions often lead to seemingly insoluble differences that cannot be neutrally resolved, and therein lies the rub. Plantinga does not throw in the towel as a consequence. He rather indicates that we should not give up on reason or discussion, nor should we necessarily throw out our deeply held convictions because they are not held by others, by most others, or by major philosophers. Major philosophers do not agree with themselves either. Given that one's faith represents the deepest, ultimate basis of one's life, Plantinga said, "[t]he Christian philosopher does indeed have a responsibility to the philosophical world at large; but his fundamental responsibility is to the Christian community, and finally to God."[29] Plantinga has not done particularly well in showing how the dialogue is to continue.[30] He has done a service, however, in pointing to the problems of the traditional view of the separation between philosophy and theology, where philosophy is rational, meaning that is it objective and has no presuppositions, and theology is not rational, meaning that it can never achieve such rationality because of its presuppositions and passion. His "advice" to Christian philosophers to be bolder and more straightforward in indicating the influence of their faith presuppositions is a point well taken. They cannot avoid the influence in any case; what is important is to be self-aware and self-critical of their presuppositions.

In light of Plantinga's position, Ricoeur's sometime view that his philosophy is separable from his religious beliefs seems naïve and curiously "modern." It is especially ironic since it should be clear by now that the main tenor of his thought runs against such a separation. Where such a

29. Ibid., 262.

30. I refer here to the fact that Plantinga himself, while developing his views further in terms of warrant, has a difficult time avoiding fideism, implying that, in religion at least, only Christians can have faculties that are properly functioning, which does not do justice to the deep interchanges that have always occurred between theology and other people, religions, and disciplines, whether foundational or ad hoc. In my view, Plantinga's thought makes much more sense in the context of hermeneutical philosophy than in his tradition of analytical philosophy. See Alvin Plantinga, *Warrant: The Current Debate* (Oxford: Oxford University Press, 1993); Alvin Plantinga, *Warrant and Proper Function* (Oxford: Oxford University Press, 1993); Alvin Plantinga, *Warranted Christian Belief* (Oxford and New York: Oxford University Press, 2000).

concern is valid is to protect a legitimate pluralism of interests and disciplines, as one finds in the Yale school. This is the appropriate dimension of Ricoeur's philosophical asceticism. His concern is also comprehensible in light of a desire to maintain his primary role as a philosopher and not as a theologian, particularly on the French scene. The concern is understandable, but it should not lead to violation of his fundamental philosophical position. Yet it seems to do so at several points.

Occasionally Ricoeur implies that faith has less to do with knowledge than does philosophy or science. As we have seen, Ricoeur terms his thought a "post-Hegelian Kantianism." He means by this, among other things, that he refuses the Hegelian claim for absolute knowledge of the totality and retains the basic Kantian strictures on knowledge.[31] In his earlier work, he depicted the philosophical impact of religion on philosophy in terms of hope.[32] As we saw, he utilized the religious image of "the Last Day" to function as a limit to Hegelian philosophies of history. The upshot for religion is that, in Kantian fashion, he identified it with the spheres of "hope" and "freedom" and consequently refrained from gracing it with the appellation of "knowledge."[33] In accord with Kant, Ricoeur argued that the philosopher's relation to religion is one "within the limits of reason alone."[34] In the preface to *History and Truth,* Ricoeur apologizes for one essay "because it goes much further than the others . . . toward a profession of Christian faith and thereby breaks a certain modesty which to me seems essential to philosophical dialogue."[35] As we saw in the discussion of Ricoeur's epistemology, he brings knowledge and truth into conjunction with hope in the phrase "I hope that I am within the bounds of truth."[36] In contrast, following Kant, he appeals to a "regulative feeling . . . which is reason but not knowledge."[37] Peter Joseph Albano says after consideration of this issue in Ricoeur's thought:

> Throughout all this, it is not entirely clear to me that Ricoeur understands the cognitive value of religious symbols as more than the statement of possibility, in effect as illusion, albeit necessary illusion (Kant)—as neither true

31. Ricoeur, "Freedom in the Light of Hope," 166–80; Paul Ricoeur, "Science and Ideology," in *Hermeneutics and the Human Sciences: Essays on Language, Action, and Interpretation,* ed. John B. Thompson (Cambridge: Cambridge University Press, 1981), 242–46.

32. Paul Ricoeur, *History and Truth,* trans. Charles A. Kelbley, Northwestern University Studies in Phenomenology & Existential Philosophy (Evanston, Ill.: Northwestern University Press, 1965), 11.

33. Ricoeur, "Freedom in the Light of Hope."

34. Ibid., 166.

35. Ricoeur, *History and Truth,* 7.

36. Ibid., 54.

37. Ibid., 6.

> nor false because scientifically unverifiable, as referring to nothing other than possible ideals or states of being without objective substance.[38]

As we saw earlier in the discussion of reference, Ricoeur is understood by some, such as Kevin Vanhoozer and William Placher, to be too subjective and "existentialist" when it comes to religion. Religion is therefore understood in largely noncognitive terms, or perhaps better, religion has cognitive implications that cannot be redeemed in the present. These questions are sharpened when we remember that Ricoeur sometimes also pictured science as cognitive in a way that other disciplines are not. In that case, religion has little chance to be seen as "knowledge" of reality.

We also saw that the subjectivist interpretation of Ricoeur could not be maintained in light of Ricoeur's general epistemology, which is certainly not objectivist but has its own "ontological vehemence" concerning the world, as well as the self, to such an extent that it is startling in a postmodern philosopher. Perhaps Ricoeur's split between philosophy and religion along with his occasional noncognitive remarks about faith lend themselves to this misinterpretation. If one merges his remarks about the reference of faith to his general epistemology, as these critics do, then one can end up with a subjectivist appraisal. Ironically, these critics are correct in merging the philosophical and religious epistemologies, but the consequence flows in the opposite direction. Rather than the subjectivity of faith undermining knowledge, a postmodern epistemology undermines a subjectivist or fideist approach to faith.

Given Ricoeur's thought as a whole, there is no strong reason to separate religious faith from his hermeneutical epistemology. As we have seen, the basic characteristics and dynamics are the same for all knowledge. With a more consistently postmodern appropriation of Ricoeur, we can see that, from science to faith, the dynamics of knowledge persist, that is, the hermeneutical contours of his epistemology flow throughout. In fact, one can argue that the fundamental paradigm of interpretation that shapes hermeneutical philosophy is taken supremely from the dynamics of interpretation of religious texts. This does not collapse religious knowing into a flat, one-size-fits-all epistemology for every area of reality. The arena of religious faith rightly contains elements of risk and of hope that are intensified beyond any other area. Since these, however, according to Ricoeur himself, are characteristics of all knowing, why should religious knowing be demarcated as an entirely different entity? The emptiness of the

38. Peter Joseph Albano, *Freedom, Truth, and Hope: The Relationship of Philosophy and Religion in the Thought of Paul Ricoeur* (Lanham, Md.: University Press of America, 1987), 166.

subjectivist criticism in general epistemology thus carries over into the religious realm. We have seen that Ricoeur is no more bracketing out the issue of God's reality than he is the reality of the world or of other people. There are actually no grounds within his own philosophy for him to deny the claim to knowledge of faith either. To clarify Ricoeur's religious epistemology as solidly cognitive renders him more consistent and more postmodern at the same time.

Drawing on these various threads from the Yale school, Plantinga, and a more consistently postmodern Ricoeur, philosophy and theology may be both connected and distinguished in the following way: They are alike materially in having the same sources, that is, our basic presuppositions and experiences. We bring ourselves and our horizon to philosophy and to theology, and they are obviously influenced by our deepest commitments and most significant experiences.

They can be distinguished formally, however, in three ways. They have different primary "publics," to use David Tracy's term.[39] Philosophy attempts to speak to everyone, not just people of faith, although one might narrow its public to the *academy.* It thus makes its arguments as public as possible. This does not mean everyone will be persuaded; far from it, as the history of philosophy shows. Philosophy can allow for the inclusion of religious elements as long as they are backed. This does not mean objectivist proof but reasons and evidence that may or may not be convincing. Theology, by contrast, speaks primarily to the public of the *church.* As Barth particularly emphasized, theology comes from the church and is given back to the church; it serves the church. It presupposes the life of faith and need not try to "ground faith" in the beginning, as is the case with philosophy.

The second formal difference lies in the primary norm. Philosophy appeals to *public reason.* Theology does as well, but it appeals in most cases to *scripture* as a primary norm. That is, a theological position can appeal to scripture as warrant without having to defend scripture's authoritative position to the wider public. As David Kelsey has indicated, the authority of scripture is virtually analytical for theology, even though the way in which the authority of scripture is utilized can vary greatly.[40] If scripture is not as authoritative, usually key religious experiences, such as Schleiermacher's feeling of absolute dependence, are appealed to as authoritative.

39. See David Tracy, *The Analogical Imagination: Christian Theology and the Culture of Pluralism* (New York: Crossroad, 1981), chap. 1, "A Social Portrait of the Theologian," where he deals with the three publics of theology: society, academy, and church.

40. David H. Kelsey, *The Uses of Scripture in Recent Theology* (Philadelphia: Fortress Press, 1975).

Philosophy would have to provide warrant for such appeals; theology begins with them without further ado.

The third formal difference follows from the first two. When disciplines are directed to different audiences and to different norms, they develop different traditions over time and are institutionalized in different ways. The concrete ways in which philosophy is done in the academy and theology is done in the academy and in the church have incredible formative power. For example, philosophy traditionally treats the problem of evil and suffering as a focus without presupposing the Christian context or even the existence of God. Theology deals with it as a subsidiary point under the doctrine of providence. The "flavor" of the treatments of virtually the same issue by a theologian and by a philosopher can vary tremendously. As a result of their differing traditions and ethos, as Plantinga has also observed, philosophy has been preoccupied particularly with *foundational* issues when it has overlapped with theology, such as the existence of God, the basic nature of God and of faith, as opposed to finer points of Christology or of Trinitarian theory. Theology, of course, deals with the *comprehensive* issues of the church. Plantinga has suggested that Christian philosophers could branch out, but they still have tended not to do so. Thus, philosophy and theology tend to have a different primary focus.

With this framework in mind, a postmodern approach to the relationship of philosophy and theology can be developed. It should not collapse one into the other or subordinate one to the other. Neither should it separate them absolutely. The criticism of Vanhoozer and others stems from this kind of collapsing of the two together. These critics tend to subsume Ricoer's philosophy into his theology, interpreting him as subjective in theology, and to regard his overall project as too subjective. Vanhoozer says, "It is also evident that his hermeneutic philosophy as a whole is slanted in favor of 'the idealism of the word event' where new forms of self-understanding arise in front of poetic metaphors and narratives."[41] In fact, Ricoeur's *philosophy* is open to strong historical affirmations as well as to universal human possibilities revealed in poetic literature. These critics interpret his *theology* as idealistic, and this is then read back into his philosophy. Especially in light of the previous section's treatment of Ricoeur's notion of the summoned self in faith, summoned by God, attesting to the particularities of Christian revelation, one can defend a less idealistic and existentialist interpretation in favor of a more realistic and historical interpretation. Nevertheless, as Vanhoozer recognizes, Ricoeur is less a

41. Kevin J. Vanhoozer, *Biblical Narrative in the Philosophy of Paul Ricoeur: A Study in Hermeneutics and Theology* (Cambridge: Cambridge University Press, 1990), 279.

theologian than a philosopher. While not easy to interpret, his philosophy is much more developed and explicit, whereas his theology is more suggestive and implicit. In light of Plantinga's approach, we must recognize that Ricoeur's faith presuppositions inform his philosophical reflection. At the same time, his philosophy is not the same as his theology.[42] Maintaining this nuanced distinction means that Ricoeur's philosophy is open to appropriation by a variety of theological perspectives. For the most part, the appropriations of Ricoeur by mainline theologians such as David Tracy, Langdon Gilkey, and Hans Küng are good examples.[43] It is also true, however, that more conservative theologies, such as those of Vanhoozer, Stanley Grenz, James McClendon, and Ted Peters, are very compatible with Ricoeur, or at least the interpretation of Ricoeur that I have given here.[44]

Philosophy and theology are to be neither equated nor segregated; rather, they are distinctive resources for each other. When they are put into dialogue, both are usually transformed. The question of whether their integrity might be lost in the process is part of the risk that belongs to our incarnate situation. We are only deceiving ourselves if we think we are not influenced by our own horizon; rather than being relegated to relativism or skepticism, however, a philosophy such as Ricoeur's shows how such influence can promote rather than hinder the integrity of meaning. From

42. Noting this distinction resolves the "ambiguity" that Vanhoozer finds in Ricoeur's treatment of philosophy and theology. See Vanhoozer, *Biblical Narrative,* 285. Vanhoozer worries, "It is the very success of his approximations that has given rise to our suspicion that Christianity is for Ricoeur only an illustration of philosophical truth." Just because there is a connection or "approximation" does not mean that one has to be collapsed into the other. If, in fact, Ricoeur goes in the direction of a liberal or idealist theology, it does not mean that his philosophy requires "that Christianity is only an illustration of philosophical truth." One could equally argue, as some have against Plantinga, that his revelational theology has subsumed his philosophy. A better balance is to see that they unavoidably share presuppositions but still can maintain their own integrity in the same person. For example, I do not think Plantinga's notion of warrant leads ineluctably to his own conservative Reformed theology, with an emphasis on Satan as the cause of all natural evil, although obviously his Calvinist heritage has shaped his philosophizing. Indeed, I think one could end up with a liberal theology on the basis of Plantinga's epistemology.

43. See Langdon Gilkey, *Naming the Whirlwind: The Renewal of God-Language* (Indianapolis: Bobbs-Merrill Co., 1969); Langdon Gilkey, *Reaping the Whirlwind: A Christian Interpretation of History* (New York: Crossroad, 1976); Hans Küng, *On Being a Christian,* trans. Edward Quinn (Garden City, N.Y.: Doubleday, 1976); Hans Küng, *Does God Exist? An Answer for Today,* trans. Edward Quinn (Garden City, N.Y.: Doubleday, 1980).

44. See Vanhoozer, *Biblical Narrative*; Kevin Vanhoozer, *Is There a Meaning in This Text? The Bible, the Reader, and the Morality of Literary Knowledge* (Grand Rapids: Zondervan Publishing House, 1998); Stanley J. Grenz and John R. Franke, *Beyond Foundationalism: Shaping Theology in a Postmodern Context* (Louisville, Ky.: Westminster John Knox Press, 2001); Stanley J. Grenz, *Renewing the Center: Evangelical Theology in a Post-Theological Era* (Grand Rapids: BridgePoint, 2000); James Wm. McClendon Jr., *Doctrine: Systematic Theology* (Nashville: Abingdon Press, 1994); Ted Peters, *God—The World's Future: Systematic Theology for a New Era,* 2d ed. (Minneapolis: Fortress Press, 2000).

the modernist paradigm, such a hermeneutical situation may seem impossible and more than a little disquieting. From another paradigm, it represents our God-given situation, for which we are thankful. Most of us in the meantime are in between, performing the challenging exercise of keeping our eyes on both paradigms. This is part of what makes the current situation one of extraordinary challenge and ferment.

Ricoeur and Contemporary Theology

In this contemporary situation for theology, when our footing constantly threatens to slip, we can welcome aid from any quarter. The purpose of this book has been to propose Ricoeur's hermeneutical philosophy as just such a timely aid, and now it is time to reflect on what it offers on this side of the enterprise.

The current theological situation is widely regarded as one of change in a "time of troubles." It is not just that the world around theology is changing; the framework for doing theology itself is changing. It is not a situation of taking a timeless message in a timeless form and applying it; rather, the situation calls, as it always has, to apply a message of universal truth that arose in a particular situation, that we inherited from a different situation, and that we now want to appropriate in yet a very different situation. I characterized the current content as one facing the challenges of postmodernism, pluralism, and praxis. In response, I have attempted to show that Ricoeur's philosophy is one of the most viable postmodern philosophies for theology. It raises one of the sharpest critiques to modernity while not throwing the baby out with the bathwater. It retains on the far side of modernity radically revised conceptions of objectivity, truth, and reality. The issues of pluralism and praxis are also deeply embedded in Ricouer's philosophical reconstruction, as signaled by his continuing concern to deal with the conflict of interpretation, with the role of the other, with the will, and with practical appropriation.

I characterized the theological legacy also as one deeply shaped by modernism, including the most conservative theology—sometimes the ones most deeply affected—as well as liberal theologies who proudly point to contemporary influence. Many theologians for good theological reasons have embraced aspects of postmodernism, pluralism, and praxis as deeply consonant with the gospel. Sometimes the historical challenge calls us away from the gospel; at other times it may call us to discern aspects of the gospel that we have missed or neglected. The current situation, as most, has elements of both.

For those looking to relate or fuse the gospel with the contemporary horizon, I have suggested that Ricoeur's hermeneutical philosophy is a somewhat neglected resource. At the least, its full potential has hardly begun to be tapped. Why this is the case may be clearer at this point than before. He has often been appropriated piecemeal, without a clear conception of his larger philosophical project. He offers an extraordinary range of detail across a broad swath of issues, but he has often neglected the synthetic and summarizing task. It is only with his more recent work that he has filled in the few remaining gaps, making it easier to see his work as a congruent whole, including particularly the deep connection of his religious affirmation of testimony with his general epistemology of attestation.

One of the strengths of Ricoeur's philosophy at this point is that it is as comprehensive a philosophy as any in the twentieth century. It is probably also apparent that Ricoeur's philosophical project is still unfinished and open to multiple interpretations, a point that is not inconsistent but fully predictable in light of his own views. It is not incumbent on theologians to adopt any philosophical or psychological or sociological approach lock, stock, and barrel. The reader will note that I have appropriated Ricoeur in a critical way. While taking him as the more comprehensive thinker, I have modified his thought in the direction of Gadamer at several points. I have noted several places where he reveals his role as a transitional figure between modernity and postmodernity. He is clearly a major critic of the modern project, and he offers one of the substantial, if not the most substantial, comprehensive philosophical responses to it. Yet he at times reveals remnants of modernity in his thought, some of which he has later modified and some of which he has never reconciled with the larger direction of his thought. Nevertheless, on these occasions of finding discrepancies in his thought, I have tried to point to ways in which his thought could be made more coherent. At other places, I have simply interpreted him in a certain way that the surplus of meaning in his thought makes possible but not necessary. It is conceivable that he himself would not take his thought in the direction that I have, but again, it is a tribute to his thought that he predicts this dynamic. What I have tried to offer is an "appropriation" or "application" of Ricoeur, to use his words, that offers a distinctively postmodern philosophy, with great breadth and depth, that has remarkable congruence with the current theological task.

The intriguing leitmotiv from the beginning is that hermeneutical philosophy and theology share a similar paradigmatic model, namely, that of interpreting a significant text. We can see how fecund this model is as a basis for an entire philosophy in Ricoeur, which illustrates the significance of metaphorical models for any kind of thought, whether it be philosophy, theology, or science. This is again a point of coherence of Ricoeur's method and his content, both relating to the newly appreciated cognitive significance of metaphor.

What also contributes to the surprising affinity in Ricoeur's philosophy and contemporary theology is simply the fact that he combines in the same person, the same *ipse*-identity, if you will, a major contemporary philosopher and a deeply committed Christian who is well versed in contemporary theology and biblical studies. We noted the tension in his thought as he has tried to keep these separate, seeing valid reason for such a distinction at a certain level but finally seeing here an example of a residue of modernity. So, despite his protestations but consistent with his overall philosophy, we can affirm that there has been dialogue and "interweaving" between Ricoeur's deepest religious and philosophical convictions. This may be uncomfortable for Ricoeur, but it is a boon for theologians who are seeking ways, as ad hoc as they may be, to relate theology to the contemporary scene.

Beyond the basic hermeneutical heuristic, hermeneutical philosophy as developed here dialogues with theology in several other ways. It explicitly contributes to theological hermeneutics itself. Ricoeur's integrated hermeneutic that moves away from foundationalism, allows for critical methodology, but finally points to a holistic, second, postcritical understanding is significant for interpretation of scripture and of classic Christian texts. It offers, in fact, a critical way of reading theology. Even if they are usually second-order reflections, theological texts require to be read in terms of the hermeneutical arc. They need to be read with a critical eye but also to be appropriated holistically. They may achieve the status of a religious classic and grasp us with great power. Ricoeur's arc prompts us to test our appraisals but also to move beyond criticism—given that criticism comes all too easily when evaluating what someone else says about God—to critical appropriation.

In particular, Ricoeur's hermeneutical emphasis on the epistemological uniqueness and significance of metaphor and narrative, which are so basic to the church's scripture and life, even in the formation of theology itself, is a resource that is only beginning to be fully explored. Rather than being relegated to being ornaments of religious language and theology, metaphor and narrative can be seen sometimes as the key to the cognitive disclosiveness of religious language. Despite the development of narrative theology, many questions remain concerning whether it is justified and how it is to be elaborated in theology. There are few resources as rich as Ricoeur's in responding to these questions.

Ricoeur's hermeneutical arc is most helpful, however, as a broad framework for conceiving theological methodology. What we are looking for is a way of affirming theology but not exalting it. We need to see it not as a replacement but as a support and aid for the wider life of faith. In the contemporary context, we see renewed emphases on primary sources such as scripture, the practices of faith, and the pietistic religious experience of conservatives or the more general religious experience of the liberal tradition. From the perspective of the model envisaged here, these are protected as first-order expressions of Christian faith, and even though theology is clearly a second-order discipline, it is not, so to speak, "out of order." Theology should be able to enhance these primary expressions by reflection and critical examination, but not at the expense of replacing them. The hermeneutical arc should pass through theology but not end at theology. Ricoeur's hermeneutical philosophy thus can provide a framework, or at least a heuristic, for a productive relationship of theology with the life of faith.

In relation to theology's dialogue with other disciplines, Ricoeur's framework helps avoid the danger of overemphasis and underemphasis, a balance that history teaches us has been difficult to find. Such an approach calls for critical analysis and a public dimension to theology, thus avoiding a fideistic, closed stance, without abandoning itself to external control. It still allows for theologians to develop the distinctiveness of scriptural authority in a variety of ways but helps avoid the dangers of biblical positivism on the one hand and subservience to the historical-critical method on the other. It also offers ways to think about the primacy of the public of the church that are not divorced from the public of the academy. In this model, theology must begin with the church, its scripture, and its practices. Then, in accordance with Ricoeur's hermeneutical arc, it must be tested by the church—and others, such as the academy and other religions—in an ongoing hermeneutical spiral.

Ricoeur's anthropology, which in a sense is the focus of his entire philosophy, also resonates with movements in theology. Theology's recovery of a holistic, embodied self is also in its nascent stages and has yet to be fully appropriated in Christian formation, education, ministry, preaching, and counseling, not to mention the speculative understanding of the afterlife. Such an embodied and social understanding of the self as Ricoeur's offers a constructive dialogue partner to theology as theologians try to rethink the way in which they have tended to denigrate the body and the world in favor of the "soul." The conception of a social self particularly relates to the church's concern to relate to the often rootless and alienated modern person.

In another area, Ricoeur's epistemology offers a postmodern way of reformulating faith and reason in creative ways. It offers an integrated look at faith and reason that does not disparage faith at the expense of reason or lapse into fideism. In fact, it is almost unique in being sharply postmodern and yet allowing for robust claims to truth, to reference, and to ontology. I have argued that, rather than these claims being passé or disallowed by postmodernism, when they are suitably reconceived in the chastened hermeneutical manner of Ricoeur, it is more genuinely postmodern to allow for them. The skepticism and despair of some postmoderns then appear to reflect more the entrenched dualism of modernity than an authentically new paradigm. We are only in the beginning stages of reconceiving theology in light of these seismic shifts. What is promising is that the shifts are in the direction of the church's mode of expression, not away from it as during the Enlightenment.

In short, Ricoeur's thought has manifold ties to the role of theology in the church. It supports the integrity of the theological task as a rational enterprise, not in the monolithic, propositional sense of modernity but in its own distinctive way of being reasonable even as it is self-consciously both figurative and faithful. To integrate even further, the hermeneutical epistemology that is rooted in an incarnational, embodied self-in-community has rich implications for understanding how theology relates to faith itself, its beginning, and its nurturance. In other words, discipleship and evangelism may not look the same in this light; nor will education and missions, nor theology and apologetics. Interreligious dialogue, as we discussed, can be reshaped to allow for both conviction and critique. Perhaps one of Ricoeur's best contributions can be to integrate the dimension of critique that comes from Nietzsche, Freud, Marx, and Habermas with the critique that comes from the prophets and the Christian tradition. His hermeneutic of suspicion thus intertwines both biblical and contemporary strands in an integral way. He also allows, however, for a moment beyond critique, but one that is genuinely "post," not "pre." He helps us see that the critical moment is deeply biblical, Christian, and theological.

It is also deeply coherent with Ricoeur's philosophy and his purposes that his thought be critically appropriated by the theologian in a variety of ways. Both liberal and conservative can find this framework helpful. It is true that it is incompatible with modernist and foundationalist approaches, whether conservative or liberal, which in principle avoid pluralism and leave praxis outside the theological task. What Ricoeur does best is provide a dialogue partner with theologians who feel they cannot avoid the landscape informed by postmodernity, pluralism, and praxis. Even then, the surplus of meaning certainly applies to his own philosophy, especially as it is creatively appropriated by a community that claims to have experienced the grace of God. Light is shed on what might seem to be an impossible task at the outset, namely, theology's attempt to reflect on God and at the same time engage the new postmodern situation while avoiding pitfalls of the past. Some navigational illumination at least points to a possible path amid some treacherous shoals. In the spirit of Ricoeur's stance, we would not want to say that this is the only helpful prolegomenon, or that it says everything, or that it cannot be improved. Probably the most helpful approach in the present is to draw on several approaches with their various strengths and weaknesses. What I have wanted to convey is that Ricoeur's hermeneutical philosophy offers a more substantial and full-blown framework than is commonly supposed, without some of the weaknesses that are commonly supposed. The true test lies in its usefulness and fruitfulness, which leaves it up to the appropriation of the reader and the wider community of faith.

While no philosophy can predict, explain, or comprehend the surplus of grace that is the gospel, it can be open to it and even seek to think about it. As reflected in one of Ricoeur's favorite aphorisms from Kant, "The symbol gives rise to thought," Ricoeur understands that even the excess of grace has a certain logic. If not, it would be ineffable, as the mystics say, and theologians, not to mention philosophers, would be relegated to mute silence. The fact is, grace gives much to think about. Its excess lies in being not too little but too much. The challenge of a philosophy for a Christian theologian is whether it allows room at all for the gift of grace. If it does, as Ricoeur's attempts to do, it has a chance to be a gift itself to the theologian.

INDEX